SAVING
DEMOCRACIES

SAVING DEMOCRACIES

U.S. Intervention in
Threatened Democratic States

Edited by Anthony James Joes

Westport, Connecticut
London

Library of Congress Cataloging-in-Publication Data

Saving democracies : U.S. intervention in threatened democratic states
/ Anthony James Joes, editor.
    p.   cm.
   Includes bibliographical references and index.
   ISBN 0–275–96304–7 (alk. paper)
   1. United States—Foreign relations—1989– . 2. United States—
Foreign relations—1945–1989. 3. United States—Military policy.
4. Intervention (International law). 5. World politics—1945– .
6. Democracy—History—20th century. I. Joes, Anthony James.
E840.S28 1999
327.73—dc21   99–22112

British Library Cataloguing in Publication Data is available.

Library of Congress Catalog Card Number: 99–22112
ISBN: 0–275–96304–7

First published in 1999

Praeger Publishers, 88 Post Road West, Westport, CT 06881
An imprint of Greenwood Publishing Group, Inc.
www.praeger.com

Printed in the United States of America

The paper used in this book complies with the
Permanent Paper Standard issued by the National
Information Standards Organization (Z39.48–1984).

10 9 8 7 6 5 4 3 2 1

Contents

Preface

The collapse of the empire of Josef Stalin in 1989 soon precipitated the disintegration of the empire of Peter the Great. Thus the global political system found itself undergoing another period of profound transformation, the third in this century.

In the early post-Soviet years, expectations of the rapid spread of political democracy and free economies abounded. These expectations soon led to dismay as unforeseen troubles and challenges emerged at every turn. The era of communism was finished apparently, but its implosion had unleashed long-suppressed ethnic and religious rivalries, hatreds, and wars. More than one country saw its government simply disintegrate. Anarchy afflicting one society threatened to spread to its neighbors. The threat of or the enacting of internal and international violence raged in nearly every quarter.

These surprising and alarming developments coincided with the emergence (or recognition) of potentially quite large ethnoreligious movements and groups professing virulent hostility to the United States and to the entire West. In the view of some, the clash of ideologies was about to be superceded by the clash of civilizations.

The seemingly uncontrollable violence of the nineties, following so quickly upon the euphoria of the immediate post–Cold-War period, produced a paradoxical nostalgia for the exaggerated (and oxymoronic) "stability of the Cold War Era." As the millennium approached, the world of the Reagan presidency seemed very far away. American society hovered indecisively between the burden of continued world leadership and the temptation of neoisolationism.

A DEMOCRATIC VISION

In the midst of these perplexities, an influential segment of American opinion perceived the post–Cold-War mission of the United States to be that of helping to construct or protect democratic governments around the globe. To some, this seemed like the venerable Wilsonian vision of making the world safe for democracy and making democracy the dominant system of political organization in that safe world. But even hard-bitten realists of various hues felt able to support such a mission, if on a selective basis and in less-than-classically Wilsonian rhetoric. However, the exact requirements for safeguarding or helping to establish democratic governments abroad remained undetermined, and convincing proofs that such a pursuit is truly in the best interests of the United States remain undeveloped.

The historical record on this subject seems to offer insufficient guidance. In the early days of the East–West confrontation, President Harry Truman provided assistance to the governments of Greece and the Philippine Republic when those at least quasi-democratic states found themselves beset by insurgencies. But in fact the United States has had much more experience assisting governments that were anything but democracies to fight off insurgencies or revolutions. That seeming paradox arose in part because outside of the North Atlantic basin, there were (and are) few states whose democratic credentials were beyond being challenged. Nor should it be forgotten that even in the depths of the Cold War, not every democratic individual or state was an admirer or even a friend of the United States. And today, Russian democrats can quite comfortably advocate reassembling under one flag the territories of Peter's Empire—or perhaps Stalin's.

TO DEPLOY U.S. FORCES

Most important, perhaps, the possibility of active U.S. support for an endangered democratic government immediately and inescapably raises several contentious questions about U.S. ground forces, such as whether to commit them, to commit them alone or in cooperation with those of other states, in symbolic or overwhelming numbers, or for a limited or an indefinite period. One might recall that in Viet Nam, U.S. ground forces operated in tandem not only with hundreds of thousands of South Vietnamese troops but also with many tens of thousands of South Koreans, Australians, Thais, and others. A similar situation existed later in Somalia. Such precedents are hardly encouraging.

With regard to the protection and propagation of democratic regimes, where should the United States be heading? Where *is* the United States heading? Where do U.S. interests in this policy area lie, and how can we know? Clearly, these are fundamental questions upon which a great deal hinges. Equally clearly, the answers are far from obvious to large segments of the American polity.

Hence the present volume, which grew out of a conference on the subject of U.S. support for endangered democratic states, sponsored by the U.S. Army War College and Saint Joseph's University, held at the latter institution in 1997. The contributors to the volume are drawn from military, intelligence, and academic backgrounds (some are from all three). Their essays analyze the experiences and capabilities of the United States and also of several other societies on the vital questions at hand. The broad diversity of focus and analytical approaches these essays display recapitulates in itself the diversity of the challenges faced by the United States as it grapples with the issues involved in safeguarding endangered democracies around the globe.

ACKNOWLEDGMENTS

The editor and authors wish to thank the U.S. Army's Strategic Outreach Program, and especially its director, Colonel John R. O'Shea, without whose support this book would not have appeared. Thanks also to Major Lisbon Williams, USA, for his encouragement and efficiency.

SAVING
DEMOCRACIES

1

Force, Peace, and Democracy

Harvey Sicherman

The proclamation of the end of the Cold War was hardly completed before U.S. military forces were again on the move: to Somalia, to Haiti, to Bosnia. American experiences in these interventions were troubling. A principal cause of U.S. unhappiness arose from the unexpected, difficult, and controversial relationship between peace keeping and nation building.

The United States has a long history of using force to assist democracy. Virtually every war since the Revolutionary War has been justified as necessary to secure its survival (the War of 1812), extend liberty (the Mexican War, Civil War, and Spanish–American War), or defeat a tyranny threatening to democracy—our own or that of an allied people (World War I, World War II, the Korean War, and the war in Viet Nam). Fighting in the name of democracy is as much part of American military culture as the strategy of massive force employed for complete victory.

Alongside this record, however, there lies another, more complex story. U.S. military forces have been used to defend governments that were, at best, only potentially democratic. During the Cold War, these efforts on behalf of "friendly tyrants" were often controversial, but at least could be justified by the larger framework of the contest with the USSR.[1] Thus, the pro-American authoritarian regime was graded favorably because of its possible evolution toward democracy, an option denied to states that fell under Soviet sway.

Once the Cold War ended, this rationale disappeared. Both the Bush and the Clinton administrations attempted fresh visions, but neither succeeded. Bush's "New World Order" ended even before his presidency. Clinton's "Democratic Enlargement" proved to be a theme rather than a policy. As a result, the civilian leaders could give little political guidance on when and where to intervene. "Policy" became instead a series of case-by-case crises.

That left the Pentagon in an unusually strong position to influence the issue of when and how to use force. Military thinking was dominated by the so-called "Weinberger–Powell Doctrine," which demanded clear missions and the use of overwhelming force in a popular cause in order to avoid not only another Viet Nam but also another Beirut: the 1983 "peacekeeping" mission in Lebanon that ended with the deaths of 241 marines. This doctrine, eminently serviceable for the Desert Storm operation against Iraq in 1991, could say little about lesser contingencies except "Don't do them." Otherwise, the military had only the old and not very ennobling tradition of the Marine Corps's *Small Wars Manual*, a midthirties summation of the encounters in Haiti, Cuba, the Philippines, and Nicaragua. But in the nineties, what would be the justification for armed U.S. intervention to assist an embattled government with which it had no alliance and for which there was no obvious larger strategic virtue? Would the prospect of potential democracy alone be enough to justify the risk of American lives? Finally, even if these hurdles were overcome, could U.S. forces produce the desired results?

This article reviews three outstanding cases where the United States wrestled with such dilemmas: Somalia, where intervention was eventually justified in the name of a potential for democracy; Haiti, where U.S. force was used in the name of restoring democracy; and Bosnia, where U.S. troops took on the task of defending the concept of multiethnic democracy. Each case offers pointers for both American statesmen and soldiers as they face the perils of an incoherent era known only as the "post–Cold-War world." Overall, they teach a singular and predictable lesson: U.S. military forces can produce peace far more readily than democracy.

THE SEARCH FOR DOCTRINE

The unexpected demise of the Soviet Union, and with it, the end of the Cold War, pitched the United States onto entirely unfamiliar ground. There was not too much time to rejoice. Saddam's attack on Kuwait punctured the illusion that the absence of conflicting ideologies meant the absence of conflict. But the American victory over Iraq, coming atop the victory over communism, ushered in another false dawn: that democracy and free-market capitalism were inevitable and that the United States, as the sole remaining superpower, could encourage these trends without much risk.

President George Bush held aloft the vision of a "new international order" even before the Soviets were safely in the grave. The phrase and even the idea, however, were byproducts of the effort to stir public support for Desert Storm. Never fleshed out beyond cliché, the "order" disappeared when it became clear that the campaign of 1992 would be waged over domestic policy.

The new president, Bill Clinton, did not pretend to offer international expertise. His critique of Bush's foreign policy had been sporadic and calculated to appeal to interest groups: more aid for Russia (internationalists); a tough approach on Bosnia and China (human rights groups); less pressure on Israel (the Jewish community); more action on Haiti (Afro-Americans and Floridians). Once in office, he sounded the theme of trade as the key foreign policy item on an agenda plainly devoted to domestic affairs, promising to focus on the economy "like a laser."

Clinton's lack of foreign policy experience was accentuated by his uneasy relationship with the military. Accused of draft-dodging during the Viet Nam War, the new commander in chief began badly by attempting to change the rules on homosexuals in the services. His White House staff was widely regarded as antimilitary. It took the prestige of General Powell himself to effect a reconciliation of sorts at the 1993 Memorial Day ceremony for Viet Nam veterans.[2]

Clinton's appointees at the Departments of State and Defense were more experienced, although their experience was out-of-date. From Secretary of State Warren Christopher on down, they were the men and women whose views were formed by the traumas of the Johnson and Carter administrations. Junior officers during Viet Nam and middle rank or higher during the late seventies, they had seen two presidencies wrecked by the unsuccessful use of force abroad. The Viet Nam War, "the seminal event of our generation" as Richard Holbrooke wrote, was never far from their minds.[3] Nor was "Desert One," the botched operation to rescue the Iranian hostages in 1980 that had so harmed Carter and provoked the resignation of his secretary of state, Cyrus Vance. Christopher, then deputy secretary, had been the key figure in subsequent negotiations with the Khomeini regime over the hostage release.

While making a point of elevating trade to high virtue in foreign policy, Christopher took pains in his confirmation testimony to say that he had learned important lessons about the relationship between diplomacy and military power. "I do believe," he told the senators, "that the discreet and careful use of force in certain circumstances—and its credible threat in general—will be essential to the success of our diplomacy and foreign policy."[4] Thus did Christopher separate himself from the prevailing view that the Carter-era veterans were totally averse to military action. A commitment to a neo-Clausewitzian view of international conflict was an odd note to sound at a moment when the really seminal event—the Cold War—had just ended. But it found a ready echo at the Pentagon.

Despite Bush's assertion that Desert Storm had cured America of the Viet Nam Syndrome, that conflict still preoccupied the generals, especially the chairman of the joint chiefs, Colin Powell, himself a Viet Nam veteran. In 1983 he had been instrumental in drawing up what became known as the Weinberger principles. These followed the Lebanon catastrophe, where 241 marines were killed by a truck bomb while on "peace-keeping" duty in Beirut. The essence of this "doctrine" was to demand that the military be assigned a clear mission, be given the overwhelming force to achieve victory, and be supported by the American people in the enterprise. Although Powell had initially been a very reluctant warrior in Desert Storm, that operation exemplified the kind of war the Pentagon wished to fight.

The Weinberger–Powell Doctrine, like Desert Storm itself, was actually a return to traditional American ways. Successful American campaigns, whether those of Ulysses S. Grant, John Pershing, or Dwight Eisenhower, used overwhelming force to defeat the enemy and relied on a noble cause to sustain public support. Limited campaigns with limited objectives were synonymous with unhappy outcomes in Korea and Viet Nam; U.S. troops did best at crusades, not peace keeping. The only service with another tradition—the marines, who had done "pacification" in places like Haiti and Nicaragua—was the exception rather than the rule, and even they looked to the great Pacific campaigns of World War II for their inspiration, rather than to these minor contingencies.

The Clinton people and the Pentagon people were bound to have an uneasy relationship because each saw in the other an unwelcome reminder of failures past. But if the soldiers expected these particular civilians to avoid the use of military force, they were badly mistaken. The Clinton administration soon began to deploy the military abroad far more frequently than its predecessors. As Pentagon budgets and forces were still shrinking (about 35% since 1991), this meant much greater wear and tear on both men and machines, including operating rates three to four times higher than during the Cold War.[5]

These deployments did not derive from a grand strategic design that either measured the relationship between force and diplomacy or, for that matter, tried to coordinate them. Clinton had no broad ideas on American international objectives. Christopher, a lawyer by training, and also cautious by temperament, preferred to deal case by case, avoiding broad concepts. UN Ambassador Madeleine Albright filled the vacuum with talk of "assertive multilateralism," a concept justifying American action through the United Nations, especially in Somalia. It was not until September 21, 1993, after much criticism, that National Security Advisor Anthony Lake (followed by Clinton himself at the United Nations on September 27) enunciated as America's new purpose the doctrine of "enlargement"—the expansion of the ranks of democratic and free-market nations. In Lake's view, a dominant America should resist the attempts of various rogue states such as Iraq or Iran to ambush the calvacade of progress toward a more peaceful world made possible by the end of the Cold War.[6] Yet within three weeks of these bold pronouncements about a world not only safe for democracy but increasingly democratic, the administration suffered the disaster in Somalia. And as a consequence of that disaster, a heavy defeat was dealt to both enlargement as the objective and assertive multilateralism as the method.

SOMALIA: ENGINEERING A NATION

Somalia had been described by Lake in his speech to be almost peripheral and, along with other points of conflict such as Bosnia, not issues that "define our broader strategy in the world." This begged the obvious question of why American troops were fighting and dying in a place not deemed vital to any U.S. interest. Yet in many respects, the Somali enterprise did represent "democratic enlargement," namely, the use of American forces to engineer a protodemocracy in a small African state.

Two potent myths have emerged from the U.S. experience in Somalia. One was "mission creep": the idea that the United States had somehow stumbled onto a new objective without realizing it. A second was UN command: the idea that U.S. troops under UN direction had been led into an avoidable fiasco. Both are false. There was no mission creep; after an initial humanitarian intervention, Washington, including the Pentagon, had entered open-eyed into "nation building." Nor had the United Nations commanded the campaign to capture General Aideed, thought to be the main obstacle to the creation of a new Somali state. The commanders, forces, and plans were almost exclusively American, including the fatal raid that ended the entire mission. Yet somehow it came about that the United States was driven from the battlefield of choice by a ragtag army led by a general who would have preferred to be an American client.

This took some doing, not least because Somalia was a strange place for a post–Cold-War bout of American social engineering. It had been briefly important as a barrier to the Marxist-run and Soviet-assisted former American ally, Ethiopia. The end of the Cold War, however, spelt doom for the long-time Somali dictator, Siad Barre, who, deprived of American patronage, soon fell to mounting clan opposition. But the victors turned upon each other, and by 1992, a bad harvest and civil warfare threatened mass starvation. The usual UN- and NGO-sponsored programs proved ineffectual, partly because much of the food was stolen or diverted by the clans and their ubiquitous armament, the so-called "technicals"—heavy machine guns mounted on the beds of small trucks. (The relief organizations listed their bribes to the clans under "technical services," hence the name.)

None of this might have mattered much to the United States except that CNN and other Western TV networks began to cover the starving Somalis. Their pictures persuaded President Bush to launch a humanitarian mission in his last month of office, its purpose being to alleviate famine. General Powell supported the operation but gave it his own doctrinal twist. A massive American force of 26,300 landed to glaring TV coverage. Simultaneously, the former U.S. ambassador, the experienced diplomat Robert Oakley, let the clans know that the United States would *not* do what they feared: select one leader to be chief and disarm the rest. America was neutral—its only enemy: starvation.

There were other doctrines at work too. Among the services, the marines in particular believed in the "biggest, baddest junkyard dog" thesis. Humanitarian mission or not, their idea was to secure peace by biting, not just barking. The marine commanders, veterans of the 1983 Beirut disaster, gave their men aggressive rules of engagement. They understood, better than Washington, that big ships, loud noises, and a few good men—or even many good men—would not necessarily impress clans recently experienced in vicious urban warfare. Anticipating trouble in a near-combat situation, the heavily armed marines killed hundreds of Somalis through protective sniping as they actively patrolled their sectors.

These three factors soon produced success: (1) a mission that favored no clan, (2) overwhelming force, and (3) aggressive reaction to challenges. By mid-April, the food shortages had been alleviated, and supplies were being efficiently distributed.

It was at this point that Somalia took on a very different meaning. Arguably, the U.S. action bought a season of food but no permanent freedom from famine. Only an end to the civil war could reestablish the state. UN Secretary General Boutros-Ghali had therefore sought to use the American presence to create a new Somalia. This meant picking one clan leader over the others or persuading them to work together. Either choice might require a long-term military presence.

Urged on by Ambassador Albright, the UN Security Council gave the Somalia operation a new purpose—nation building. As Albright approvingly said of UN Security Council Resolution 814 (March 26, 1993), "With this resolution we will embark on an unprecedented enterprise aimed at nothing less than the restoration of an entire country as a proud, functioning and viable member of the community of nations."[7] This enormously ambitious undertaking—a kind of UN mandate for Somalia—greatly disturbed General Powell, who wrote later that he had heard of "nation building" once before—in Viet Nam.[8] He was happy enough to see the UN "take over" while most U.S. forces were withdrawn, once the humanitarian mission had been completed.

The small remaining army contingent took the peace keeping slogan seriously. They took a diplomatic approach to challenges and did not employ light-armored cars or tanks, equipment that the marines regarded as highly effective in urban warfare.[9] As Oakley later observed, "The departure of the heavily-armed, aggressively patrolling Marines from South Mogadishu obviously had a much greater psychological effect on the Somalis, especially the Somali National Alliance [Aideed's group] than the continued presence of the Quick Reaction Force from the [army's] 10th Mountain Division."[10]

The result was to turn the Powell Doctrine—and military sense—on its head. At the very moment when most U.S. forces had left, Washington committed itself to a much larger mission, one likely to encounter fierce opposition from the warlords who would lose influence. Chief among these was General Muhammad Aideed.

Aideed's claim to power was his primary role in the overthrow of Siad Barre. He also controlled strategic areas of Mogadishu. In 1993, he had enough strength to prevent others from winning but not enough to win it all himself. Aideed liked Americans and America. His son, later his successor, who was educated in the United States, had joined the marines and participated in the original humanitarian mission of December 1992.[11]

Aideed, seeing the negotiations for a national coalition deprive him of his prize, got the United Nations' attention by ambushing a

Pakistani contingent sent to remove his blockades of UN food distribution routes. In retaliation, the United Nations authorized a reward for Aideed's head. The hapless Somali was now directly in the path of the U.S.-powered, "assertively multilateral" UN mission to "fix" Somalia.

In 1989, the U.S. invading force in Panama had taken three days to find General Noriega in territory they knew well. Mogadishu was a much more haphazard place, and U.S. intelligence was less well informed. When Aideed might have been taken fairly easily in June, the local U.S. commanders did not feel strong enough and called for reinforcements. When the elite Army Rangers arrived six weeks later, Aideed could not be found, and instead, a summer's miniwar of attrition began between the U.S.-led UN forces and the warlord's adherents.

General Powell and his doctrine could not affect the situation. Unable to persuade the Clintonians of the folly of "nation building," he still supported the insertion of the Rangers because the local commanders were begging for it. Meanwhile, Congress had begun to stir over the costs and purposes of Somalia, leading Secretary of Defense Aspin to approve some reinforcements but not others, especially an armor component. Fed up with a decision-making process he described as "graduate student bull sessions," Powell retired on schedule in the fall of 1993, telling the president in his last meeting, "We can't make a country out of that place [Somalia]. We've got to find a way to get out, and soon."[12]

The stage was thus set for the raid of October 3. In the late afternoon, helicopter-borne Rangers attacked a building in downtown Mogadishu and seized several of Aideed's most important deputies. A clean escape was foiled when groundfire brought down a Blackhawk helicopter and then another sent to rescue it. When the Rangers attempted to recover their dead and wounded, they found themselves surrounded by large numbers of Aideed's men. A devastating fire fight followed. Several UN relief attempts failed, and coordination among the American and UN forces was poor. Only by 4 A.M. the next morning did the embattled Rangers manage to escape.[13] Eighteen Americans were killed and seventy-three wounded; the Somalis lost more than five-hundred dead and a thousand wounded.

The raid resembled in miniature the 1968 Tet Offensive in Viet Nam—a heavy defeat for the enemy, but a political disaster for the United States. Aideed's forces could not afford any more "victories" of this kind; a thousand of his best fighters had been lost, a large part of his total real effectives. And the United States could hardly have expected to wage this kind of war without casualties. Yet the damage to American prestige had been great; greater still was the sudden revelation that a Somali democracy could not be "engineered" without considerable loss of American life.

In December 1992, TV footage of starving Somalis led Americans to urge their government to "get in." In October 1993, TV film of a Somali mob dragging the body of a dead American soldier led Americans to urge their government to "get out." Clinton could not explain why American lives should be lost to build a democracy in Somalia, and he folded quickly under pressure.

Gone were the brave words about assertive multilateralism or nation building. Instead, the United Nations itself was blamed for beguiling the United States into the folly, leading Secretary General Boutros-Ghali to declare, "If it helps the Americans solve [their problems] by blaming me, I'll be a scapegoat."[14] Christopher confessed that "we got undue focus on the military side of this . . . right up to and including the President. . . . We were not sufficiently attentive." Clinton himself explained later, "I don't think we fully appreciated . . . just how much [the management of Somalia] . . . had been abandoned when we turned it over to the UN mission."[15] Presidential Decision Directive 25, intended to codify assertive multilateralism, was revised to incorporate the new, much less willing American attitude toward UN peacekeeping; it was dubbed "deliberative multilateralism," and it virtually precluded U.S. participation in most such missions.[16] The Secretary of Defense, Les Aspin, took the heaviest blows because of his apparent lack of detailed knowledge of the mission and his failure to send armor. The Somalia fiasco contributed to his resignation a few months later.

The president and the secretary of state believed what they said, but what they said was at variance with the facts. They had agreed, at Albright's urging, to the "nation-building" objective; the Pentagon had contrived, under the guise of the United Nations, an operation controlled by American officers top to bottom, using U.S. troops as the point of the spear. Once Washington discovered that Aideed, the strongest warlord, was in the way, the choice had to be made: crown him or eliminate him. The administration deliberately chose the latter. To have pursued Aideed and nation building—a greatly expanded mission—while simultaneously *reducing* the size of the force, was a blunder equalled only by the White House's shallow commitment to the entire exercise, for it required only one military reverse—the raid—to frighten the president out of the mission.

Somalia badly shook the new administration. Those Alberto Coll called the "values-driven globalists" remained ascendant but much more respectful of the arguments of the "interests-driven realists," if only because the American people seemed to support the caution of these antiinterventionists.[17] The idea of sacrificing U.S. lives (30 dead, 175 wounded overall) and treasure ($2 billion plus) on behalf of a potential democracy or even a stable state in Somalia had been repudiated. The new formula for assertive multilateralism was discredited and with it the United Nations, especially Secretary General Boutros-Ghali. (Albright herself skillfully led the charge against the United Nations and in the process earned a unique relationship with the world body's foremost American opponent, Senator Jesse Helms.) The "Viet Nam veterans" who peopled Clinton's security team seemed unable to coordinate military power and political objectives, at least in their own minds, as Christopher's comment suggested.

The Pentagon, even under General Powell, had somehow gone along for another Beirut-style ride, accepting a far-reaching mission to assist a policy of social engineering without popular support and with forces seemingly inadequate for the task. But the service chiefs did not conclude from this episode that they could simply block such exercises in the future; after all, Powell himself had not been able to stop this one. Smarting from the blow to their prestige, the army quickly adopted marine-style tactics.[18] Significantly, the next case study—Haiti—was to combine the Somali lesson with a renewed dose of Powellism in the size and variety of the forces employed.

HAITI: RESTORING DEMOCRACY

Haiti, a small Caribbean country, shared many characteristics with its neighbors. Its culture, like its mixed-race population, contained colonial French, Spanish, and African strains, not the least of which was a Roman Catholicism overlaying a voodoo religion still widely practiced. The U.S. Marine Corps had spent nineteen years in Haiti (1915–1934) for the purpose of restoring order, and many of its *Small Wars Manual* lessons were drawn from that less-than-happy experience.

For some three decades, the Duvaliers, "Papa Doc" and "Baby Doc," had run the country. "Baby Doc's" voodoo had been regarded as far less potent than his father's, the ultimate proof being that the older Duvalier died while still in power, while the son was forced to flee to France after a popular uprising in 1986. An election of sorts in 1990 brought to power a one-time Catholic priest, Bertrand Aristide, on a platform of redistributing the wealth of the mostly impoverished plantation-style economy. But the soldiers and the plantation masters evicted Aristide in December 1991 before he could seize their property. American sanctions followed and a sharp decline in the economy, accompanied by yet another reign of terror, stimulated a massive flow of desperate refugees. Despite protest by various human-rights groups, the Bush administration used the U.S. Navy to collect the unfortunate Haitians, sending them to the base at Guantánamo Bay, Cuba, where only those who could prove political oppression were allowed asylum in the United States. Beyond this, the United States brought diplomatic and economic pressure on the regime to restore democracy, if not the erratic Aristide.

Clinton had criticized this policy, and, under American prodding, both the Organization of American States (OAS) and the UN Security Council upped the ante with an oil and arms blockade in June 1993, which produced the so-called Governor's Island Agreement of July 2, providing for Aristide's return. Then ensued a long haggle over the conditions, while the continued economic blockade produced a fresh explosion of refugees. The Black Congressional Caucus protested the Clinton policy and so did the politically potent state of Florida, most affected by the Haitian immigration. A scheme to send unarmed American military police under UN auspices to prepare the way for Aristide went badly awry on October 11, 1993, when armed Haitian irregulars, shouting that "another Somalia" awaited the mission, prevented them from landing. This humiliation galvanized the Pentagon to prepare a serious "Powell-style" intervention.

The Haiti operation was facilitated by an act of comic opera that turned out well. Former President Jimmy Carter, who held a kind of subcontract on U.S. foreign policy in Clinton's first term, volunteered to lead a mission consisting of himself, leading Democratic Senator Sam Nunn and recently retired General Colin Powell to persuade the Haitian junta not to oppose the U.S. landings. (Powell's role was apparently to make sure that Carter—"sometimes a wild card" in Clinton's words—did not foul it up by letting the Haitians off the hook in order to negotiate.)[19] Once in Port-au-Prince, by Powell's account, the team brought home to the leading general, Raul Cedras, that the invasion was certain and the only choice either exile or defeat. The nearly forty hours of discussion were often in French and were about military honor. There were surreal touches: A Haitian colonel refused Carter's hand because it had touched Aristide, contaminating it with the former priest's "spirit." Finally, Powell told Cedras what he faced. It would not be only the Army Rangers, although that surely would have sufficed to seize the country, but also would be other forces such as two aircraft carriers, two-and-a-half infantry divisions, twenty thousand troops, helicopter gunships, tanks, artillery, and armored cars. When it became clear to the Haitians that the massive force had begun to move, they capitulated.[20]

Haiti was quickly transformed from a brutal, if inept, military dictatorship into a kind of international trusteeship. Swarms of

UN civil servants and other experts descended. The U.S. and other UN detachments found themselves completely in charge of public order and in some cases local government altogether.

Both the army and the marines applied lessons learned from the recent fiasco in Somalia. The army used light tanks in the towns to intimidate those who might resist. The marines noticed the police still attempting to retain their authority through random whippings of the population who stood watching them march past, and they put a stop to it. Marine scout-snipers also developed intelligence about the ringleaders among the more aggressive police. Not long after their entry into Cap Haitien in northern Haiti, the marines and police fired at each other; the police lost several. This established the American credentials for serious work.[21]

The announced objective of the invasion was to "restore" democracy in the person of Bertrand Aristide, not to create a new colony. Democracy in Haiti was a relative term. Those who knew Aristide well also knew that by 1995, there was not much democrat left in him. American diplomats and soldiers were also resolved to be neutral among the competing civilian factions on the island once the Cedras clique had been forced into exile. This translated into a policy of letting Aristide finish his term; providing for new, free elections for a new president and legislature; preventing a bloody settling of scores between the Aristide camp and its local opponents; and plentiful economic aid to jump-start the badly damaged island economy. Thus political stability plus economic growth would allow a quick exit from Haiti—or so the theory went.

Seventeen months after the invasion, a presidential election was staged on December 17, 1995. Approximately 87.5 percent voted for René Préval, Aristide's handpicked successor. This event was duly hailed by Washington, but it seemed not to have excited the Haitian population: Only 30 percent of those eligible cast ballots, versus the 60 percent who participated in the election of 1990. Still, Brian Atwood, USAID administrator, claimed, "The democratic process is taking hold."[22]

Two billion dollars spent and one election held, however, did not spell stability for UN Secretary General Boutros-Ghali. On January 15, 1995, General David C. Meade, the U.S. commander of all UN military forces in Haiti, wrote to the UN Security Council that "a secure and stable situation" existed, allowing responsibility to be shifted from the United States to a UN command. Two days later, Boutros-Ghali reported to the UN Security Council on a "very fragile" situation. He insisted that an international police force be retained to "train, guide and monitor" a reconstructed Haitian police. Public order and security depended on an international backstop of retrained Haitian army soldiers (the Interim Public Safety Force) and police. Seizures and rewards were also employed to collect weapons—a kind of "demilitarization" of the local gangs and militias.

As in Somalia, the UN "command" was less than met the eye. A third of the resident international force was to be American, and Washington clearly called the shots. In this case, Washington wanted out as quickly as possible; and in January 1996, after the presidential elections were declared a victory for democracy, the United States drew down its troop level (then 2,200 of 5,800 in the multinational force) to a minimal 200 "engineers." While Préval took office peacefully, economic progress on the island remained elusive, and a stalemated political system prevented wholesale reform of the government-dominated economy. Even advocates of continued American aid for Haiti have admitted that "improvements in the Haitian quality of life have not yet taken place."[23] Virtually all observers believed that a withdrawal of the U.S. contingent would lead to a rapid return to chaos. That may be happening on the installment plan, even *with* the American presence, for both political murders and crime (transshipments of cocaine) in Haiti are again on the rise.[24]

The Haiti intervention had produced a tenuous stability ornamented with the forms of democracy, although not its substance. Its motivation, unlike Somalia, was not an experiment in nation building but a refugee crisis that affected American domestic politics. Also unlike Somalia, the U.S. military performed the mission using overwhelming force and tactics that, at least in the army's case, were based on lessons learned from the Mogadishu disaster.

In addition to the Powell Doctrine's presence in the form of a huge force, the Pentagon, aided by congressional and public pressure, also influenced the administration's "endgame." This meant an "exit strategy": a timetable to get out, not only to get in. The timetable device assured Americans and the military that there would not be a long-term commitment of large forces to little Haiti. In a way, this also helped to protect the troops; would-be troublemakers had reason to wait out the U.S. occupation rather than pick a fight. But, as the UN leadership and others understood, the exit strategy did not encourage the local politicians to cooperate or assure even short-term success in laying the grounds for enduring stability. That took second place. Instead, the symbolic success, especially an election, would provide the signposts for an exit of American troops. A similar strategy could be seen in our third case, Bosnia, where it proved ultimately impossible to apply.

BOSNIA: MULTIETHNIC DEMOCRACY?

Yugoslavia, like Somalia, was a state that depended on the rarefied oxygen of the Cold War. For over three decades, its communist dictator, Josef Tito, had maneuvered skillfully between Washington and Moscow, extracting aid and political support. He proved equally adept at controlling the Croat, Muslim, and Serb populations, defusing a potential danger by granting a limited autonomy to the Albanians, who formed the majority in the historic Serb heartland of Kosovo.

Yugoslavia survived Tito's death in 1980 for over a decade, finally coming to grief when the end of communism, economic reform, and ambitious politicians fatally disrupted its internal balance. Former communists, such as Tudjman of Croatia and Milosevic of Serbia, transmuted themselves into extreme nationalists, further aggravating historic animosities. Finally, in 1991, the Slovenians and the Croatians broke away and the Yugoslav army, under Milosevic's direction, acted to create a Greater Serbia, by seizing territory and then supplying local Serb populations in parts of Croatia and Bosnia with the arms and training to hold it. Bosnia-Herzogovina, dominated by the Muslim-led government of Alija Izetbegovic, found itself the crucial transit point between the Serb holdings in Croatia and Serbia itself.

Izetbegovic's declaration of neutral independence did not prevent war. The Bosnian Serbs, led by the former psychiatrist Radivan Karadic and Yugoslav army general Ratko Mladic, declared their own independence. They pursued a strategic plan of uniting the Serb areas in Croatia (the Krajina region) and Bosnia with Serbia itself, a military objective facilitated by "ethnic cleansing"—the removal of the Muslim and Croatian population in their path. Sarajevo itself was soon besieged and massacres there and elsewhere, familiar to students of the Balkans but shocking to everyone else, provoked revulsion throughout the West. The Serbs lacked the strength, however, to complete the job; their offensives stalled in the outskirts of Sarajevo, the Posavina corridor to the north, and the Croatian-held Dalmatian coast to the south. This grinding war of attrition guaranteed a daily diet of telegenic atrocities.

Yugoslavia had been an "American account" during the Cold War, but as the state broke down, the United States eagerly handed it off to the Europeans. The Bush administration, seeking a "soft ending" to the rivalry with the USSR, feared a breakup would set a bad precedent and argued against Croatian and Slovenian independence. When it happened, Secretary of State Baker declared that Washington "had no dog in the fight."[25] This suited the Europeans well enough at the outset. The French, British, and Germans wanted to demonstrate that Europe's "hour" had arrived and that "internationalizing" the breakup by recognizing the new states would convince Belgrade not to fight. When this failed, French President Mitterand invoked historic Franco–Serb ties to no avail; Milosevic was interested only in those who would help him and took only Washington seriously. The British, French, and others then offered troops to a UN-sponsored effort to gain a cease-fire in Croatia. But these forces (UNPROFOR, or UN Protection Force), numbering eventually 38 thousand, only allowed the Serbs to consolidate their conquests and proved helpless to prevent the ethnic cleansing of Bosnia itself. They had no mandate except to monitor a cease-fire and facilitate humanitarian assistance. Its commanders, unable to deploy in a militarily sensible way, found the troops hostage to the more aggressive Serbs, who were prepared to attack and to seize UN units who opposed their movements.

These events stupefied Western statesmen, who had never imagined that the end of the Cold War would "reverse history," reviving a nineteenth-century nationalism that in 1914 had ignited World War I. But 1991 was not 1914; NATO and postcommunist Russia guaranteed that conflict over Sarajevo would not provoke another European war. To resolve this nineteenth-century problem, diplomats resuscitated a nineteenth-century model: the Concert of Europe that produced the Congress of Berlin and a Balkan settlement that lasted from 1878 until 1914.

Through much of 1992, the United States, the United Kingdom, France, Germany, and Russia met in the so-called "Contact Group" (the name derived from the diplomacy that produced a successful settlement in southern Africa during the 1980s). A map, devised by former U.S. Secretary of State Cyrus Vance and former British Foreign Secretary David Owen, rebalanced the Bosnian ethnic arrangement in a complex set of miniprovinces or cantons, giving the Croats and the Muslims 51 percent of the area and the Serbs 49 percent. The Serbs rejected it. But the Contact Group, unlike the Congress of Berlin, was not composed of nineteenth-century powers, and they were not prepared to enforce their will, especially against the Serbs.

The Clinton administration, strongly critical of the Bush policy, began with an ambitious plan called "lift and strike." The arms embargo on Yugoslavia, imposed in 1991, would be lifted to benefit the Bosnian government; meanwhile, NATO aircraft would strike the Serbs to end the siege of Sarajevo. Christopher's presentation of these ideas was undercut by well-founded accounts of Clinton's second thoughts about the "historic" Bosnian quagmire, and little came of it all, except serious tensions within the Western alliance.[26]

As various observers soon realized, NATO itself was suffering mounting damage from the Bosnian crisis. During the Cold War, the alliance had struggled with "out of area" issues in Algeria, Suez, and Viet Nam. This was compounded by the very different military capabilities among the members, only very few of whom could project force. Eventually, a formula was devised that allowed for the use of forces dedicated to NATO "out of area" but not with formal alliance involvement. Those who could act, did; the others were expected to support such action or at least keep quiet. Thus, for example, NATO endorsed the Gulf War in 1991 but did not participate in it as an alliance.

This formula was not used in Bosnia. Beginning in 1992, NATO agreed to enforce the embargo by sea and air. Later it imposed, with UN authorization, a "no-fly" zone. While the French and British provided ground forces under UN control, the Americans provided most of the sea and air forces under NATO officers but subject to UN rules of engagement. These complex and often absurd arrangements trapped NATO in a new mission without either the unified control or central purposes of its Cold War-era organization. It was a frustrating and debilitating experience.

Somalia and Haiti reinforced the Pentagon's basic reluctance to involve U.S. forces in Bosnia where the Serbs, heirs to the huge arsenal of the supposedly formidable Yugoslav army, might offer serious opposition to any intervention. Washington squirmed in this stalemate, refusing to offer U.S. troops or to lift the embargo, while it berated the Europeans and the United Nations for cowardice and winked at secret arms shipments to the Bosnians by the likes of Iran.[27]

This paralysis might have continued indefinitely if the Bosnian Serbs had not resolved on a final offensive in the spring and summer of 1995 to crush the rump of the Muslim state altogether. Their attacks on UN "safe-zones"—isolated Muslim enclaves—and increased shelling of Sarajevo finally brought NATO air raids on May 25; two days later the Serbs seized several hundred UN troops (including a French contingent) and publicly humiliated them. Newly elected French President Jacques Chirac was enraged by this spectacle. In his view, NATO had to get tough with the Serbs or get out. Then on June 2, an American F-16 was downed by Serbian fire. The pilot, Scott O'Grady, was rescued by a special American helicopter-borne unit that exchanged fire with the Serbs.

Five weeks later, the Clinton administration ran out of maneuvering room in Bosnia. Chirac's threat to withdraw invoked an earlier American pledge to use ground troops if necessary to extricate the UN force. Simultaneously, Senate Republican Leader Bob Dole secured a congressional resolution to lift the arms embargo, an act that in itself could trigger the withdrawal of the British and French from Bosnia. NATO's plan (Ops 40-104) to rescue these soldiers had already been approved by the Alliance Council, but it was not until the end of the Chirac visit on June 14 that Christopher, Assistant Secretary for European Affairs Richard Holbrooke, and finally Clinton himself, fully understood what was happening.[28] The choice of whether or not to use American ground forces was no longer in Washington's hands. More than 20 thousand Americans would be needed to conduct a humiliating retreat; the alternatives were to betray NATO or to engage U.S. military might more directly in an effort to stop the war, which meant at this point, stopping the Serbs.

While Washington dithered, the Serbs acted. Their destruction of the UN enclave in Srebrenica (July 5–16), including the massacre of over 7 thousand male Muslims despite the presence of a sizable Dutch UN force, finally galvanized NATO into action. The London Conference on July 21 authorized vigorous military action unless the Serbs desisted. They did not, moving instead to capture the Bosnian town of Bihac, to better secure their connection to the Krajina region of Croatia.

NATO's task in making the Serbs heel benefited from the unexpected Croatian offensive in early August that rapidly rolled over the Serbs in Krajina. This sudden change in the balance of power was accompanied by a heavy and effective NATO bombing campaign that began after a new Serb shelling of Sarajevo killed dozens of civilians. Although Washington and the Europeans publicly opposed the Croat attack (while Holbrooke privately urged Tudjman to continue it), the Serbs wilted under the combined air and ground pressure, quickly agreeing to a cease-fire. This set the stage for the Dayton Conference proposed by the United States.[29]

The conference, held November 1 through 21, 1995, at Wright-Patterson Air Force Base in Dayton, Ohio, assembled the Croatian Tudjman, the Bosnian Izetbegovic, and the Serb Milosevic. The latter agreed to represent the Bosnian Serbs, thus confirming that Belgrade was the key to controlling the conflict. The Contact Group was also present where it paid the full price for Europe's irresolution. Although the Europeans were still providing most of the money and two-thirds of the troops, they functioned primarily as bystanders. The Americans ran the show.

The agreements that emerged from this often tragicomic transaction reflected the history of the Balkans. Only two methods had ever pacified the area: a local balance of power or imposition by an outside power. Dayton would produce a mixture of these methods.

The division of territories between the Muslim-Croat Federation and the Serb Republic within Bosnia and Herzogovina reflected mostly the cease-fire lines, the local balance. On top of that came an international army called IFOR, or "Implementation Force." In 1878, British Prime Minister Benjamin Disraeli, architect of the Congress of Berlin, estimated that "nothing short of an army of 50,000 of the best troops would produce anything like order in these parts."[30] One hundred seventeen years later, a NATO-led force of 60 thousand disembarked to do the same job. After intensive negotiation, Russia agreed to join it, but only on the condition that the NATO commander, an American admiral, function with respect to the Russian commander as an American officer, not a NATO one.

In addition to this mix of local and international balances of power, Dayton also bore another hallmark: the gap between the political aspirations of the agreement and the role of the military in helping to bring these about. This was entirely the product of a split U.S. administration, where the political rhetoric exceeded the military's commitment, and the White House would not, or could not, impose a coherent line. Even before the conference, Clinton had complained, "I am frustrated that the air campaign is not better coordinated with the diplomatic effort."[31] Holbrooke wrote later that the NSC system had broken down, and it seems never to have recovered.

Bosnia had been torn apart by the most vicious of civil wars. Half the population had been displaced. Hundreds of thousands had been killed, most of them civilians. Now outside powers proposed to revive a "multicultural democracy" patterned on the prewar tolerance of the once polyglot but now mostly Muslim city of Sarajevo. The same formula used in Haiti—democracy, civility, and economic aid—would be applied. Among the necessary conditions: a return of refugees to their homes; common state institutions; disarmament of some and rearmament of others (the Muslims); and the capture of war criminals.

Yet the obligations of the IFOR were not to do any of these things. The Pentagon agreed to police the cease-fire and limited force zones, but it refused any obligation to assist in the return of refugees, to arrest indicted war criminals, or to do "police actions." Furthermore, both the generals and the White House agreed to a one-year timetable. Thus, IFOR would not threaten anything currently held by the combatants nor erode the lines of division. There would not even be a formal coordination between the new high commissioner (the Swedish statesman Carl Bildt) and the military commander of IFOR.[32] The creation of a multiethnic mixed democracy in Bosnia would be left to diplomatic persuasion and money, neither of which had prevented war in the first place or brought about the peace.

In announcing the Dayton Agreement, Clinton had chosen rhetoric remarkably similar to that of his predecessors. The United States would be using military force with its NATO allies (and others) to bring peace and democracy. He also put a timetable on it, attributed to the Pentagon: "Our joint chiefs of staff have concluded that this mission should and will take about one year." Holbrooke put a different cast on it, telling *The New Yorker* (November 6, 1995), "My worst nightmare is a decent interval and then anschluss."

Subsequently, Clinton was forced to abandon the deadline because he feared that the removal of foreign troops would produce just that: a division of Bosnia between Croatia and Serbia. Holbrooke himself regarded the civilian side of Dayton as a failure until he returned to government service in 1996 and 1997 and pushed for military supported intervention against Serb obstruction and the seizure of war criminals. Nor was there much hope on the ground that democratic elections would provide the neon sign to the exit. The first general election held in 1996 as part of the plan to finish up the operation quickly returned all the leaders, Croat, Muslim, and Serb, who preached the division of Bosnia and had condemned it to war in 1992. By 1998, the deputy chief of the High Representative, the U.S. diplomat and former Air Force officer Jacques Klein, was telling Washington visitors, "Forget about exit strategies. We are the life-support system."[33]

At latest reckoning, 35 thousand soldiers (about 6,500 American) garrison a divided country, where 50 thousand or so foreign experts and humanitarians minister to a variety of troubles. Five billion dollars have been spent on the troops and $1.5 billion on economic aid. The three-headed Bosnian presidency heads an administration increasingly dependent on foreigners and foreign decisions: the Chief of the Central Bank is a New Zealander; a former Los Angeles policeman is deputy chief of the international police force. Meanwhile, few refugees have returned and many ugly incidents still remind everyone that the Bosnian Serbs want out and the Muslim-Croatian Federation hardly functions except under international pressure. At the end of August 1998, Secretary of State Albright could be seen actually campaigning on behalf of the anti-Karadic candidate, Mrs. Bitjan Plâsic, in the forthcoming general Bosnian elections. The Bosnian enterprise had turned into a new kind of international trusteeship, with the United States serving as chief trustee.

To nearly everyone's surprise, the U.S. military had come through over two years of duty in Bosnia without a single casualty. Part of this was due to the rigid separation of the U.S. forces from the population. American forces also held the crucial Posavina Corridor area.

A possible flash point in the form of Brcko, a small town in the narrowest part of the corridor, was defused when the U.S. mediator appointed by Dayton decided that the Serb-held but originally Muslim town should remain under "international supervision." Another threat to U.S. troops was sharply reduced when on February 17, 1996, special forces raided the camp of Iranians and Arab "volunteers." The Bosnian leader Izetbegovic then had to make good on his Dayton promise to rid his country of such would-be terrorists if he wanted American training for the Muslim-dominated Bosnian army.[34]

The American forces were also quick to impose the limited force arrangements. A high degree of area intelligence was attained, a precondition to letting the locals know that the United States would not be blind-sided. General Nash put it this way: "We don't have arguments. We hand them pictures and they move their tanks."[35] Yet there could be no doubt that this very effective self-protection and the narrow scope of military responsibility fenced IFOR off from the attempt to reconstruct the country. Early in the mission, for example, when Sarajevo was reunified, foreign troops stood by while the Serb-held part of the city was torched at Karadic's instructions, often against the will of the Serb residents. This "ethnic self-cleansing" demonstrated that whatever the aspirations of Dayton, the Serbs wanted no part in a multiethnic Bosnia, and it was a serious blow to U.S. policy.[36]

American soldiers had not died for Bosnia, but several American civilians lost their lives, especially in the upper reaches of the administration. Even as Holbrooke threw his diplomacy into high gear, on April 19, 1995, a road accident on the treacherous track over Mt. Igman into Sarajevo killed three of his closest assistants: Robert Frasure, his deputy at state; Joseph Kruzel, senior deputy assistant secretary of defense; and Air Force Colonel Nelson Drew, of the National Security Council Staff. A year later, Secretary of Commerce Ron Brown, a close friend of the president; Assistant Secretary of Commerce Charles Meissner; and thirty-three others perished when their plane crashed into a mountain while trying to land in Dubrovnik.

MODELS, NATION BUILDING, AND MILITARY FORCE

As noted earlier, the three cases of Somalia, Haiti, and Bosnia hardly reflect a well-thought-through doctrine that fit America's post–Cold-War challenges. The Clinton administration never developed an effective guide for the use of military force in the name of democracy or even material interest. Except for the early stages alties or "quagmires." Once engaged, however, the danger of a relapse into chaos or war kept Washington tied to the longer-term "nation building" efforts. This in turn required the U.S. to create a "trusteeship" with much deeper American involvement in controlling local events than was ever contemplated. And U.S. military forces would still be needed to assure peace, if not to aid more directly in promoting democracy.

Ironically, then, whether Washington likes it or not, the use of American military power on behalf of "democracies" such as those found in Somalia, Haiti, and Bosnia inevitably entails some "nation building." To avoid this, Washington could abandon the pretense that its intervention is for democratic purposes and find justification in coarser economic or political interests. But if the U.S. does argue that American soldiers should be risked for democracy in such countries, then the only issue is whether American military power will be coordinated with nation building or, as in Bosnia, will be largely exempt in order to avoid trouble. Here the *Small Wars Manual* should have the last word: "Formulation of foreign policy in our form of government is not the function of the military."[37] Instead, the forceful coordination of political and military efforts is a function of presidential leadership.

NOTES

1. Adam Garfinkle and Daniel Pipes, eds., *Friendly Tyrants: An American Dilemma* (New York: St. Martin's Press, 1991).

2. See Colin Powell with Joseph E. Persico, *My American Journey* (New York: Ballantine Books, 1996), pp. 565–566. See also pp. 549–550 on the homosexual issue.

3. Richard Holbrooke, *To End a War* (New York: Random House, 1998), p. 92.

4. Warren Christopher, *In the Stream of History: Shaping Foreign Policy for a New Era* (Stanford, Calif.: Stanford University Press, 1998), p. 27.

5. See U.S. General Accounting Office, *Military Readings: A Clear Policy is Needed to Guide Management of Frequently Deployed Units* (Washington, D.C.: U.S. Government Accounting Office, April 1996). See also John Hillen, "Superpowers Don't Do Windows," *Orbis* 41, no. 2 (Spring 1997): 43–245.

6. Quotes are from Lake's speech, "From Containment to Enlargement," at the Paul H. Nitze School of Advanced International Studies, Johns Hopkins University, Washington D.C., September 21, 1993.

7. *Facts on File*, April 1, 1993, p. 224.

8. Powell, *My American Journey*, p. 565.

9. See quote from *Small Wars Manual*: "Tanks are particularly valuable in assaulting towns and villages, and in controlling the inhabitants of an occupied hostile city." Quoted in Thomas E. Ricks, *Making the Corps* (New York: Charles Scribner's Sons, 1997), p. 182.

in Somalia when the new administration decided to "build
tion," events on the ground more than thoughts in Washii
shaped U.S. policy.

These events also influenced overall strategic thinking in th
government but did not yield a coherent result.

1. Somalia heavily damaged the hastily devised "enlargement" the
   the emphasis on "assertive multilateralism" through the U
   United States then rediscovered its regional allies, especially
   in Bosnia and resorted to thinly disguised unilateral action ir

2. All three crises inspired yet more conditions and requiremei
   the Weinberger–Powell Doctrine, that would supposedly ink
   disciplined U.S. military interventions. But, in almost pervei
   ion, the more policy makers emphasized the rhetoric of restr
   less it seemed to matter. Instead, events deprived Washingt
   choice: a military accident in Somalia; refugees in Haiti; Chii
   and the Serbs in Bosnia; and public opinion squalls through

3. Powellism survived in the Pentagon in the form of resistanc
   military power on behalf of "nation building" or "democracy
   that went beyond simply securing a cease-fire or acting in self-į

4. The services themselves, especially the army, began to a
   cally to situations that were termed "peace keeping" but
   sembled more the marine "small-war" tradition.

   It is difficult to conclude too, that after the Somalia disa
action drew its primary motivation from the theme of d
There was no real democracy to restore in Haiti, and th
multiethnic state was mostly a nostalgia for old Sarajı
push came to shove, the Clinton administration placed
portance on the need to avoid casualties or a prolonged
the objective of creating democratic societies. Ironicall
bols, if not the substance, of democracy also served aı
markers for the exit of U.S. forces.

   From this cat's breakfast there still emerged a rough
American military intervention: delay, delay; when pre
fast and hard; do not try to change the balance on the
much; stay out of harm's way, if possible; hold an elec
pour in money; recruit allies and friends to help hold 1
then, proclaim victory near the exit without looking ba
trouble with this formula was that it did not work; it
neither democracy nor a quick exit and probably ha
objectives by failing to coordinate military action v
purpose. Democracy in Haiti or Bosnia could never
day or a decade, especially if the superior military fc
to the United States was not applied to the project fo

10. Ibid., p. 183.

11. *Facts on File*, August 15, 1996, p. 587.

12. Powell, *My American Journey*, pp. 560, 572.

13. An excellent review of the battle may be found in Mark Bowden, "Blackhawk Down: An American War Story," *Philadelphia Inquirer*'s investigation, November 16–December 14, 1997.

14. *The New York Times*, October 10, 1993.

15. *The Washington Post*, January 31, 1994.

16. See *Philadelphia Inquirer*, May 6, 1994, and *The New York Times*, May 6, 1994.

17. For a perceptive discussion of the Pentagon's role in Somalia, see Alberto R. Coll, "Somalia and the Problems of Doing Good," in *Close Calls*, ed. Elliott Abrams (Washington, D.C.: Ethics and Public Policy Center, 1998).

18. Ricks, *Making the Corps*, pp. 183–184.

19. Powell, *My American Journey*, p. 598.

20. Ibid., p. 584.

21. See Ricks, *Making the Corps*, pp. 268–272, for an illuminating account of the marine portion of the invasion.

22. See John Sweeney, "Stuck in Haiti," *Foreign Policy* 102 (Spring 1996): 146. This issue also features a debate between Sweeney and Robert I. Rotberg entitled, "Clinton Was Right."

23. Robert I. Rotberg, "Clinton Was Right," *Foreign Policy* (Spring 1996): 140. Rotberg's article, "Haiti's Past Mortgages Its Future," *Foreign Affairs* (Fall 1988), offers a good review of the country's complexities.

24. See *The Economist*, February 28, 1998, p. 39.

25. Quoted in Richard Holbrooke, *To End a War*, p. 27. See also James A. Baker, III with Thomas M. DeFrank, *The Politics of Diplomacy* (New York: G. P. Putnam and Sons, 1995), p. 483; Warren Zimmerman, *Origins of a Catastrophe: Yugoslavia and Its Destroyers* (New York: Times Books, 1996); and David C. Gompert, "The United Sates and Yugoslavia's Wars," in *The World and Yugoslavia's Wars*, ed. Richard Ullman (New York: Council on Foreign Relations, 1996).

26. See Elizabeth Drew, *On The Edge: The Clinton Presidency* (New York: Simon and Schuster, 1994), p. 157. Clinton and others claimed to have been influenced by Robert Kaplan's *Balkan Ghosts: A Journey Through History* (New York: Vintage Books, 1993), an odd conclusion given Kaplan's very brief references to Bosnia and his preface explicitly condemning Serb war crimes. These readers—including William Cohen, then a senator—seem to have willfully misread Kaplan's attempt to explain the weight of history on current attitudes as justification to stay out of an "age-old" conflict.

27. Five hundred troops were deployed as part of a UN force stationed on the Macedonian border to discourage the spread of the war.

28. See Holbrooke, *To End a War*, pp. 66–68, for an account of the administration's disarray on this point.

29. Ibid.

30. Quoted in Larry Wentz, *Lessons from Bosnia: The IFOR Experience* (Washington, D.C.: Institute of National Security Studies, CCRP, 1997), p. 9.

31. Holbrooke, *To End a War*, p. 145.
32. Ibid., p. 276.
33. Quoted in *The Wall Street Journal*, August 26, 1998.
34. Holbrooke, *To End a War*, p. 334.
35. Wentz, *Lessons from Bosnia*, p. 412.
36. Holbrooke, *To End a War*, p. 336.
37. Quoted in Ricks, *Making the Corps*, p. 184.

2

From Counterinsurgency to Peacemaking: New Applications for an Old Approach

Thomas R. Mockaitis

Sending American forces to Somalia and Bosnia produced much disquiet and debate at home. The following article identifies a principal cause of the lack of satisfactory results from those operations— the U.S. Army's reluctance to recognize important similarities between traditional counterinsurgency and "peace-keeping operations" to end civil conflicts. That reluctance, a legacy of the Viet Nam conflict, is unfortunate, because more "peace-keeping" interventions are certain to occur.

Few tasks have been more problematic for conventional forces than those at the low end of the conflict spectrum. This discomfort can clearly be seen in the evolution of terms used to describe such tasks. "Counterinsurgency" gave way to "low-intensity conflict," which yielded to "operations other than war," a catchall phrase designed to group all activities perceived as other than the military's proper role.[1] The discomfort of conventional forces with unconventional war is of course understandable. Such conflicts deprive regular armies of most of the advantages that numbers, mobility, and firepower convey upon them, tie them down in protracted engagements with imprecise goals and no definite end date, and often expose them to intense political criticism.

While all armies share distaste for unconventional wars, the U.S. military finds them particularly repugnant. American culture and the U.S. political system are not especially conducive to the con-

duct of such operations, so much so that America's armed forces
might be forgiven for eschewing them altogether were it not for a
simple, inescapable fact: Unconventional war has been the most
prevalent form of conflict in the twentieth century and is likely to
remain so into the twenty-first. A brief historical overview of U.S.
military activities reveals the persistence of unconventional involvement which, although it has gone by many names, amounts to
counterinsurgency. Despite a certain predilection to consider such
activity as exclusively tied to communist-backed wars of national
liberation, insurgency has survived the end of the Cold War. The
ethnic conflicts that have racked Somalia and the former Yugoslavia are cases in point. Peace operations in these countries have had
far more in common with counterinsurgency than with traditional
UN peace keeping, though few in the military seem willing to ac-
knowledge the similarity. Analysis of American participation in
peace operations in these two countries reveals both the persistence of some bad habits from the Cold War and some real signs of
change. They also suggest the continued relevance of counterinsurgency as a model for intervention in civil wars. America's response
to the new peace operations can only be understood in terms of its
counterinsurgency experience.

Given the lack of precision used to define conflicts at the low end
of the spectrum, it is worth considering the nature of insurgency
and counterinsurgency. Insurgency combines guerrilla warfare and
subversion to weaken and ultimately conquer a state from within.
Operating from a position of numerical and material weakness,
insurgents work within a disaffected population by winning adherents to their cause, attacking government facilities, and using terrorism to dramatize their cause. While the armed elements of an
insurgency will attack isolated military posts or small units, they
avoid combat with superior forces. With their hit-and-run tactics,
they hope to provoke government forces into committing atrocities
that further alienate the general population. In the Maoist model,
the insurgents will build a rural base area and ultimately over-
whelm the government concentrated in the cities. "Counterinsur-
geny," as the name suggests, seeks to defeat the insurgents. Success
at this difficult type of warfare requires the same combination of
military and nonmilitary means employed by the insurgents. Government forces must of course defeat the armed guerrillas, but they
should concentrate on removing the causes of unrest upon which
the insurgency feeds.[2]

While the U.S. military faced insurgencies in the first half of the
twentieth century, their exposure remained far more limited than
that of Europe's imperial powers. Indeed some of the most valuable

counterinsurgency lessons can be gleaned from British and French efforts to first maintain and later disengage from their global empires.[3] In contrast, U.S. intervention was confined to the army's war with Emilio Aguinaldo's guerrillas in the Philippines in 1899 and a series of Marine Corps incursions into the countries of Central America and the Caribbean in the 1920s and 1930s.[4] Carefully analyzed, these conflicts might have provided the basis for sound counterinsurgency doctrine, but they were too limited to offset the overwhelming conventional war mentality instilled by World War II, which seemed to demonstrate that mobility, firepower, and above all, logistics could solve any military problem. Not surprising, the U.S. military carried this conventional war mentality into the unconventional conflicts of the Cold War. Unfortunately, the Greek Civil War (1946–1949), the Korean Conflict (1950–1952), and the Huk Revolt in the Philippines (1950–1954) provided atypical examples that reinforced this mentality.[5] The denouement came in Southeast Asia.

Without digressing into a lengthy discussion of what was clearly a hybrid war involving both conventional and unconventional operations, it must be noted that Viet Nam left the U.S. military with a profound dislike of anything resembling counterinsurgency. This distaste was quickly transformed into doctrine, which asserted that primary responsibility for defeating an insurgency must rest with the host country, with the United States providing assistance and training.[6] The very term "counterinsurgency" was subsumed into the larger category of "low-intensity conflict," an unfortunate label that categorized all interventions according to the level of force employed and provided soldiers with an uncomfortable euphemism for their experiences. From the late 1970s to the end of the Cold War, the United States would provide assistance to threatened regimes, largely in the form of military training and foreign aid, both military and civilian, while eschewing any direct involvement by U.S. ground forces. This indirect approach came to be known as assistance for "Foreign Internal Defense," a term still in the military lexicon. Direct involvement in such conflicts would be covert. Consistent with this new approach, the post–Viet Nam era witnessed a dramatic increase in Special Forces, which numbered almost 21,000 by 1990, and the creation of a Special Operations Command in 1982.[7]

During the 1980s the reality of military activity generally matched the rhetoric of nonintervention. The most prominent operations of the era were the 1983 invasion of Grenada to parry an alleged communist threat and the 1989 invasion of Panama to remove its narcotics-trafficking leader General Manuel Noriega. Both actions conformed to the kind of wars the U.S. military wished to fight: short, sharp engagements with clear, attainable goals and firm political support. Under the umbrella of its new low-intensity conflict doctrine, the U.S. military assisted the government of El Salvador's counterinsurgency campaign against FMLN guerrillas while simultaneously conducting a covert insurgency against the Marxist government of Nicaragua via the contras. This indirect approach supported foreign-policy goals without American casualties, but it came at a price. The United States found itself backing some very unsavory characters who committed atrocities such as the infamous massacre at the Salvadoran village of El Mozote by the American-trained Atlacatl battalion in 1981. The School of the Americas at Fort Bragg, where most Latin American militaries train, has come under considerable criticism and demands that it be closed.

The one exception to the indirect approach occurred in Lebanon. In 1983 the Reagan administration deployed the marines to Beirut as part of a multinational force to stabilize the situation following the Israeli invasion and withdrawal of the Palestine Liberation Organization. Although technically a peace operation rather than a counterinsurgency campaign, Lebanon would reveal the similarity between such operations and counterinsurgency. The bombing of the U.S. Marine barracks with over two-hundred fatalities led to a precipitous withdrawal and underscored the traditional dislike for intervention in civil conflicts of any type.

The anticounterinsurgency mentality survived into the post–Cold-War era, hanging like a shadow over America's first midlevel regional war since Korea. The decision to halt the 1991 ground offensive against Iraq after only one-hundred hours may well have been influenced by a desire to avoid becoming embroiled in a protracted, insurgent-style conflict. Had Operation Desert Storm pushed on to Baghdad, Iraq would probably have collapsed into anarchy and civil war involving both separatist Shiah rebels in the south and Kurds in the north. U.S. forces throughout the theater might have found themselves in the position of an advanced unit entering an Iraqi village only to find themselves confronted by locals asking for everything from food and water to band-aids.

Given America's long-standing reluctance to become embroiled in civil wars and the disastrous results of those interventions, the willingness to deploy large numbers of ground troops first to Somalia and then to Bosnia requires considerable explanation. If the U.S. military had little experience in counterinsurgency, it had none in peace keeping. When Dag Hammarskjold sent the first UN emergency force to the Sinai Peninsula in 1956, he established what became the pattern for future operations. The need for impartial interposition forces in volatile parts of the world, where neither superpower trusted the other to go, determined that American and Soviet troops could not take part in peace-keeping missions. The task fell predominantly to the Nordic countries, the Canadians, the Pakistanis, and the Indians, all of whom developed considerable expertise in this highly specific type of military activity.

America's lack of experience with peace keeping, combined with its disinclination to become involved in unconventional conflict of any kind, shaped the response to Somalia and Bosnia. Analysis of these two operations reveals an initial failure to recognize in peace enforcement the same inherent dangers of counterinsurgency, and a corresponding reversion to a more limited role in order for U.S. forces to avoid those dangers. In Somalia, the United States took on a complex mission only to be dragged into the shooting war, while in Bosnia, American troops interpreted their task so narrowly as to raise serious doubts as to whether the peace that they enforced will survive their withdrawal. Both operations reveal a remarkable continuity between how the United States approaches counterinsurgency and how it approaches peace operations, without much effort to make past experience inform current practice.

Ironically, U.S. willingness to participate in UN interventions grew out of the same Gulf War experience that seemed to caution against such interventions. Following the cease-fire, Saddam Hussein moved his remaining forces north to crush a Kurdish revolt, causing thousands of Kurds to flee to inhospitable mountainous areas in northern Iraq and southeastern Turkey, where they faced death from exposure, starvation, and disease. The humanitarian crisis prompted a combined UN–Gulf War coalition operation to protect the Kurds. The international body provided observers while the coalition declared a no-fly zone over Northern Iraq and deployed 8 thousand troops to move the Iraqis out of the region and create a secure environment for the delivery of humanitarian aid.[8] Observers have been quick to point out that the mission was the first instance of the United Nations deploying a peace-keeping force under Chapter VII to intervene in the affairs of a sovereign state because those affairs threatened international peace and security.[9]

The Bush administration seemed enamored of its role as peacemaker in the "New World Order," and the military was not immune to this enthusiasm. Lieutenant Colonel John P. Abizaid's 1993 article "Lessons for Peacekeepers" captured the Gulf War confidence in the American ability to conduct peace operations:

Provide Comfort's American command and control, limited objective and flexible rules of engagement proved highly successful. . . . The fact that we were planning on staying and were serious about using force, if necessary, was never lost on the local Iraqi commanders, many of whom had the unhappy experience of meeting American firepower in the south.[10]

For all of its accomplishments, *Provide Comfort* provided a very misleading example from which to draw conclusions. Compared to the challenges of Somalia and Bosnia, clearing northern Iraq was a relatively straightforward operation. With their overwhelming superiority in air power, U.S. and coalition forces could easily compel Iraqi withdrawal in the open desert terrain. Once this goal had been achieved, the troops had little to do but maintain a buffer zone. Given the enormous prestige of the American-led alliance and the strong desire of the international community to aid the Kurds, *Provide Comfort* could hardly have failed. The operation certainly conjured up no demons from the counterinsurgency era.

On the contrary, the Kurdish experience probably encouraged intervention in Somalia the following year. After a protracted civil war to oust the dictator Said Barre, the African nation imploded. By January 1991 the political and social infrastructure had collapsed, and the country was reduced to incessant fratricide between warring factions vying for control of clan territories. The resultant disruption of communications, transport, and virtually every other national activity interfered with food production and distribution. Between November 1991 and January 1992, 300 thousand people died and 4.5 million (over half the population of the country) faced starvation.[11] The Somalis appealed to the United Nations for help, and the Security Council responded, recognizing in the situation a "threat to international peace and security" and authorizing a massive relief effort.[12] However, as the nongovernmental organizations (NGOs) quickly discovered, aid cannot be delivered in an atmosphere of anarchy. Food shipments either never made it off the docks of Mogadishu or were looted en route to distribution centers. Perceiving the need to protect food convoys, the Security Council now authorized deployment of first military observers and then five-hundred troops as part of the United Nations Operation in Somalia (UNOSOM).[13] Because the United Nations remained committed to the traditional model of peace keeping, which requires consent of the parties for any troop deployment, the soldiers were not sent for some time, and in any case there were too few soldiers to do much good. Those NGOs that delivered aid did so with the assistance of hired Somali gunmen who protected their convoys.

By the fall of 1992, the crisis had drawn international attention and produced calls for greater action. Without resources, however, Secretary-General Boutros Boutros-Ghali could do nothing. In November these resources were provided from a most unlikely source. Lame-duck President George Bush offered almost 30 thousand troops as the core of a Unified Task Force (UNITAF) under American command to safeguard humanitarian aid shipments and restore some semblance of order to war-torn Somalia. Although he would have preferred a purely UN operation, Boutros-Ghali had little choice but to accept the American offer. The Security Council approved UNITAF on December 3, giving it a Chapter VII mandate to "use all necessary means to establish as soon as possible a secure environment for humanitarian relief operations in Somalia."[14]

Other than designating the operation as enforcement rather than peace keeping, the mandate remained vague. In a letter to President Bush, Boutros-Ghali insisted that in addition to protecting humanitarian aid, UNITAF should make sure that "at least the heavy weapons of the organized factions are neutralized and brought under international control and that the irregular forces and gangs are disarmed" and that a secure environment be created "throughout Somalia."[15] Certainly the term "counterinsurgency" must have crossed the mind of someone reading this document because the United States refused to accept such a challenging and open-ended commitment. The UNITAF mission statement set more modest goals:

To secure the major air and sea ports, key installations and food distribution points, to provide open and free passage of relief supplies, provide security for convoys and relief organization operations, and assist NGOs in providing humanitarian relief under UN auspices.[16]

Once he had secured control of Mogadishu port and airport, the force commander, Marine Lieutenant General Robert Johnston, translated the mission statement into an even more precise set of guidelines, issuing four "nos" to the Somalia warlords: "no technicals [trucks mounted with crew-serviced weapons such as heavy machine guns]; no banditry; no road blocks; no visible weapons."[17] He demonstrated resolve to enforce these rules in a series of sharp fire-fights, and the clan leaders soon avoided direct confrontations with UNITAF.

By limiting its objectives to what could reasonably be attained with the available forces under the circumstances prevailing in Somalia, UNITAF not only saved millions of people from starvation but pioneered some invaluable experiments in peace operations. From past counterinsurgency experience the marines had apparently learned the limits of military power because in Somalia they used force as a means to an end, not as an end in itself. Through daily meetings with representatives of the principal factions, they apprised the Somalis of their movements with the clear warning that interference would not be tolerated. Contact continued even following incidents of conflict. This measured approach reduced the loss of life on both sides and convinced the Somalis that UNITAF had a job to do and would not take sides in the confllict. Since that job was the delivery of humanitarian aid, the military recognized the need to work closely with the numerous NGOs. The marines created a Civil–Military Operations Center (CIMOC) in Mogadishu to coordinate the activities of and exchange information between UNITAF forces and the relief agencies. Although far from perfect, this approach took an important step toward building the kind of trust from which true cooperation flows.

Although no one seems to have made direct comparisons between UNITAF and previous U.S. experience with counterinsurgency, the American-led mission to Somalia had signs of past lessons writ large upon it. From the outset, the defense establishment insisted on and obtained clear, attainable objectives. U.S. forces entered the operational environment adequately armed and with robust but reasonable rules of engagement. By refusing to take on broad, open-ended tasks such as forcibly disarming Somali factions, they avoided the kind of military actions that turn an acquiescent population into a hostile one. In short, the mission conformed to most of the guidelines for intervention prescribed by the low-intensity conflict literature of the 1980s. It conformed in one other unfortunate respect as well—it did not stay in place long enough. In the aftermath of Viet Nam, the U.S. military insisted that foreign interventions should be of limited duration. Given the mercurial nature of American public opinion, which is prone to demanding intervention and then insisting on withdrawal the minute anything goes wrong, this short-term approach is understandable. However, it hampers the ability of a military force to conduct counterinsurgency or peace operations effectively, since the belligerents can simply wait the United States out.

Perhaps recognizing that the situation in Somalia remained precarious but not wishing to continue its deployment, the United States opted for a hybrid solution that combined the worst elements of a UN and a purely American-led operation. UNITAF would hand the mission over to a newly created UN operation, dubbed UNOSOM II, but would maintain a significant contribution to the mission: 3,000 support and 1,150 combat troops in a rapid reaction force.

Because of the American refusal to place its soldiers under UN or any other command, the rapid reaction force would be led by Major General Thomas Montgomery, who would also serve as deputy force commander under Turkish General Cevik Bir. As further insurance, the United States secured the appointment of retired Admiral Jonathan Howe as special representative to Somalia and, therefore, head of UNOSOM II.[18]

Far from ensuring U.S. control of the mission, these complex arrangements not only violated the unity of command that had helped make UNITAF successful but actually reduced U.S. flexibility. Under the new arrangements the United Nations would have primary responsibility for planning and implementation, but U.S. forces would be implicated in any decisions that UNOSOM II made. They would also have the capacity to act outside the UN chain of command, and as events played out, the temptation to do so would prove irresistible.

The situation began to deteriorate even before the U.S. troops withdrew. Marines on the streets of Mogadishu noticed that guns which had been absent for months started to reappear as the date for transfering responsibility for the mission back to the United Nations approached. The Somalis strongly disliked Boutros-Ghali, who as foreign minister of Egypt during the Barre era was suspected of supporting the dictator. The clan leaders may also have been aware that Boutros-Ghali would push the disarmament issue as the Americans had not. He made clear his intention of doing so in his report to the Security Council preparatory to the launching of UNOSOM II. While acknowledging the contribution made by UNITAF, the Secretary-General noted that a secure environment had to be achieved. He insisted that in addition to monitoring cease-fires and delivering humanitarian aid, the UN troops must also "maintain control of heavy weapons . . . [and] seize small arms of all unauthorized armed elements."[19]

As the British had learned in Palestine, disarming a hostile population is not only impossible but needlessly provocative. The trick of both counterinsurgency and peace operations is to provide positive inducements to get people to turn in their weapons, which they will only do when the environment is sufficiently secure. To forceably disarm the belligerents when such security does not exist is to court disaster, and UNITAF had wisely refused to attempt it despite the urging of Boutros-Ghali.

Ironically, the Secretary-General now proposed to implement his disarmament policy with a much smaller and weaker force. While UNITAF had deployed 38 thousand troops to control about 40 percent of Somalia, UNOSOM II would have only 20 thousand to implement a much more dangerous mandate throughout the entire country. The force would also be more heterogeneous and therefore harder to control. The twenty-one troop-contributing countries provided units of varying quality, many of whom did not have interoperability, and most of whom consulted their home countries about UN orders. These factors complicated command and control. As one observer noted,

The sheer size of the headquarters communications and control components became amazing. Any national loop involved translators, dedicated communications systems, and liaison officers, all of whom were required to ensure that tasking and reporting were clearly understood. These people, in turn, required logistic support, space, communications, and information management resources.[20]

Reduced troop strength, cumbersome command and control, an independent U.S. contingent, and stiffening Somali resistance did not bode well for implementing a more vigorous mandate. Nonetheless the Secretary-General got his way, and UNOSOM II was authorized under Chapter VII.[21] The troops pushed the envelope on the weapons issue, and the denouement was not long in coming. Within a month of UNOSOM II's deployment the forces of General Mohamed Farrah Aideed slaughtered 25 Pakistani peacekeepers and wounded 57 others, including 3 Americans from the Rapid Reaction force, sent in to bail out the peacekeepers. The UN troops had gone to inspect an arms depot at Radio Mogadishu without giving the Somalis adequate warning, thus creating the plausible suspicion that they had come to seize the station itself.[22]

Rather than produce a serious reappraisal of the UNOSOM II mandate, the fifth of June incident led to calls from the Security Council for sterner measures against General Aideed. The council duly passed an enabling resolution that not only reiterated the right to use force but added this phrase: "including against those responsible for publicly inciting such attacks, to establish effective authority of UNOSOM II throughout Somalia, including to secure the investigation of their actions and their arrest and detention for prosecution."[23] Only the United States had the firepower to implement such stern action, but in doing so they would repeat the mistakes of Viet Nam and Lebanon. Nonetheless, American helicopter gunships swooped in over south Mogadishu while ground troops seized the radio station in an operation lasting from June 12 to 14. Three days later they launched a series of attacks against Aideed's supply depots, which lasted until June 25.

These military actions had several unfortunate consequences. They killed a lot of innocent Somalis, turning an acquiescent populace into an actively hostile one. Because of this hostility, the NGOs had to be moved into secure areas for their own protection, breaking a vital link with the populace. The raids also replaced the United Nations with the United States as the most likely target for Somali violence. All these consequences might have been lessened, however, if only UNOSOM II had followed the example of UNITAF. Having hit the gunmen hard, they should have negotiated. Instead the United Nations persisted in turning the entire mission into a witch hunt for Aideed. This approach of course led to increased attacks on UN personnel in general and Americans in particular.

These attacks, coupled with the continued UN pressure to capture Aideed, produced one of the most tragic incidents of the conflict: the raid of October 1993. Following a series of incidents involving remote-controlled mines that killed and wounded U.S. service personnel throughout August, the Clinton administration agreed to a raid by Delta Force commandos and army rangers to capture Aideed. Many experienced soldiers pointed out that without precise intelligence, such a raid would be unlikely to succeed, a point dramatized on August 30 when the strike team captured an empty warehouse that was supposed to have been a headquarters. Any student of counterinsurgency would have drawn the same conclusion. Planners of the mission would have done well to read British General Frank Kitson's classic work, *Low-Intensity Operations*, in which he observed that defeating insurgents "consists very largely in finding them."[24]

This lack of precise information on Aideed's whereabouts notwithstanding, the Clinton administration gave the go-ahead for a raid at an available opportunity. That opportunity came on October 3, when 142 commandos supported by helicopters struck at the clan leader's headquarters in south Mogadishu. The strike went off without a hitch with the force capturing 25 of Aideed's associates (though not the general himself). In the ensuing withdrawl, however, a Blackhawk helicopter crashed. Not wishing to leave the crew to the mercy of Somalis, the Rangers moved in to rescue them. In the ensuing firefight, 18 Americans and over 300 Somalis died. Because the U.S. forces in Somalia lacked tanks and armored personnel carriers, they had to contact the UN headquarters for these vehicles. Since the United States had not notified the headquarters of the raid, the UN commanders were caught unaware. The resultant delay contributed to the fatalities.

The October 3 incident spelled the beginning of the end for UNOSOM II and accelerated U.S. disillusionment with peace operations. President Clinton announced that U.S. forces would be withdrawn in December, and several other nations followed suit. With reduced manpower and dwindling commitment to the mission, the Security Council retreated to a Chapter VI mandate, and UNOSOM II bided its time for another year. The Somalia episode ended optimistic discussion of a "New World Order." The mission cast a long and tragic shadow over other conflicts in which the United States could have played a more prominent role. When in April 1994 the UN commander in Rwanda, Canadian General Romeo Delaire, requested a small force of 5 thousand soldiers to stop the killing, no one would supply them. For want of a single infantry brigade, genocide occurred. Ironically, a mission like UNITAF could have worked wonders in Rwanda, but having found in peace enforcement something very reminiscent of counterinsurgency, the United States remembered its historic dislike of such missions. The experience of Somalia would place severe limits on the timing and nature of the U.S. intervention in the former Yugoslavia.

American reluctance to commit troops to the worsening situation in the Balkans was not a direct result of either the Somalia debacle or fear of embroilment in a civil war, though both contributed to this hesitancy. Just as Somalia was to have been the United Nations's New World Order debut, former Yugoslavia presented the new Europe with a chance to go it alone without the aid of its powerful NATO ally. European critics of U.S. policy in the Balkans forget that both the European Union and the Committee for Security and Cooperation in Europe had asked the United States to stay out.[25] Still, the physical and human terrain of the Balkans must have given those with counterinsurgency experience pause, for here was an intervention that threatened to become a protracted, desultory conflict with no clear objectives or end states. In the immediate aftermath of the Gulf War, Chairman of the Joint Chiefs of Staff Colin Powell spoke for the U.S. military: Asked about the possibility of a U.S. deployment in the former Yugoslavia, he observed, "We do deserts; we don't do mountains."

As the conflict spread from Croatia to Bosnia, accompanied by horrific tales of rape and murder, the United States could not escape the same "CNN factor" that had drawn it into Somalia. The UNPROFOR mandate changed from protecting humanitarian aid deliveries to defending safe areas from Bosnian Serbs, who by the summer of 1992 were undeniably the aggressors. The multinational force soon consisted of more than 40 thousand troops, lightly armed and operating under a Chapter VI peace-keeping mandate even though there was no peace to keep. During the first three years of the mission, the United States participated in a manner consistent with its noninterventionist policy of the 1980s. American ships patrolled the Adriatic as part of Operation Sharp Guard to prevent contraband military supplies from reaching the belligerents while American warplanes kept the skies over Bosnia clear of Serb aircraft in Operation Deny Flight and occasionally conducted strikes when Serb tanks and artillery fired from within the heavy-weapons exclusion zones around the safe areas. Such participation presented very little risk of casualties, but also had little impact on the war.

As the situation in Bosnia deteriorated during the fall of 1994 and the winter of 1995, the United States called for more vigorous air action against the Serbs. The European allies pointed out that their soldiers and not Americans would become targets for retaliation if bombing occurred. Their fears proved justified in May 1995 when Bosnian Serb forces detained hundreds of peacekeepers, using some as human shields. It became increasingly clear that UNPROFOR would have to upgrade to an enforcement mission with adequate strength and firepower or be withdrawn altogether. The United States would commit ground troops to an expanded mission only if certain conditions were met:

1. a clear definition of command and control of the operation.
2. the command entrusted to NATO.
3. a definite timetable, allowing the United States to determine the duration of its participation.
4. a clear political and military strategy.
5. an expression of support from American Congress.
6. knowledge of what the operation would cost and assurance that other countries would "do their bit."[26]

The operative word was "clear," as it had been for all interventions since Viet Nam.

While the United Nations and NATO contemplated contingencies, events once again got ahead of the planners in Brussels and New York. In July, Bosnian Serbs overran the safe areas of Zepa and Srebrenica, massacring thousands of Bosnian men in the worst example of ethnic cleansing thus far. U.S. satellite photos identified mass graves, and the United Nations provided further evidence of extensive human rights violations.[27] The United States and its NATO allies determined that any further provocation must be met with a strong and asymmetrical response. In preparation for extensive airstrikes, UNPROFOR pulled its units out of exposed positions. Meanwhile a rearmed and American-trained Croat army recaptured the Krajina in early August, producing yet another exodus of refugees. On August 28, the anticipated provoking incident occurred in Bosnia when five mortar rounds struck the Sarajevo marketplace, killing thirty-seven people. In retaliation the United States and its NATO allies launched a month of airstrikes while the artillery of the NATO Rapid Reaction force on Mt. Igman established dominance around Sarajevo. Under cover of this bombardment, the Bosnian Fifth Army Corps advanced out the Bihac pocket, driving the Serbs back toward Banja Luka. Faced with overwhelming force, the Serbs agreed on October 5 to a UN-brokered cease-fire that went into effect on October 12. The warring factions met in Dayton, Ohio in November to draw up a peace plan.

The signing of the Dayton Accords in Paris a month later made UNPROFOR obsolete and began a new period of extensive U.S. commitment to Bosnia. The Security Council passed a resolution approving the creation of a multinational Implementation Force with a Chapter VII mandate.[28] The U.S. decision to commit 20 thousand troops to IFOR carried with it the risk of protracted involvement in civil conflict. While the demonstration of overwhelming NATO military power had cowed the Serbs into submission, IFOR faced considerable risk of having to carry out difficult internal operations if it chose to forcibly implement all provisions of the Dayton Accords. The framework agreement insisted on free and fair elections, the return of over 2 million refugees, and the apprehension of indicted war criminals.[29] Reminiscent of counterinsurgency plans that require rebuilding a country from within, this framework would require a comprehensive, unified effort by IFOR, the United Nations, the European Union, the Committee for Security and Cooperation in Europe, and a host of NGOs. The repatriation of refugees and apprehension of war criminals could only be accomplished with the threat and probably the application of force. Both the Framework Agreement and the UN enabling resolution authorized IFOR to use such force "to help create secure conditions for the conduct by others of other tasks associated with the peace settlement."[30] However, the mandate was sufficiently vague as to allow considerable room for interpretation. Rather than risk confrontation, IFOR generally avoided implementing the most difficult clauses of the accord. Commenting on the accomplishments of the mission, soldiers noted, as they did at the Florence meeting in the summer of 1996, that although the military side of the operation was going well, the civilian side was not—a claim tantamount to saying, "We don't have to worry, the leak is in the other end of the boat."

Responding in a manner highly consistent with historical experience, U.S. forces defined their role in the narrowest terms, insisting that their job was to patrol the zone of separation along the "inter-entity boundary" and to render support services with the cooperation of local authorities. Internal security within the entities themselves, including guaranteeing the security of returning refugees, would be the responsibility of each entity and the UN police monitors. Thus the Serbs were allowed to burn down Sarajevo suburbs while IFOR troops watched. NATO soldiers have also generally declined to apprehend war criminals, although one was captured and another killed by British special forces in the summer of 1997. This cautious approach prevented any serious infringement of the cease-fire during IFOR's first twelve months and has allowed its continued deployment at reduced strength and under a new name, the Stabilization Force (SFOR). While sticking to a limited task prevents American casualties, it also reduced the likelihood that the Dayton Peace Accord would survive the final troop withdrawals scheduled for July 1998. At the very least, failure to arrest indicted war criminals and to repatriate refugees demonstrates that ethnic cleansing has worked.

While the future of UN peace operations, and the U.S. involvement in them, remains uncertain, some tentative conclusions may be drawn from the experience of the past five years. To begin with, peace operations to end civil conflict have far more in common with counterinsurgency than they do with traditional UN peace keeping. Ironically, U.S. Army doctrine recognizes this fact without making the salient comparison. The latest peace-keeping manual notes that

Peace operations may often take place in environments that are less well-defined than in war. The identity of belligerents may be uncertain and the relationship between a specific operation and a campaign plan may be less clear than would normally be the case in combat. . . . Such operations often do not involve large professional armies or even organized groups. . . . Instead loosely organized groups of irregulars, terrorists, or other conflicting segments of a population may predominate. These segments will attempt to capitalize on perceptions of disenfranchisement or disaffection within the population.[31]

The peace-keeping manual goes on to note the primacy of civil action over military action and concludes that "overemphasis on firepower may be counterproductive."[32] This description reads like a classic definition of counterinsurgency from any manual written during the Cold War. However, the army still avoids any direct comparison between the two types of conflict, continuing to relegate counterinsurgency to a different publication under the heading "Aid to Foreign Internal Defense."

Failure to make a clear comparison between counterinsurgency and peace operations has prevented the United States from applying past lessons to current problems. The American military recognizes a similarity between Somalia and Bosnia on the one hand and its experience of counterinsurgency on the other without considering how the experience of the one might inform conduct of the other. In Somalia, UNITAF pursued a comprehensive strategy, but for too short a time, while UNSOM II succumbed to the old reliance on firepower to solve any problem. In Bosnia, the United States stayed the course for a lengthy period but perhaps interpreted its mission too narrowly for success. This inconsistency reflects a military in transition struggling to adapt past experience to changed circumstances within limits set by American politics and society.

Post–Cold-War conditions virtually guarantee the continued likelihood of civil conflicts occurring in areas of concern to the United States and the corresponding need for an intervention capability. The recent *Quadrennial Review* acknowledges this reality. While concluding that the cornerstone of U.S. strategy for the next decade must be the ability to fight simultaneously two major theater wars, the *Review* also recognized the need to conduct "Small Scale Contingency Operations," such as peace keeping and peace enforcement.[33] In preparing for such operations, the U.S. military could benefit from its own counterinsurgency experience and that of other nations, which might provide a suitable model for effective intervention in a variety of civil conflicts. The ancient Roman adage, "Let those who wish for peace prepare for war," might be adapted for the contemporary world to read "Let those who wish for peace prepare for peace keeping."

NOTES

1. Thomas R. Mockaitis, "Unconventional War," in *America's Armed Forces: A Handbook of Current and Future Capabilities*, ed. Sam Sarkesian (Westport, Conn.: Greenwood Press, 1996), p. 387.

2. Ibid., pp. 388–389.

3. There is an extensive and still growing body of literature on this subject. See, for example, Charles Townshend, *Britain's Civil Wars: Counterinsurgency in the Twentieth Century* (New York: St. Martin's Press, 1986); Thomas R. Mockaitis, *British Counterinsurgency, 1919 to 1960* (New York: St. Martin's Press, 1990); and *British Counterinsurgency in the Post-Imperial Era* (New York: St. Martin's Press, 1995).

4. See Brian McAllister Linn, *The U.S. Army and Counterinsurgency in the Philippine War, 1899–1902* (Chapel Hill: University of North Carolina Press, 1989). With the exception of the Coco Patrol in Nicaragua, marine interventions in Latin America have received considerably less attention.

5. Larry Cable, *Conflict of Myths: The Development of American Counterinsurgency Doctrine and the Vietnam War* (New York: New York University Press, 1986), pp. 38–41, 62–68.

6. Rod Paschal, "Low-Intensity Conflict Doctrine: Who Needs It?" *Parameters* 15, no. 3 (Autumn 1985): 42.

7. Michael McClintock, *Instruments of Statecraft: U.S. Guerrilla Warfare, Counter-Insurgency and Counter-Terrorism, 1940–1990* (New York: Pantheon Books, 1992).

8. Michael M. Gunter, "The Kurdish Peacekeeping Operation in Northern Iraq," in *Peacekeeping and the Challenge of Civil Conflict Resolution*, ed. David Charters (Fredericton: Centre for Conflict Studies, University of New Brunswick, 1994), p. 107.

9. Ibid. Although technically correct, this conclusion overlooks the operation in the Congo, which although launched under Chapter VI, took on an enforcement role.

10. John P. Abizaid, "Lessons for Peacekeepers," *Military Review* 73 (March 1993): 15–16, 19.

11. *United Nations Peacekeeping*, United Nations Department of Public Information, DPI/1306/Rev.3-June 1994-7M, p. 98.

12. Security Council Resolution, UN document, S/RES/733, 23 January 1992.

13. Security Council Resolution, UN document, S/RES/751, 24 April 1992.

14. Security Council Resolution, UN document, S/RES/794, 3 December 1992.

15. "Letter Dated 8 December 1992 from the Secretary-General to President Bush of the United States Discussing the Establishment of a Secure Environment in Somalia and the Need for Continuous Consultations," in *The United Nations in Somalia, United Nations Blue Book Series, VII* (New York: UN Department of Public Information, 1996), pp. 216–217.

16. UNITAF mission statement, quoted in Kenneth Allard, *Somalia Operations: Lessons Learned* (Washington, D.C.: National Defense University Press, 1995), p. 16.

17. Report on Activities of UNITAF, UN document, S/24976, 17 December 1992, p. 36.

18. For a detailed discussion of these command and control arrangements and the problems inherent in them, see Richard Hayes, *Command Arrangements for Peace Operations* (Washington, D.C.: National Defense University, 1995).

19. Further Report of the Secretary-General Submitted Pursuant of Paragraphs 18 and 19 of Resolution 794 1992, UN document, S/25354, 3 March 1993, p. 13.

20. Hayes, *Command Arrangements*, p. 50.

21. Security Council Resolution, UN document, S/RES/814, 26 March 1993.

22. Details of the mission from *Report of the Commission of Inquiry Established Pursuant to Resolution 885 (1993) to Investigate Armed Attacks on UNOSOM II*, UN document, S/1994/653, 1 June 1994.

23. Security Council Resolution, UN document, S/RES/837, 6 June 1993.

24. Frank Kitson, *Low-Intensity Operations: Subversion, Insurgency and Peacekeeping* (London: Faber and Faber, 1971), p. 65.

25. Spyros Economides and Paul Taylor, "Former Yugoslavia," in *The New Interventionism 1991–1994: United Nations Experience in Cambodia, Former Yugoslavia, and Somalia*, ed. James Mayall (Cambridge: Cambridge University Press, 1996), p. 65.

26. Dick A. Leurdijk, *The United Nations and NATO in Former Yugoslavia, 1991–1996* (The Netherlands Atlantic Commission, 1996), p. 90.

27. Report of the Secretary-General, UN document, S/1995/755, 30 August 1995.

28. Security Council Resolution, UN document, S/RES/1031, 15 December 1995.

29. General Framework Agreement for Peace in Bosnia Herzegovina, signed in Paris, 14 December 1995.

30. The Framework Agreement, cited in Leurdijk, *United Nations and NATO*, p. 124.

31. *FM 100–23: Peace Operations* (Washington, D.C.: Headquarters, Department of the Army, 16 April 1994), iii.

32. Ibid.

33. William Cohen, "Report of the Quadrennial Review," http:\\www.defenselink.mil\PUBS\QDR.

3

Can Traditional UN Peace Keeping Be Saved?

Frederick H. Fleitz, Jr.

Much controversy has surrounded recent UN peace-keeping missions, in large part because they have been greatly expanded from their intended characteristics—to include near-consensus support and minimum use of lethal force. Some peace-keeping missions have actually been "peace enforcing," that is, involving real combat. American soldiers in UN missions may be especially at risk from violent groups who seek media coverage.

• • •

United Nations peacekeeping missions have hit hard times. Since the end of the Cold War, the use of lightly armed soldiers to police cease-fires or monitor elections has given way to ambitious attempts to impose peace on hostile forces determined to keep fighting, as in Somalia and Bosnia. . . . There should be a shift back toward more limited objectives like policing cease-fires. . . . UN peacekeeping does what it can do very well. It makes no sense to continue eroding its credibility by asking it to do what it cannot.
The New York Times, Editorial, January 12, 1995

By early 1995, due to a string of peace-keeping failures in Somalia, Yugoslavia, and Rwanda, the world began to reassess the much-publicized effort to use new types of UN-collective action to address post–Cold War global conflicts.[1] These setbacks were the result of an attempt to transform UN peace keeping—a conflict resolution mechanism designed to address a narrow range of conflicts during the Cold War—into a conflict resolution mechanism that could resolve a wider range of conflicts by expanding its mandate, rules of engagement, and armament. In effect, the concept of peace keeping was expanded considerably beyond its previous province of noncoercive operations deployed with the consent of warring parties to operations that were half traditional peace keeping and half UN warfare. The failure of the these new operations—hereafter referred to as "expanded peace keeping"—damaged the United Nations as well as traditional peace keeping. Indeed, while its accomplishments and capabilities were modest, "traditional" peace keeping's ability to monitor truces and cease-fires helped end several wars, lower regional tensions, and strengthen U.S. allies.

While the debate over the future of UN peace keeping is still unsettled, evidence and experience suggests that expanded peace keeping is a flawed approach to conflict resolution, which has shown little ability to promote international security, places international troops—especially U.S. troops—at unnecessary risk, and threatens to discredit the fairly successful traditional peace-keeping model.

MULTILATERAL CONFLICT-RESOLUTION EFFORTS: COLD-WAR MODELS

Peace Keeping

Peace keeping is a unique conflict-resolution mechanism invented by UN Secretary-General Dag Hammarskjold and Canadian UN Ambassador Lester Pearson when they proposed the UN Emergency Force (UNEF) to help end the 1956 Suez War.[2] Usually deployed by the United Nations, the UNEF peace-keeping model showed a moderate ability to promote international security, advance U.S. interests, and maintain friendly governments. Over time, peace keeping was generally understood to include unarmed military observers, such as the UN Truce Supervision Organization (UNTSO), deployed to Palestine in 1948, as well as forces like UNEF, which were lightly armed and permitted to use military force in self-defense. While the precise definition of peace keeping has been long debated, the United Nations came up with one of the most widely used formulations in 1990:

As the United Nations practice has evolved over the years, a peacekeeping operation has come to be defined as an operation involving military personnel, but without enforcement powers, undertaken by the United Nations to help maintain or restore international peace and security in areas of conflict. These operations are voluntary and are based on consent and cooperation. While they involve the use of military personnel, they achieve their objectives not by force of arms, thus contrasting them with the "enforcement action" of the United Nations.[3]

Peace keeping was the result of both the superpower conflict and the tenacity of the nation–state system. The superpower conflict had frozen the UN Security Council, which has primary responsibility for addressing threats to international peace and security under the UN Charter. However, the UN's collective security ideals also had suffered due to the refusal of UN members to cede sovereignty to the United Nations by placing some of their military forces at the disposal of the Security Council, as called for by Articles 43 and 45 of the UN Charter, or by permitting the activation of the UN Military Staff Committee, as stipulated in Article 47.[4]

UN peace keeping's legal basis was designed to skirt the Security Council permanent member veto and the restrictions of the UN Charter. Chapter VII of the charter, "Action with Respect to Threats to the Peace, Breaches of the Peace, and Acts of Aggression," might appear to be the logical legal basis for peace keeping. But this was not possible, since a Chapter VII mandate would have implied collective action to compel parties engaged in a dispute to cease hostilities and comply with Security Council decisions, something neither the superpowers nor state-parties to disputes would agree to. The United Nations is forbidden by Chapter I, Article 2 of the charter from intervening in domestic matters *except* under Chapter VII.[5] To avoid this problem, UN Secretary-General Dag Hammarskjold argued that peace keeping drew its legal basis from several areas of the UN Charter, but mainly from a notional "Chapter 6 1/2."[6] Hammarskjold apparently did not believe that peace keeping could be properly termed a Chapter VI activity (nonmilitary mediation and negotiation) and once said, "Peacekeeping is not a job for soldiers, but only soldiers can do it."[7] While Hammarskjold's "Chapter 6½" interpretation gained some supporters, it remained controversial and was debated for decades. For example, Secretary-General U Thant noted in a speech in 1970 that the United Nations was still sharply divided over the specific provisions (see Table 3.1) of the UN Charter under which peace-keeping missions were undertaken.[8] In 1990, UN Secretary-General Boutros-Ghali seemed to lean toward Hammarskjold's interpretation when he said that "peacekeeping is a missing link between Chapters VI and VII."[9]

Despite a vague definition and a questionable legal basis, the traditional UN peace-keeping model pioneered by Hammarskjold

Table 3.1
Traditional Peace-Keeping Missions (Data as of March 13, 1998)

	Start/End Dates	Authorized Size	Total Cost ($ millions)
UNMOGIP (India-Pakistan)	1948–present	44	$105
UNTSO (Palestine)	1948–present	270	491
UNEFI (Sinai/Gaza Strip)	1956–1967	6,073	214
UNOGIL (Lebanon)	1958	591	4
ONUC (Congo)	1960–1964	19,828	400
UNSF (W. New Guinea)	1962–1963	1,576[a]	
UNYOM (Yemen)	1963–1964	189	2
UNFICYP (Cyprus)	1964–present	1,257	840
UNIPOM (India/Pakistan)	1965–1966	96	2
UNEFII (Sinai/Suez)	1973–1979	6,973	446
UNDOF(GolanHeights)	1974–present	1,049	662
UNIFIL (Lebanon)	1978–present	5,200	2,661
MFO(Sinai)[b]	1982–present	2,500	650
UNIIMOG (Iran/Iraq)	1988–1991	399	190
UNGOMAP (Afghanisan/Pakistan)	1988–1990	50	14
UNTAG (Namibia)	1989–1990	7,500	400
UNAVEMI (Angola)	1989–1991	70	16
ONUCA (Central America)	1989–1991	1,098	89
ONUSAL (El Salvador)	1991–1995	300	107
MINURSO (W. Sahara)	1991–present	1,700	272
ONUMOZ (Mozambique)	1992–1995	7,100	520
UNASOG (Libya/Chad)	1994	9	67

Source: UN Department of Peacekeeping Operations, UN Peacekeeping Internet Homepage, http://www.un.org/Depts/dpko/, U.S. General Accounting Office.

[a]The governments of The Netherlands and Indonesia bore the full costs of this operation.
[b]Not a UN operation.

became a coherent conflict-resolution doctrine during the Cold War. Nations the world over knew what peace keeping was and understood its limitations. They also understood the minimum conditions necessary for a peace-keeping mission to function. While scores of experts over the last forty years have postulated a torrent of conditions that purportedly need to be present for a peace-keeping mission to succeed, the conditions devised by James H. Allen, a former Canadian peacekeeper, are perhaps the most useful. Allen lists three prerequisites for peace-keeping efforts: acceptance, impartiality, and minimum use of force.[10]

Acceptance means that parties to a dispute consent to the deployment of a peace-keeping force and agree to cooperate with it. Parties to a dispute must desire a peace-keeping presence to help reduce tensions and agree to peace negotiations; that is, there must be a peace to be kept. The acceptance requirement reflects the crucial distinction of peace keeping from peace enforcement: Peace-keeping missions are not occupation forces or military interventions. They recognize the sovereign rights of state-parties to disputes. Because peace keepers are sent with the consent of warring parties, they must leave if a party to a dispute withdraws its consent.[11]

Acceptance is crucial to the safety of peace keepers. Warring parties agree to accept a peace-keeping force because it does not pose a military threat. Peace keepers are thus lightly armed or unarmed and could easily be captured or killed by former warring parties. But because peace keepers are deployed with the acceptance of former warring parties, they are generally not in danger. This arrangement worked remarkably well during the Cold War, during which peace-keeping casualties were relatively low.

Impartiality refers to the need to use peace-keeping troops that are acceptable to warring parties and that have no stake in their dispute. Impartiality includes fair, unbiased treatment of parties to a dispute, openness, and the prompt investigation of complaints. Impartiality is crucial to promoting mutual trust and decreasing tensions. Rod Paschall, former head of the U.S. Military History Institute and drafter of the first peace-keeping doctrine for U.S. armed forces, gives a good description of how impartial peace keepers can lower tensions: "If a peacekeeper's conduct is impeccable and recognized as impartial, former warring parties will begin to register written or verbal protests about violations with peacekeepers rather than making their point with bullets or shells fired on an enemy.[12]

Confusing the impartiality factor is the erroneous assertion that UN peace keeping was invented *solely* to keep the superpowers out of regional conflicts. While there is no doubt that the United States and the Soviet Union were excluded from peace-keeping missions during the Cold War for this reason, many other states considered biased or politically sensitive also were excluded from Cold War peace-keeping efforts, including Bulgaria, Cuba, Israel, Romania, South Korea, Spain, Germany, and Japan.[13] Moreover, it is clear that when UN Secretary-General Dag Hammarskjold drew up rules for UNEF I in 1956, he wanted to ensure that all UNEF participants were neutral and acceptable to warring parties, and he was just as insistent in excluding France and Britain from UNEF as he was the Soviet Union and the United States.[14] Renowned UN scholar Inis L. Claude, Jr. suggested in 1994 that this principle still has merit when he wrote that peace-keeping contingents should be "voluntarily supplied by states acceptable to the parties as sufficiently evenhanded to be trustworthy."[15]

John R. Bolton, assistant secretary of state for international organizations during the Bush administration, is a vocal proponent of this view, arguing that a Cold-War "Perm Five Convention"—an informal agreement among the Security Council's veto members to avoid participating in peace-keeping missions—was a key to peace-keeping successes during the Cold War because it recognized that great powers could never be viewed as truly disinterested and neutral in peace-keeping situations. He has argued that the October 1993 tragedy in Somalia, when eighteen U.S. troops supporting the UNOSOM II peace-keeping mission were killed in an ambush, proves that the Perm Five Convention is still valid today.[16] Canadian General Lewis MacKenzie, former commander of the UN Protection Force in Yugoslavia, goes further, arguing that the risk to U.S. peace keepers is so severe that U.S. combat troops should be kept out of peace-keeping operations for their own safety. He has stated "You don't get your picture on the cover of *Newsweek* killing Canadians. You've got to kill Americans."[17]

U.S. experiences in Lebanon, Somalia, and Bosnia illustrate the seriousness of this problem. On February 17, 1988, Lieutenant Colonel William R. Higgins, USMC, was kidnapped, tortured, and executed by Lebanese terrorists while participating in a UN Truce Supervision Organization mission in southern Lebanon. The Higgins tragedy stunned U.S. policy makers, most of whom were not aware that lightly armed American soldiers were being sent on patrols in southern Lebanon. The October 3, 1993 killing of eighteen U.S. Army Rangers supporting the second UN Operation in Somalia (UNOSOM II) had a similar effect and led to the withdrawal of American troops and the subsequent collapse of the operation. The net effect on U.S. foreign policy of the Higgins and UNOSOM II tragedies cannot be underestimated and will likely continue to influence U.S. policy makers for many years to come.

Minimum use of force reflects the fact that peace-keeping forces are not sent to compel parties to a dispute to work toward peace—the forces are present to facilitate a peace settlement and usually to help maintain a truce. Peace keepers are permitted to use force in self-defense, although in the case of sniper fire, they historically avoid engagement if possible for fear of being seen by parties in a dispute as a combatant—such a development would undermine the fragile trust peace-keeping forces must maintain to remain viable. While a peace-keeping force could not defend itself against a determined attack by a nation–state army, such an attack has never occurred. Nor is this likely; it would constitute an attack on the United Nations and result in international condemnation and possible massive retaliation by UN members. It is for this reason that a peace-keeping force sometimes is described as a symbolic international presence.

A Useful but Limited Tool

There is no doubt that UN peace keeping has been a valuable conflict resolution mechanism during the Cold War. As trusted and neutral arbiters, UN peace keepers played a crucial role in reducing tensions in numerous conflicts around the world. Peace keeping advanced U.S. interests on many occasions during the Cold War, especially in the Middle East, where six operations deployed between 1948 and 1978 promoted the security of Israel, one of America's closest allies. Cold-War model peace-keeping efforts have aided other important U.S. allies, such as Turkey, Greece, Pakistan, and Morocco. Table 3.2 illustrates how several long-standing peace-keeping operations have benefited U.S. interests.

However, despite its accomplishments, peace keeping has major weaknesses, which define the limits of its usefulness in promoting international security. The most important is its inability to bring about negotiated settlements to disputes. The capabilities of peace-keeping forces also are at the mercy of a bloated, corrupt UN system.

Perpetual Holding Actions

Meeting the minimum conditions for a peace-keeping operation does not necessarily mean the operation will achieve its ultimate purpose—bringing about a final negotiated solution to an international conflict. By the mid-1960s, it became apparent that peace-keeping operations tended to remove the impetus for parties in a dispute to resolve their conflicts; the peace-keeping force itself became the solution. As a result, few UN peace-keeping operations have ever completely fulfilled their mandates. Five out of thirteen peace-keeping forces in existence in January 1993 had been deployed fourteen years or more. Two were first deployed in the 1940s.

This state of affairs was not necessarily a bad outcome, at least during the Cold War. UN members tolerated the inability of peace-keeping forces to bring about negotiated solutions because deploying these operations indefinitely was better than war, and they were inexpensive and few in number. Some observers viewed peace-keeping operations as a way to prevent conflict from breaking out between two unfriendly states, until the time was ripe to solve their dispute.

UN Mismanagement, Bureaucracy, and Fraud

UN peace keeping's greatest weakness has been the UN system, one of the world's most backward and corrupt bureaucracies. Due to centralization, overstaffing, cronyism, featherbedding, and na-

Table 3.2
U.S. Foreign Policy Interests Served by Long-Standing Peace-Keeping Operations

Operation (Year first deployed)	U.S. Interests Served
UNTSO (1948) (Palestine)	• Contributes to Middle East stability by helping to reduce tensions between Israel and its neighbors. • Operates in areas of southern Lebanon where UNIFIL is not deployed. • Implements the remaining 1949 Arab–Israeli armistice agreements.
UNMOGIP (1948) (India/Pakistan)	• Contributes to stability in South Asia by helping to reduce tensions between India and Pakistan. • Demonstrates continued UN support for settling the Kashmir question by peaceful means.
UNFICYP (1964) (Cyprus)	• Contributes to stability in southern Europe by helping to prevent civil war on Cyprus and hostilities between Turkey and Greece. • Withdrawing UNFICYP would increase tensions and could spark a costly regional war. • Encourages continued diplomatic efforts to reunify Cyprus by peaceful means.
UNIFIL (1978) (Lebanon)	• Contributes to Middle East stability by addressing the humanitarian crisis. in southern Lebanon. • Withdrawing UNIFIL would be likely to increase the influence in southern Lebanon of Hizbollah, an Iranian-supported terrorist group.
UNIKOM (1991) (Iraq–Kuwait)	• Contributes to stability in the Persian Gulf by helping to maintain the integrity of the Iraq–Kuwait border. • Helps safeguard international access to the Persian Gulf. • Underscores the international community's determination to block any outlet for Saddam Hussein's expansionist ambitions.
MINURSO (1991) (Western Sahara)	• Contributes to stability in North Africa by preventing a return to hostilities in Western Sahara that could involve Algeria and Morocco. • Supports Morocco, a longtime U.S. friend and ally.

Source: Adapted from U.S. General Accounting Office, *UN Peacekeeping: Status of Long-Standing Operations and U.S. Interests in Supporting Them*, GAO/NSIAD-97-59 (Washington, D.C.: U.S. Government Printing Office, April 1997), p. 26.

tional quotas on hiring and assigning contracts, UN peace-keeping logistical planning and procurement wastes millions of dollars every year and has seriously hindered most Cold-War peace-keeping missions. In response to these problems, savvy peace-keeping commanders in the field quickly learned how to work around the UN system, a practice that led to even less accountability and more potential for corruption. Most traditional peace-keeping efforts were able to function despite the UN system during the Cold War since they had relatively simple mandates, were generally not sent into war zones, and did not cost very much.

Peace Enforcement

Peace enforcement[18] is a conflict-resolution model intended by the founders of the United Nations to address threats to international security through the use of military action against a recalcitrant state that has breached the peace. It is therefore the antithesis of peace keeping, not a variation of it. Peace enforcement is based on Chapter VII, Article 42 of the UN Charter, which stipulates that the Security Council may take "such action by air, sea, or land forces as may be necessary to maintain or restore international peace and security." Chapter VII, Article 45 refers to such an effort as a "combined enforcement action." In 1994, NATO agreed to a more concise definition by describing peace enforcement as missions that "generally employ conventional combat operations to achieve their objectives" and states that "the classic peace enforcement operations have been the Korean and Gulf Wars."[19] The ongoing NATO-led IFOR–SFOR mission in Bosnia also is an example of peace enforcement.[20]

Confusion over the peace-enforcement model has resulted from recent decisions to add war mandates to peace-keeping missions, such as allowing peace keepers to call in airstrikes against recalcitrant parties, attempting to forcibly disarm combatants, using military force to deliver humanitarian aid, and attempting to hunt down and arrest a "warlord." Because these functions were attempted by forces with peace-keeping mandates and weaponry, they did not constitute actual peace enforcement but "expanded peace keeping," which will be discussed in the next section.

NEW MULTILATERAL CONFLICT-RESOLUTION MODELS

Expanded Peace Keeping

Traditional peace keeping was predicated on the consent and cooperation of warring parties. Disputants had to desire peace and voluntarily agree to stop fighting. Expanded peace-keeping efforts reject these requirements; instead they are intended to use force to resolve conflicts. Consent of the disputants is not necessary. Such a revolutionary change in UN conflict resolution practice was a product of an internationalist euphoria which swept through the West between 1989 and 1993 due to the end of the Cold War. This euphoria generated greater expectations for the United Nations, in the belief that improved relations between Washington and Moscow would allow the world organization to pursue and evince the collective security ideals envisioned by the UN's founders. Expanded peace keeping was the principal manifestation of this belief, and it was given ambitious mandates, including guaranteeing the delivery of humanitarian aid, putting an end to civil wars, and building nations (see Table 3.3). Over twenty expanded peace-keeping missions have been created since 1991, more than the total number of peace-keeping forces deployed in the previous forty-six years of the UN's existence.

Analyzing expanded peace keeping is difficult because of divergent schools of thought on the subject and the wide range of terms used to describe it. Advocates of the traditional peace-keeping model regard expanded peace keeping as the discrete enlargement of traditional peace-keeping mandates to address specific post–Cold-War conflicts and crises. But other experts view expanded peace keeping as a natural evolution in conflict resolution and evidence of movement toward globalism and international interdependence. Advocates of more expansionist concepts of peace keeping have devised many names for this type of conflict resolution, including "next generation," "second generation," "enhanced," and "aggravated" peace keeping.[21] More than a dozen new definitions have cropped up. Different UN theorists have assigned the same terms vastly different meanings. Table 3.4 gives some of the most widely used new definitions.

The newest moniker for the expanded peace-keeping model is "multidimensional peace keeping." Advocates of this term believe it best describes post–Cold-War UN missions; they contend that it includes a host of nonpeace-keeping functions, such as distributing aid and monitoring elections (see Table 3.4). However, an examination of prior peace-keeping operations indicates that this rationale is erroneous because Cold-War peace-keeping missions have long performed many of these duties. For example, UNFICYP, deployed in Cyprus since 1964, established a humanitarian and economics branch to provide emergency humanitarian assistance. UNIFIL, deployed in Lebanon since 1978, has long been engaged in civilian administration, humanitarian activities, and rebuilding infrastructure. UNIFIL also operates a hospital for the local population in southern Lebanon. UNSF, deployed in west New Guinea from 1962 to 1963, built a police force, performed civilian administration, and helped organize civilian elections.[22]

Table 3.3
Expanded Peace-Keeping Missions (Data as of March 13, 1998)

	Start/End Dates	Authorized Size	Total Cost ($ millions)
UNIKOM (Iraq–Kuwait)	1991–present	1,082	400[a]
UNAVEM II (Angola)	1991–1995	655	175
UNAMIC (Cambodia)	1991–1992	1,504	—[b]
UNTAC (Cambodia)	1992–1993	22,000	1,600
UNPROFOR (Yugoslavia)	1992–1995	45,000	4,600
UNOSOM II (Somalia)	1993–1995	26,000	942
UNOMUR (Rwanda)	1993–1994	81	15
UNOMIG (Georgia)	1993–present	122	180
MICIVIH(Haiti)[c]	1993–1996	100	?
UNOMIL (Liberia)	1993–1997	300	85
UNMIH (Haiti)	1993–1996	1,500	316
UNAMIR (Rwanda)	1993–1996	5,500	437
UNMLT(Cambodia)	1993–1994	20	5
MINUGUA (Guatamala)	1/97–5/97	132	50
UNMOT (Tajikistan)	1994–present	57	12
UNAVEM III (Angola)	1995–6/97	4,220	890
UNPREDEP (Macedonia)	1995–present	1,106	525
UNCRO (Croatia)	1995–1996	7,000	300
UNIMIBH (Bosnia)	1995–present	2,022	167
UNTAES (Croatia)	1996–1/98	5,177	350
UNMOP (Croatia)	1996–present	28	10
UNSMIH (Haiti)	1996–present	1,500	56
MONUA (Angola)	7/97–present	1,326	50[d]
UNTMIH (Haiti)	8/97–11/97	250	20
MIPONUH (Haiti)	12/97–present	300	28[d]
UNCPSG (Croatia)	1/98–present	233	24[d]

Sources: Project on Peacekeeping and the United Nations, U.S. General Accounting Office, UN Peacekeeping Department of Peacekeeping Operations, UN Peacekeeping Internet Homepage, http://www.un.org/Depts/dpko/, October 1997.

[a]Since 1993, the government of Kuwait has paid two-thirds of the costs of this mission.

[b]The cost of this operation was included in UNTAC.

[c]Joint UN–OAS operation.

[d]Estimated annual cost.

The main difference between traditional and expanded peace-keeping missions is the carte-blanche authority to use force in order to achieve compliance with UN dictates the latter enjoys. Also, expanded peace-keeping missions do not require the consent of parties in disputes before they are deployed. These changes attempted to address a major shortcoming of traditional UN peace keeping: the ability of parties in disputes to use national sovereignty and the UN Charter's nonintervention clause to prevent the international community from attempting to relieve human mis-

Table 3.4
Pick Your Definition

New Peacekeeping Definition	Proposed by	Description and Requirements
Second Generation Peacekeeping	John MacKinlay and Jarat Chopra, Brown University, 1993	"A range of contingencies sometimes erroneously described as peacekeeping . . . does not necessarily have consent of all warring parties . . . may take rigorous steps to achieve its goals, possibly including heavy weapons, airstrikes, and warships."[a]
"Chapter VII" Peacekeeping	Clinton Administration, 1993	"Actions involving the use of the threat of force to preserve, maintain, or restore international peace and security or address breaches of the peace or acts of aggression. Such operations do not require the consent of the state(s) involved or other parties to the conflict."[b]
Multidimensional Peacekeeping	Henry Stimson Center, 1995	"Primarily involves the settlement of internal conflicts . . . usually has the full consent of local parties, although may be authorized to use force against local elements."[c]
Second Generation Peacekeeping	U.S. Ambassador Edward Marks, 1966	"A multi-dimensional activity combining traditional peacekeeping with extensive civilian responsibilities."[d]
Peace Support Operations	John MacKinlay, Brown University, 1996	"Operations and activities of all civil and military organizations deployed to restore peace and/or relieve human suffering. Peace support operations may include more forceful military actions required to establish peaceful conditions."[e]
Aggravated Peacekeeping	U.S. Department of Defense, 1997	"Operations undertaken with nominal consent, but which are complicated by intransigence, banditry, or anarchy."[f]
Peace Restoration and Conflict Management Operation	United Nations Department of Peacekeeping Operations, 1997	"New and tentative concept for operations which are forced by realities in the field to turn into Chapter VII operations, such as when humanitarian convoys need to be defended by force or arms or exclusion zones by airstrikes."[g]

[a]John MacKinlay and Jarat Chopra, *A Draft Concept of Second Generation Multilateral Operations 1993* (Providence, R.I.: Thomas J. Watson Institute for International Studies, 1993), p. 4.

[b]*PDD-25* (Clinton administration policy on UN peacekeeping), cited in George Mason University Peacekeeping Center Internet Homepage, http://ralph.gmu.edu.cfpa/peace/definitions/a_g/html, August 1997.

[c]William J. Durch, *UN Peacekeeping, American Policy, and the Uncivil Wars of the 1990s* (New York: St. Martin's Press, 1996), p. 4.

[d]Edward Marks, *Complex Emergencies: Bureaucratic Arrangements in the UN Secretariat* (Washington, D.C.: National Defense University Press, 1996), p. 9.

[e]John MacKinlay, *A Guide to Peace Operations* (Providence, R.I.: Thomas J. Watson Institute for International Studies, 1996), p. 2.

[f]U.S. Department of Defense Joint Publication 3-0, cited in George Mason University Peacekeeping Center Internet Homepage, http://ralph.gmu.edu.cfpa/peace/definitions/a_g/html, August 1997.

[g]United Nations Department of Peacekeeping Operations, UN Peacekeeping Internet Homepage, http://www.un.org/Depts/dpko/glossary/html, August 1997.

ery in areas beset by civil conflict or dire humanitarian disasters.[23] This was a radical departure from traditional peace-keeping experience and practice: It abandoned the neutral, nonthreatening reputation of traditional peace keeping and tended to turn UN troops into combatants in internal conflicts. There were no minimum conditions to abide by; the UN made up its own rules and conditions as it went along.

A Failed Experiment

In 1993, conventional wisdom held that the expansion of peace-keeping mandates and missions were an evolutionary improvement in UN conflict resolution. By 1995, it became apparent that these expansions were a disastrous experiment (see Table 3.5). In Yugoslavia, a four-year, $5 billion peace-keeping mission culminated in the execution of hundreds—perhaps thousands—of Muslim civilians and soldiers in areas supposedly under the protection of the UN; 370 peace keepers taken hostage and used as "human shields"; and a humiliating withdrawal.[24] A second UN Operation in Somalia (UNOSOM II) suffered a similar fate after its ambitious efforts to build a nation out of chaos and disarm combatants led to the killing of eighteen U.S. soldiers, and put the UN at war with armed Somali clans.

The expanded peace-keeping model hinged on two crucial assumptions: First, that fundamental changes in the international system due to the end of the Cold War to enable the long-dormant collective-security ideals of the United Nations would finally be enacted, and second, that UN peace keeping's limited achievements during the Cold War were solely due to the superpower conflict. These assumptions proved to be false.

First, while the international system had changed, it had not changed as much as some experts believed. Expanded peace keeping required nation–states to cede sovereignty to the United Nations and to recognize that, unlike in the Cold-War era, sovereignty was no longer inviolable. But the nation–state system is still intact after the Cold War, and there are no signs of its demise. On the contrary, an outbreak of civil wars and secessions in the early 1990s suggested that the world actually moved *away* from global integration and interdependence. For example, the number of UN members has *increased* by 28 countries or 17 percent since 1992; 19 are new nation–states formed due to secessions. UN members—especially states participating in peace-keeping missions—resisted fully supporting expanded peace keeping for fear of creating precedents that would encroach on their national sovereignty.

Table 3.5
Mandates and Records of Major Expanded Peace-Keeping Missions

Operation	Years	Mandate	Results
UN Transitional Authority in Cambodia (UNTAC) Peak size: 22,000	1991–1993	Oversee transition to democratic government, separate warring parties, run an interim government, conduct national elections, disarm warring parties.	The $1.6 billion UNTAC mission improved living conditions, and ended the fighting for several years. It failed to carry out four-party elections or to disarm combatants. As a result, Cambodia returned to civil war in 1997.
UN Mission in Rwanda (UNAMIR) Peak size: 5,500	1993–1996	Contribute to security of Kigali, monitor cease-fire, assist humanitarian relief, contribute to security of refugees, provide security for relief operations.	Due to its small size and fierce ethnic rivalries, was not able to bring peace to Rwanda. UNAMIR was widely—and probably unfairly—condemned in April 1994 when it stood by and did nothing while ethnic Hutus slaughtered 250,000–500,000 Tutsis.
UN Angola Verification Missions (UNAVEM II and III) About 4,800 total troops	1991–1997	Monitor transition to democracy and incorporation of UNITA into Luanda government.	While the UNAVEM traditional peacekeeping mission succeeded in getting Cuba to withdraw its troops, questions about the fairness of the1993 presidential elections and bad faith by the Marxist MPLA Government prevented UNAVEM II and III from fulfilling their mandates. Not only is the civil war continuing, but MPLA forces have begun to intervene in neighboring states.
UN Protection Force (UNPROFOR) (Former Yugoslavia) Peak size: 45,000	1992–1995	Separate warring parties, provide security for humanitarian relief convoys, deter attacks against six "Safe Areas." Use airpower from regional organizations, if necessary to accomplish mandate.	Confusion over its mandate, insufficient troops, unreliable troops who refused to follow orders and often were involved in blackmarket activity doomed this $5 billion UNPROFOR operation. UNPROFOR's inconsistent use of force emboldened the Bosnian Serbs to defy it, resulting in 370 UN peacekeepers taken hostage and the execution of hundreds—perhaps thousands—of Muslims.

Table 3.5 (*continued*)

Operation	Years	Mandate	Results
UN Operation in Somalia II (UNOSOM II) Peak size: 26,000	1993–1995	Use enforcement measures to secure a safe environment, disarm warring factions, ensure delivery of aid, assist in rebuilding Somali institutions.	A confusing mandate to rebuild the country, insufficient troops and equipment, a large number of troops which refused to follow the orders of UN commanders, incompetent troops, contributed to the failure of UNOSOM II. Ill-advised orders from UN officials in New York to try to capture a tribal leader and use massive force turned UNOSOM II into a war combatant. UNOSOM II withdrew in early 1995 and the Somali civil war resumed.

Sources: U.S. General Accounting Office, *United Nations Limitations in Leading Missions Requiring Force to Restore Peace*, GAO/INSIAD-97-34 (Washington, D.C.: U.S. Government Printing Office, March 1997); UN Department of Peacekeeping Operations Internet Homepage. Center for War Peace Studies Decision Brief, *Clinton Legacy Watch #15: Invitation to Genocide in Angola*, Number 97-D, December 10, 1997.

Second, while the superpower conflict was a major reason for UN peace keeping's limited scope of applications during the Cold War, it was not the only reason. Incompetent UN troops, fraud, mismanagement, and limited commitments constantly plagued Cold-War peace-keeping missions. UN systemic problems had a far greater effect on expanded peace-keeping efforts because of their greater size, cost, and complexity. However, since most advocates of expanded peace keeping held an unrealistically favorable view of traditional peace keeping's record, they had little understanding of the UN's problems and failed to take any steps to address them.[25] Finally, unlike traditional peace-keeping missions, which due to their small numbers and size could be deployed indefinitely, expanded peace-keeping missions were large operations that did not have the luxury of time. Since nations would not agree to maintain these expensive peace-keeping efforts indefinitely, they needed to fulfill their mandates promptly, an impossible feat due to problems within the UN system.

Unchecked by reform, massive post–Cold-War expanded peace-keeping efforts yielded massive mismanagement and corruption. During the UNTAC mission in Cambodia from 1991 to 1993, UN officials and contractors committed "outright thievery" by stealing millions of dollars through phantom payrolls and work never performed, according to a 1993 *60 Minutes* investigation.[26] The 1993 to 1995 UNOSOM II mission in Somalia spurred similar reports, including the theft of $3.9 million, $76,000 in cash destroyed by mildew, and millions of dollars in contracts for vastly overpriced supplies and unnecessary contracts.[27] UNOSOM II mismanagement and corruption was so bad that U.S. Ambassador Daniel Simpson derided it in 1994 as "the world cash cow."[28]

Post–Cold-War peace-keeping efforts also continued to lack basic military competence. The UN's capacity to plan, support, and command peace-keeping missions—which was barely functional during the Cold War—broke down in 1993 due to the deployment of seven new peace-keeping missions costing over $4 billion and utilizing over 70 thousand troops, a sixteenfold increase in cost over 1988. Casualties occurred in Somalia when some peace-keeping contingents refused to follow orders given by UN commanders without first consulting with their capitals.[29] Peace-keeping troops often could not work together due to training, language, and competency problems. Many nations sent unqualified troops; one actually emptied its prisons and dispatched criminals.[30] Despite intensive pressure by the United States on the UN to reform peace keeping over the last four years, a State Department Inspector General study determined in March 1997 that the UN's peace-keeping department still lacks modern command and control, sufficient competent civilian administrators, and a responsible procurement system.[31]

The equation for post–Cold-War peace keeping was not promising: Bad assumptions plus lack of reform plus massive new operations equaled disaster. Lack of adequate planning and mismanagement led to confusion and incoherent mandates. UN troops participating in expanded peace-keeping missions claimed to be neutral but frequently attacked warring parties. Peace keepers sometimes engaged in extremely provocative actions, such as calling in airstrikes. At the same time, expanded peace keepers were given pacific rules of engagement and light equipment similar to traditional peace-keeping efforts. UN Secretary-General Boutros-Ghali explained this dilemma in a May 1995 report on UNPROFOR:

Nothing is more dangerous for a peacekeeping operation than to ask it to use force when its composition, armament, logistic support, and deployment deny it the capacity to do so. The logic of peacekeeping flows from political and military premises that are quite different from enforcement; and the dynamics of the latter are incompatible with the political process that peacekeeping is intended to facilitate. To blur the distinction between the two can undermine the viability of the peacekeeping operation and endanger its personnel.[32]

A tenuous legal basis also undermined expanded peace keeping. Chapter VII of the UN Charter, "Action with Respect to Threats to the Peace, Breaches of the Peace, and Acts of Aggression," applies where economic sanctions and military action are used against a nation–state that poses a dire threat to international security, such as Korea in 1950 and Iraq in 1991.[33] This view, adhered to during the Cold War, was given a strong legal boost in 1962 by a ruling of the International Court of Justice with respect to the UN Operation in the Congo (ONUC). Although that mission was authorized to use force by the UN Security Council and had conducted military operations against mercenaries and Katangese separatists, the court held that it "was not an enforcement action within the compass of Chapter VII of the Charter," because it was a situation within a state, initially deployed at the request of the Congolese Government, and approved by the Security Council to be a UNEF-like peace-keeping operation.[34] Nevertheless, since 1993 the council rejected this and similar long-standing precedents and began to "invoke" Chapter VII in approving several expanded peace-keeping missions, but failed to provide sufficient military force to carry out enforcement actions. This created confusing mandates for peace-keeping forces, as UN Secretary-General Boutros-Ghali explained in his May 1995 UNPROFOR report: "UNPROFOR is not a peace enforcement operation and some confusion has arisen as a result of references to Chapter VII in some Security Council resolutions relating to its mandate, particularly as regards the use of force other than in self-defence."[35]

In effect, for UNPROFOR and UNOSOM II, references to Chapter VII in authorizing Security Council resolutions actually constituted a threat of future Chapter VII enforcement action against recalcitrant parties, without giving them actual enforcement mandates. Thus, these peace-keeping soldiers were placed in the impossible situation of being incapable of fighting a war, while at the same time unable to make peace. The resulting breakdown of expanded peace-keeping missions in Yugoslavia and Somalia caused a severe loss of prestige and confidence in the United Nations, which may affect it for years to come.

Humanitarian Intervention

A second distinct conflict resolution tool created after the Cold War requires attention: humanitarian intervention. It is similar to peace enforcement except that it is deployed in response to a humanitarian emergency and not an international conflict. Humanitarian intervention is designed in part to deal with crisis areas where there may not be a functioning government. Such operations thus are deployed without the consent of parties to disputes, usually within a state, and on the basis of a "right" of the international community to intervene. It therefore moves far beyond the UN Charter, traditional peace keeping, or expanded peace keeping, in that it represents abrogation of national sovereignty when there is no risk to international peace.

The humanitarian intervention model stems from UN Security Council Resolution 688, passed in 1991, which served as the legal basis for a military operation to provide humanitarian assistance to the Kurds of northern Iraq. Resolution 688 cited Chapter VII and was the first effort by the council to define a humanitarian situation within a country as a threat to international peace. This mission, Operation Provide Comfort, was initiated over the objections of the Iraqi government *and* UN Secretary-General Perez de Cuellar, who disputed its legality under the charter.[36] The northern Iraq mission spawned other humanitarian intervention operations in Somalia (UNOSOM I and UNOSOM II) and Yugoslavia (UNPROFOR) as part of larger expanded peace-keeping efforts. Over time, it became apparent that these humanitarian interventions were actually attempts by Western countries to do *something* after a media frenzy resulted in pictures of human misery displayed on the evening news and CNN. However, since the international community simply did not have the ability, will, or organizational skill to mount decade-long rebuilding efforts, the cameras were pointed elsewhere, the so-called humanitarian "forces" left, and chaos returned.

UNOSOM II's and UNPROFOR's humanitarian intervention missions went very badly, hurting the UN's overall peace-keeping effort as well as the United Nations. A lack of consent by factional leaders to these missions and the use of force by them alienated local populaces and caused both efforts to be viewed as occupying forces and combatants. The United Nations discovered that the delivery of humanitarian aid was not a neutral act, as it could sustain losing factions under siege, thus alienating winning factions and prolonging the conflict. Since humanitarian aid was not linked to a cease-fire or a negotiated solution, it was manipulated by factions to allow them to regroup and prepare for further warfare. Not only was UNOSOM II's humanitarian aid used to enrich Somali warlords, much of it was confiscated and sold to buy more weapons to continue the war.[37]

Humanitarian interventions have proven to be poor solutions to internal conflicts. The risk of great power involvement in these efforts suggest that such crises probably are better left to smaller neutral states and nongovernmental organizations. While humanitarian intervention-like missions will occasionally be necessary to address dire humanitarian emergencies, such as countries laid waste by civil wars, recent history suggests that there is no easy way to carry out such missions cheaply, quickly, and without violent confrontations between the humanitarian intervention forces and warring parties.

SIX LESSONS TO SALVAGE TRADITIONAL PEACE KEEPING

One can walk into any college library and find newly issued books explaining how expanded peace keeping is the wave of the future of conflict resolution. The setbacks of 1993 and 1994 have failed to discredit the theoretical basis for expanded peace keeping in the eyes of many experts.

But no matter how elegant their arguments, one thing is clear: Expanded peace keeping is dead, at least for now. It had a chance to prove itself between 1992 and 1994, and it failed utterly. This failure has not only undermined popular support for all peace-keeping efforts, but for the entire UN system.

But traditional peace keeping need not suffer this fate. While post–Cold-War expanded peace-keeping failures illustrate the limits of multilateral interventionism in a world where nationalism and the nation–state system remain strong, it also suggests several lessons to maintain traditional peace keeping as a useful tool for post–Cold-War foreign policy makers.

First, peace keeping works best when it sticks to the traditional model. Such missions will be rare and should be reserved for *international* conflicts and deployed only when full consent can be obtained from parties in a dispute. Ancillary duties such as election monitoring and rebuilding infrastructures are permissible so long as the consent of warring parties is obtained, and these duties do not compromise the neutrality of the peace-keeping mission.

Second, the UN's refusal to reform and clean up waste and corruption will limit the deployment of all future UN operations. Recent pronouncements on this subject by UN Secretary-General Koffi Annan have not been encouraging.[38]

Third, expanded peace-keeping models—which combine traditional peace keeping with force to compel former warring parties to abide by diplomatic entreaties—do not work and should be abandoned.

Fourth, the events of the 1990s indicate that there is no such thing as Chapter VII peace keeping and that peace keeping and peace enforcement are mutually exclusive. It usually will not be feasible or advisable to convert a peace-keeping operation—which is by definition consensual and nonthreatening—into an offensive war-fighting force. Peace-keeping missions that plan to do so will be unable to achieve the successes scored by most traditional peace-keeping efforts, which were borne on trust, neutrality, and the consent of parties in a dispute. Such efforts also sacrifice the UN's reputation as a neutral arbiter, thus putting all existing and future UN peace-keeping missions at risk.

Fifth, U.S. troops participating in peace-keeping missions frequently are at great—and sometimes unjustifiable risk. If possible, U.S. troops probably should be limited to support roles, such as providing air transport and logistics support. If American troops must participate as UN peace keepers, they should be given specialized training—preferably conducted by a nation with significant peace-keeping experience—to learn the intricacies of peace-keeping doctrine and practice.[39] American peace keepers also must receive special training in maintaining a low visibility and avoiding terrorist threats.

Sixth, many world crises will go unaddressed. The United Nations and the United States need to recognize this and sometimes say "no" to demands for intervention. This does not mean a return to isolationism or withdrawing from the international stage, but it does recognize that there are no easy answers to many global conflicts, especially civil and ethnic wars.

At this time, there are indications that some world leaders and UN officials are considering the further application of expanded peace-keeping models. Given the experience of the past five years, more UN missions of this type stand a good chance of causing new failures that will destroy the remaining prestige of the United Nations and traditional peace keeping, which would be a pity. The traditional peace-keeping model has proven itself to be a useful foreign policy tool when used in the right circumstances, and it is certain to be needed again.

NOTES

1. The views expressed in this article are the author's alone and do not represent the views of the U.S. government or the Central Intelligence Agency.

2. Some international-relations analysts have posited that UNEF's origins stemmed from earlier UN collective security efforts such as the UN Truce Supervisory Organization (UNTSO), deployed in 1948, or the UN Special Committee on the Balkans (UNSCB), deployed in 1947. Others have argued that modern peace keeping is the descendant of collective security efforts attempted by the League of Nations in Upper Silesia in 1921 and Greece–Bulgaria in 1925. A few claim that peace keeping's ante-

cedents go back much futher to the Concert of Europe, the Treaty of Westphalia, and even the ancient Greeks. The events of 1956 suggest that Hammarskjold and Pearson operated on the fly to draw up an ad hoc plan that best fit the dire political situation of 1956, namely the Cold War and the Suez War. UNTSO appeared to fit into these calculations, in that UNEF provided a fuller rationale for UN truce-monitoring deployments. UNSCB and earlier non-UN operations appeared to have little or no influence on the formation of UNEF. The final word on this subject may come from Brian Urquhart, a former senior UN peace-keeping official, who retired in 1986 after forty years with the United Nations. He described Hammarskjold's plan for UNEF as "a conceptual masterpiece in a completely new field, the blueprint for a non-violent, international military operation." Brian Urquhart, *A Life in Peace and War* (New York: Norton, 1987), p. 133.

3. *The Blue Helmets: A Review of United Nations Peacekeeping*, 2d ed. (New York: United Nations Publication, 1991), p. 4.

4. See Leland M. Goodrich and Edvard Hambro, *Charter of the United Nations: Commentary and Documents* (Boston: World Peace Foundation, 1949), pp. 281–293.

5. Chapter I, Article 2, Section 7 of the UN Charter reads, "Nothing contained in the present Charter shall authorize the United Nations to intervene in matters which are essentially within the domestic jurisdiction of any state or shall require the Members to submit such matters to settlement under the present Charter; but this principle shall not prejudice the application of enforcement measures under Chapter Seven."

6. See *The Blue Helmets*, p. 5.

7. Chapter VI of the UN Charter, "Pacific Settlement of Disputes," specifies nonmilitary solutions to international conflicts. Article 33 of Chapter VI stipulates that disputants shall seek a solution through negotiation, enquiry, mediation, conciliation, arbitration, judicial settlement, or resort to regional agencies or arrangements or other peaceful means of their own choice. Chapter VI also permits the Security Council to intervene by *recommending* a peaceful solution. Chapter VI thus differs significantly from Chapter VII, which allows the Council to mandate solutions to international conflicts, using force if necessary. Quote is from *Nordic UN Tactical Manual* (Joint Nordic Committee for Military UN Matters, 1992), I: 17.

8. Indar Jit Rikhye, Michael Harbottle, and Bjorn Egge, *The Thin Blue Line: International Peacekeeping and Its Future* (New Haven: Yale University Press, 1974), p. 3.

9. Boutros Boutros-Ghali, "Towards a New Generation of Peacekeeping Operations," *Bulletin of Arms Control* (May 1993): 7. Some academics and statesmen—mostly in the United States—began in the early 1990s to assert that the traditional peace-keeping model is based solely on Chapter VI of the UN Charter and started referring to expanded peace-keeping forces and peace-enforcement efforts as "Chapter VII" missions. This line of argument was controversial. Despite pressure from the United States, the UN Security Council refuses to invoke or refer to Chapter VI in approving peace-keeping mandates, a practice that appears to reflect the preference of the majority of UN members to reserve the legal description

of Chapter VI actions for bona fide mediation efforts, such as good-offices missions by the UN Secretary-General.

10. James H. Allen, *Peacekeeping: Outspoken Observations by a Field Officer* (London: Praeger, 1996), pp. 137–141.

11. In practice, the UN has resisted withdrawing peace-keeping missions. UN Secretary-General U Thant reluctantly withdrew UNEF I from the Sinai and Gaza Strip in May 1967 at the request of Egypt, which was preparing for war against Israel. When Israel invaded Lebanon in June 1982, it gave the commander of UNIFIL—which was deployed in southern Lebanon—thirty minutes notice and informed him that Israel expected UNIFIL not to impede Israeli troops. UNIFIL ignored this warning and instead attempted to block the Israeli Army's advance with small obstacles. The issue of withdrawing consent also arose on several occasions in 1993 and 1994 with UNPROFOR when the Bosnian Serbs argued that the force had to leave since they had withdrawn their consent. UN Secretary-General Boutros-Ghali did not take this demand seriously.

12. Rod Paschall, "UN Peacekeeping Tactics: The Impartial Buffer," in *Soldiers for Peace*, ed. Barbara Benton (New York: Facts on File, 1996), pp. 51–55.

13. The United States and the USSR generally did not participate in any peace-keeping operations during the Cold War after 1948. The United States and the USSR however have participated in UNTSO (Palestine), since its inception in 1948 in Palestine and continue to do so. The United States also has particpated in UNMOGIP (Kashmir) since it began in 1948. List of states is from Trevor Findlay, *Challenges for the New Peacekeepers* (Oxford: Oxford University Press, 1996), p. 11.

14. One of Hammarskjold's principles for peace keeping which he drew up on the basis of his experience with UNEF was that "UN forces should not include units from any of the five permanent members of the Security Council or from any country which may be considered as having a special interest in the situation." Sydney D. Bailey, *The United Nations: A Short Political Guide* (New York: Praeger, 1964), p. 60. See also *The Blue Helmets*, p. 55.

15. Inis L. Claude, Jr., "The New International Security Order: Changing Concepts," *Naval War College Review* 47 (Winter 1994): 14.

16. John R. Bolton, Testimony before the House of Representatives Committee on Government Affairs, February 9, 1994.

17. Lewis Mackenzie, quoted in Perry L. Pickert, ed., *Intelligence for Multilateral Decision and Action* (Washington, D.C.: Joint Military Intelligence College, 1997), p. 523.

18. Some analysts have used the term "peacemaking" to refer to this type of force. For the purposes of this article, peacemaking is defined as a diplomatic, nonmilitary activity.

19. *NATO, Peacekeeping, and the United Nations* (London: British–American Security Council, September 1994), p. 35.

20. IFOR and SFOR frequently are mistakenly referred to as peacekeeping missions. This misnomer appears to stem from popular confusion

about the IFOR–SFOR mandates and the tendency of the media to describe all UN military missions as peace-keeping operations.

21. Boutros-Ghali and some UN scholars have also discussed other UN missions such as "peace building", and "preventive diplomacy," which they believe are separate missions from peace keeping. For the purposes of this chapter, these missions are considered part of expanded peace keeping.

22. *The Blue Helmets*, pp. 134, 175–185, 263–277.

23. See Note 4.

24. U.S. General Accounting Office, *United Nations Limitations in Leading Missions Requiring Force to Restore Peace*, GAO/NSIAD-97-34 (Washington, D.C.: U.S. Government Printing Office, March 1997), p. 9.

25. See Allen, *Peacekeeping*, p. xvi.

26. This episode of the CBS news program *60 Minutes* originally aired September 19, 1993.

27. Jack Anderson and Michael Binstein, "Somali Heist Followed UN Carelessness," *Washington Post*, October 19, 1995, p. B23.

28. Julia Preston, "Waste in Somalia Typifies Failings of UN Management," *Washington Post*, January 3, 1995, p. A11.

29. U.S. General Accounting Office, *United Nations Limitations in Leading Missions Requiring Force to Restore Peace*, GAO/NSIAD-97-34 (Washington, D.C.: U.S. Government Printing Office, March 1997), p. 19.

30. About 30 percent of the peace keepers sent by Bulgaria in 1992 to the UNTAC peace-keeping mission in Cambodia were convicts sent to make prison space available. *Washington Times*, December 13, 1993, p. 12.

31. U.S. Department of State, Office of Inspector General, *Report of Audit, Peace Operations Reform: Implementation of PDD-25 and Related Issues*, 7-CI-003 (Washington, D.C.: U.S. Department of State, March 1997), pp. 20, 33–35.

32. United Nations, *Report of the Secretary-General Pursuant to Security Council Resolutions 982 and 987*, no. S/1995/444, 30 May 1995.

33. Goodrich and Hambro, *Charter*, p. 271; and Robert C. Hilderbrand, *Dumbarton Oaks: The Origins of the United Nations and the Search for Postwar Security* (Chapel Hill: University of North Carolina, 1990), pp. 139, 239–240.

34. "Certain Expenses of the United Nations," International Court of Justice Reports, 1962, www.ICJ-CIJ.org, p.151ff; and Michael Akehurst, *A Modern Introduction to International Law*, (London: George Allen and Unwin, 1984), pp. 189–192.

35. United Nations, *Report of the Secretary-General*.

36. Because Iraq refused to consent to this operation, UN Secretary-General Perez de Cuellar believed Operation Provide Comfort violated Article 2 of the charter, which forbade the UN from intervening in the internal affairs of member states. Moreover, since Resolution 688 did not explicitly authorize a UN operation in northern Iraq (mostly due to Chinese objections), the Secretary-General believed the United States should have obtained the express authorization of the Security Council. See Barry E. Carter and Phillip R. Trimble, *International Law* (Boston: Little, Brown, 1995), pp. 1411–1416.

37. *The Wall Street Journal*, March 1, 1995, p. A14.

38. See "UN Cuts Not Likely to Be Painful," *Washington Times*, May 12, 1997; "Negotiations on Paying UN Debt Making Little Headway," *The Washington Post*, May 22, 1997; and "Annan Axes 1,000 Posts in First Round of UN Reform," *Diplomatic World Bulletin*, vol. no. 28, March 3–24, 1997.

39. The Lester Pearson Peacekeeping Center in Nova Scotia, Canada comes to mind as one of the best places for American peace keepers to obtain such training. Other excellent programs are offered by Australia and the Nordic countries.

4

The Changing Face of Insurgency in the Post–Cold War Era: Doctrinal and Operational Implications

Stephen Sloan

The coming decade will witness continued religious, racial, and ethnic revolt, the consequent collapse of weak states, widespread ungovernability, and the increasing importance of nonstate actors. This chapter raises some crucial questions: How will these trends change the nature of insurgency? How well will the U.S. military be able to cope with guerrilla challenges in an era of budget cutting and neglect of military needs?

The end of the Cold War has led to fundamental changes in the international political arena. Old threats have been replaced by new challenges, which have forced academics, policy makers, strategists, and those involved in the operational arts to reevaluate their thinking, as they are confronted with the transformation of the conflict environment. The tensions and accompanying challenges created by the transformation are in part the result of the interaction between highly innovative technologies associated with war fighting and the environment in which present and future conflicts will be conducted. On the one hand, Desert Shield and Desert Storm illustrated how high technology could be applied in what was, for all intents and purposes, a conventional war. But in the new threat environment, while the dangers of regional conventional war remain very real in the Middle East and North Asia, those who must address issues of national security face the daunting demands of applying high technology weaponry in a very ambiguous environment. The cohesive doctrine that was formulated to meet the Soviet threat, as it related to the spectrum of conflict, is no longer appropriate to new conditions. Those involved in formulating a national security policy must now reorient their thinking to understand the dynamics of future battlefields that will include new adversaries, values, and goals. These new demands are further exacerbated by the budgetary requirements in the post–Cold War period. The call for downsizing, the dangers of neoisolationism, and the quest for new and the revitalization of older organizations associated with collective security have forced both policy makers and senior officers and officials to engage in the painful process of redefining the roles and missions of the military. The process of redefinition has been made even more complex by the loss of clarity over what the major elements are that constitute U.S. national security. From the traditional concerns over direct military threats and economic well being have come a wide variety of other "soft" but increasingly important elements, ranging from issues associated with international human rights to the impact of potential environmental disasters.

The problems of seeking to revitalize and transform military doctrine and the operational arts to meet new and uncertain realities can be illustrated by the topic of this chapter: the changing face of insurgency in the post–Cold War era. The battle to reconcile the requirements for both continuity and change has serious implications with regard to the ability of the United States to defend its interests and project its power in the era of the "New World Disorder." The challenge is particularly complicated when answers to the following questions are sought: Has the face of insurgency changed? If so, what are the implications of this change in regard to the requirements for U.S. national security, and more specifically, the role of the military in meeting this change?

In addressing these questions, one can take two polar positions. On the one hand, a case can be made for the contention that insurgency as a mode of warfare has become less significant since the end of the Cold War. That is, with the demise of U.S.–Soviet superpower competition, the challenges created by the use of insurgency as part of a form of surrogate or proxy warfare no longer exist. Moreover, one could argue that strategies associated with "wars of national liberation" are no longer relevant in either waging or countering this form of warfare. On the other hand, a case can be made that while the Cold War may have ended, the basic strategy and tactics of insurgency are still applicable and will be utilized by those who will continue to use the techniques of unconventional warfare in pursuit of their objectives. Therefore, the U.S. military must maintain its counterinsurgency capabilities, as well as its ability to support insurgencies in order to meet changing national security requirements. Furthermore, there may be a need to adjust and refine insurgency doctrine, since what have alternately been called "small," "dirty," or "shadow" wars may not only continue, but increase in number with the transformation of the international system.

The following analysis of the character of post–Cold War insurgencies will draw on both positions. For while the conflict environment may have changed and concomitantly certain aspects of insurgency doctrine and strategy, there is a continuity with the insurgencies of the past. In other words, while there may be "a revolution in military affairs," that revolution as it is applied to understanding and either waging or countering insurgencies does not represent a total discontinuity with the past history of insurgencies. Consequently military planners would be well advised to not only refine doctrine but also recognize that the past record provides a foundation to meet the demands of present and future insurgencies. Again, the need to reconcile continuity and change is necessary in meeting these insurgencies.

POST–COLD WAR INSURGENCIES: CONTINUITIES WITH THE PAST

In addressing the changing face of insurgency it is first important to identify the major characteristics of past insurgencies. In doing so, one can assess how insurgencies have changed and therefore determine what the policy and strategic implications are in regard to either supporting or countering future post–Cold War insurgencies. The following are four commonly identified characteristics of insurgency that differentiate it from other forms of warfare. (There are additional characteristics, but these are employed as a preliminary basis for analyzing potential insurgencies.)[1]

1. *The primacy of politics.* At the outset it has long been recognized that while warfare in general is largely driven by politics, insurgencies are an integral and vital extension of a political agenda and ultimately a form of political warfare.

2. *The importance of psychological operations.* The centrality of politics is in part the result of a second aspect of insurgency—that is, the insurgents usually have inferior military capabilities compared to their adversaries. As a result, political action ranging from subversion to psychological operations are essential if the insurgent is to neutralize the greater numbers and firepower of the enemy.

3. *The resort to protracted warfare.* Especially vital in the waging of insurgency is the emphasis on protracted warfare—namely the ability

of the insurgent to wear down the will of an outwardly more powerful enemy.

4. *The emphasis of the use of unconventional forces, strategies, and tactics.* In pursuing their objectives, insurgents often seek to maximize their limited capabilities by using unconventional forces and tactics against the opposition. The skillful use of these forces in the past has negated the superior numbers, firepower, and technological advantages of the opposition.

All these elements may still be part of present and future conflicts, but in what way may they have transformed as they interacted with the changing political and conflict environment of the post–Cold War era?

CONTINUITY AND CHANGE: THE PROCESS OF TRANSFORMATION

The Continuation of the Primacy of Politics and the Rise of Apolitical Insurgencies

The emphasis on the primacy of politics in post–Cold War insurgencies will in all likelihood continue, but the direction and magnitude may change. One could make a case for the view that the "traditional wars of liberation," ideologically based on communist doctrine and utilizing the Soviet and Maoist models, are no longer practiced (with the exception of some relatively remote areas, illustrated by the case of the insurgency in Nepal, and the modification of the Maoist approach as practiced by the Sendero Luminoso in Peru). While the case can be made for the demise of these leftist revolutionary ideologies as a program for action, the fact remains that aspects of the ideology may still be applied to selective post–Cold War insurgencies. Revolutionary strategy in regard to the primacy of politics, the emphasis on superior organizational capabilities, the resort to the effective use of clandestine cadre, the stress on subversion and psychological operations, the application of unconventional tactics, and a whole host of other insurgency techniques may be used as a handbook for revolutionary takeover, even if the ultimate outcome is not the traditional Marxist–Leninist or Maoist revolution. Moreover, with the great instability within the successor state of the former Soviet Union, the possibilities of a reassertion of Marxist–Leninist ideology as a reaction to the failed attempts at democratization and a capitalistic market economy cannot be dismissed. The legacy of an ideology that led to the superpower competition may have eroded, but the potential for its reemergence, even in a weakened form, remains.

One particularly sees the continued importance of the primacy of politics as an aspect of a post–Cold War insurgency in both subnational and transnational conflicts. Both in "internal wars" and regional conflicts, the primacy of politics is present. In the increasingly strong revitalization of traditional nationalism, the resort to insurgency as part of political warfare continues—that is, a wide variety of ethnic groups have asserted or reasserted their identity by drawing on primordial loyalties that are based on profound attachments to race, region, religion, and ethnicity, in an attempt to acquire their own territory and government. This occurs within an environment where the control from a discredited center disintegrates, as in the case of the former Soviet Union, or where existing governments are unable to control their population without the support of Washington or Moscow. This reassertion may also be understood within the context of the general decline of the traditional nation–state system and the concomitant rise of nonstate actors as leading parties in the new international environment.

The power of primordial loyalties that may fuel future insurgencies cannot be understated. The ideological beliefs that form the basis for the insurgency are not predicated on abstractions of class consciouness, class conflict, or imperialism, but the most basic values associated with a combination of race, language, ethnicity, and often a historical mission to right ancient wrongs and a commitment to both a physical longing for and psychological attachment to a specific territory. These deeply embedded parochial beliefs, which often were obscured during the rivalries of the Cold War, have now surfaced and may challenge an increasingly fragile international state system. As one authority noted, the "nation can be called a 'terminal community,' for present purposes the effective end of the road for man as a social animal, the end of working solidarity between men."[2] The post–Cold War era has provided the crucible that is redefining what communities a nation–state should represent. The arbitrary boundaries imposed on various communities as a result of colonialism are now being challenged. The rule of these areas by states with low levels of legitimacy is also being threatened, now that these states no longer can benefit from being superpower surrogates or allies, as they often were during the Cold War. The disintegration of these geopolitical–legalistic entities is the manifestation of the power and the reality of long-suppressed psychological needs that have either brought people together or promoted disunity and internal conflict based on the traditional competition of loyalties. As a result, traditional nationalism has reemerged, which can lead to the outbreak of intense insurgencies. It should be noted that these parochial beliefs may not only fuel internal, localized insurgencies, but also lead to regional destabilization. This is because a number of the groups involved are not solely fighting to acquire "self-determination" within the boundaries of an existing state and in opposition to an existing government; they are also seeking to expand their quest for identity, legitimacy, and political power beyond the imposed boundaries of the past. The potential for destabilization as illustrated by the thrust of Islamic fundamentalism, while appearing to be primordial and parochial, also has a regional and indeed global appeal to those believers who would seek to indicate their ideals in an insurgency that has implications beyond a local "internal war."

The power of the primordial ideal is further amplified by the reassertion of religious belief as a guide to the new wars of liberation in the form of nonsecular insurgencies. Having rejected secular Marxist–Leninist ideology, there are those who are seeking to find their political ideals by eliminating contemporary modernity and replacing it with the reassertion of traditional values. These values often center on a religious belief that rejects what is regarded to be the corrupt and immoral practices of the West. While it is recognized that the interpretation of religious values can promote great divisiveness within a particular faith, it can also act as a profound unifier, and the primacy of politics can therefore be joined with the commitment to spread religious ideals and values into a powerful mobilizing force. This occurs in particular where there is no separation between state and church, as in the case of countries practicing Islam; the power of religion becomes a primal driving force for political action, which underscores the potential strength and endurance of those who would engage in local or regional insurgencies in the name of religion.[3] During the Cold War, it was difficult enough to engage in counterinsurgency in the "battle for men's hearts and minds." How much more difficult would it be to engage in "the battle for their souls." However, it is important to recognize that this battle should not be understood or solely stated in terms of the Islamic challenge. Fundamentalists in other religions may promote extremism in the pursuit of their own version of a nonsecular insurgency as part of their quest for spiritual self-determination. This quest is likely to intensify in the new millennium when people increasingly look backward to acquire stability and a sense of security in a technologically driven and very uncertain political order.

Yet, at the same time, while the primacy of politics may continue and indeed be intensified by religious values, that primacy may also be challenged by a new form of insurgency, one that is very difficult to analyze because its discontinuity with the insurgencies in the past. We may increasingly be faced with the development of the *apolitical insurgencies*, which are not based on traditional ideologies of the left or the right but based on primordial loyalties. These insurgencies will be a manifestation of the apparent breakdown of the nation–state as the primary unit of action in the idealized international community. The "state-centric" model has and will increasingly be challenged by the emergence of new nonstate actors, be they transnational terrorist groups, narco-terrorists, organized crime, or the continued expansion of multinational corporations, which have always ultimately ignored the boundaries of the traditional nation–state.[4] In a sense, one can make the case for historical continuity. Before the rise of the nation–state it was the prince with his mercenary army who pursued economic and political power without the need for popular legitimacy. We are now witnessing the "privatization of public violence," where the new insurgents will not be motivated by political or religious values, but a strategy of maximizing their profits by seeking to control "gray areas . . . where control has shifted from legitimate governments to new half-political, half-criminal powers."[5] These areas often face the problem of ungovernability, in that a Pandora's box is opened for very weak and virtually nonexistent governments threatened by new mercenaries who wage their private, apolitical wars in the pursuit of their monetary objectives. For them, the state, if it does survive, will primarily be used as a cloaking device to provide a modicum of legitimacy in an international political system where there is an even broader systemic crisis of legitimacy.

In sum, in post–Cold War insurgencies, the primacy of politics will take on a new and perhaps more powerful dimension, for it will be energized by the most primal beliefs. Yet, at the same time we may also be witnessing the emergence of the apolitical insurgency, which is in a sense a throwback to the past.

THE IMPORTANCE OF PSYCHOLOGICAL WARFARE AND THE AMPLIFICATION OF PSYCHOLOGICAL OPERATIONS: HIGH TECHNOLOGY AND THE "CNNDROME"

The primacy of politics in conducting an insurgency is intimately related to another major aspect of insurgent strategy, most notably the key role of psychological operations. Since traditionally the insurgents must defeat a militarily superior adversary, they must not only gain the political high ground, but magnify their limited forces by utilizing psychological operations and warfare as a force multiplier in order to mobilize support on behalf of the insurgents and erode the unity and legitimacy of the incumbent government. Moreover, the role of psychological operations has been much amplified by modern technology. Just as a small transistor radio lessened the ability of an authoritarian government to control information, now the personal computer, the fax machine and the hand-held camera have become weapons of choice by insurgents not only seeking to acquire internal legitimacy but external support. The rapidly accelerated information flow has become a potent windfall for insurgents who can practice psychological operations by not only drawing upon the revolution in communications technology, but more important, the resulting impact of the mass media, which can now reach a global audience. In this sense, what is now called "information warfare," which can be directed at destroying an incumbent's capability to govern or to counter an insurgency by neutralizing its information infrastructure, command, and control capabilities and electronically blinding its forces, can also be employed as a form of a psychological operation that can affect the support or rejection of a particular political and social order. One may even witness the development of "virtual insurgencies," where highly sophisticated small groups may create the perception of a nonexistent insurgency that could nevertheless erode the legitimacy of an already weakened government.[6] Moreover, this potential for perception management and alteration will not necessarily be aimed at a specific geographical area where the insurgency may be taking place; it may also be aimed at a far broader target, such as a global audience, which may help to determine whether governments, international organizations, and nongovernmental organizations will remain indifferent or will support either the incumbent or the insurgent.

The power of the media is aptly illustrated by what Lieutenant Colonel David C. Bradford has called the "CNNDrome." Instant media coverage, even if it is superficial or taken out of context, may help to determine the fate of insurgencies.[7] Whether acts of violence are viewed to be remote and isolated or perceived to be salient to the concerns of the global community will in part be the result of the degree of coverage the insurgents are able to acquire. Broad coverage may help them achieve a level of support and legitimacy not only within the strife zone but also from a far broader base of support. The modern insurgent must be media-wise at a time when the "battle for men's minds" may no longer be waged solely through reliance on the development of long-term ideological commitments and organizational capabilities against the existing political order. Future insurgent strategies will include the art of employing the skillful use of visuals and sound bites that may capture the attention of the global audience—an audience which may seek simple explanations for the complex violence they are witnessing on the evening news. The CNNDrome may be a very appealing propaganda tool that can be used effectively to convey a message to an audience which has neither the time nor the inclination to understand the "big picture"—an audience which exhibits an electronic version of attention deficit disorder.

THE RESORT TO PROTRACTED WAR IN AN ERA OF QUICK SOLUTIONS

It is ironic that, while the immediacy of the media may enhance the ability of the insurgents to have the capability to seize the airwaves, this ability also enhances their capability to effectively employ the techniques of protracted conflict. For, at a time when the targeted audiences in the strife zone or in the international arena are looking for simple answers and quick solutions, the insurgent knows that time may be on his side. It may be increasingly easy to wear down the resolve of the adversary; to engage in a psychological war of attrition against those who have a low threshold of commitment to understand, much less counter, dedicated insurgents resolved to pursue long-term strategic goals. The post–Cold War insurgent can very effectively apply a two-track approach by using both short- and long-term operations—to immediately seize the media high ground on one hand, and over time break the resolve of the opposition on the other. Like the director of a successful television program, the insurgent can combine powerful, immediate use attention-getting episodes that are linked to a long-term storyline, thereby creating a desire to watch the whole season of a program.

THE USE OF UNCONVENTIONAL FORCES, TACTICS, AND STRATEGIES: NEW PLAYERS AND NEW TECHNOLOGIES

Unconventional warfare has traditionally required the training and equipping of special forces capable of engaging in or countering an insurgency. This trend will in all probability continue, especially since there is a growing recognition that such forces are necessary to wage the most likely types of conflicts that will take place in the post–Cold War era. But the equipping and training of these forces continues to change. Post–Cold War insurgencies will require forces that have at their disposal a wide variety of high-tech weapons systems to be used in what have traditionally been thought of as low-tech insurgencies. The development of equipment related to global positioning systems (GPS), the availability of more sophisticated aircraft, the use of overhead platforms to meet tactical requirements, the development of nonlethal weapons and other innovations all affirm the fact that the special forces of the future must be more technologically proficient. This proficiency will also be essential since the insurgents will have at their disposal a variety of portable and lethal weapons that range from hand-held missiles to weapons of mass destruction. At the same time special forces still require a high degree of nontechnological capabilities to conduct operations in foreign environments. The need for these capabilities will be expanded as new communities with different cultures, values, languages, and religions continue to assert themselves in the changing global arena. Therefore, care must be taken to avoid the temptation of relying on "quick-fix" technological approaches at the expense of developing the necessary language and skills to effectively work in regions and countries which until now have not been at the center of U.S. national security requirements. The need for a reservoir of skilled linguists and other specialists will be vital. Therefore, planners should recognize the need for "off-the-shelf" specialists who can quickly fill the breach in the negotiation of rapidly developing conflicts. In a rapidly changing world, the ability to develop a surge capability associated with area expertise will be limited unless there is long-term planning.

Finally, even more vexing is the fact that there will be new players in the insurgencies of the post–Cold War as a result of the following factors. As noted earlier, we have witnessed the emergence of nonstate actors as key players in international politics. As a result, governments will have to increasingly learn to coordinate their security concerns with entities in the corporate and private sector. This need for coordination will certainly apply in meeting the demands of the development of apolitical insurgencies. The rise of international criminal enterprises, the continuing threats of transational terrorist groups (now increasingly engaging in violence as a form of international extortion), and the enduring character of narco-terrorists (despite the vaunted "war" against drugs) all require the development of counterinsurgency doctrines that recognize the joint need of the government and corporate sectors to face those who are minimizing their capabilities, all in an era where we have noted the coming of the "privatization of public violence." The development of such alliances will not be easy, and questions associated with reconciling issues of sovereignty and national security with privatization do not have easy answers. But more innovative approaches must be considered, for the monopoly of force or counterforce used either by governments or insurgents has increasingly been broken in an interdependent world where the line between government and nongovernment activities and capabilities has been blurred. For example, the crucial requirements for bureaucratic coordination and integration against insurgents can no longer focus primarily on interagency coordination within a government, or coordination with other governments.[8] Alliances beyond government entities and actions will have to be forged.

POLICY AND OPERATIONAL IMPLICATIONS

The changing face of post–Cold War insurgency has had serious implications for those charged with responding to the challenges of this type of conflict in the next century. While the continuity of previous insurgencies may remain, the changing nature of the conflict environment will call for new approaches from those given the task of responding to insurgencies beyond the year 2000.

While the Marxist–Leninist and Maoist strategies may be applied with less frequency and in more isolation than the concerted efforts of the "surrogate warfare" employed as an instrument of Cold War foreign policy, we are more likely to see the utilization of insurgency by primal-loyalty groups who may be seeking their own form of "self-determination." While their tactics in all probability will mirror those of guerrilla warfare, their strategies will not be based on the communist model. As previously noted, the use of class analysis, the call for insurgencies as part of international campaigns, and proclamations of "wars of national liberation" may be replaced by more localized demands for ethnic, religious, and regional liberation. While not as cosmopolitan or universal as the Marxist and Maoist models, these parochial insurgencies may be more intense than the secular models that preceded them. Since the call must be for liberation in the most fundamental senses of political community, it may energize leaders, cadres, and followers with an intensity greater than the insurgencies of the past. Fueled by religious fervor, for example, the post–Cold War insurgent may have the will and religious faith to engage in a protracted conflict against all odds. Moreover, it may be difficult to analyze the stages of these insurgencies based on past experience since they may be politically, religiously, and ideologically localized to meet the unique requirements of the culture and society in which the insurgents operate. An understanding of the uniqueness of the strategic visions of these insurgencies may not be based on the models that were employed to explain and counter or support Cold War insurgencies. One size will not fit all; consequently, there will be increased requirements for those who meet the insurgent challenge to be highly knowledgeable of the unique environment in which the insurgency takes place. Certainly current comparative theories associated with understanding and analyzing the dynamics of political violence and insurgency that were formulated during the Cold War will have to be modified if they are to effectively address the unique elements of these home-grown, internally driven conflicts.

At the same time, these primordial insurgencies may also expand outward with the strategic goal of transforming a whole region to achieve not the ideological models of the revolutionary left, but the reactionary models of a fundamentalist right that uses religious extremisms in the "battle for men's souls, not minds." The policies and accompanying rhetoric associated with countering such insurgencies through the resort to "economic development," "nation building," and "democratization," which were and are still often used to justify U.S. counterinsurgency programs may not be germane to meeting the regional, yet revolutionary, strategy of insurgents who emphasize the idealized return to fundamental religious values and the rejection of both technological and political modernity. These insurgencies driven by core beliefs may be quite intractable despite either internal or external pressures.

Perhaps even more challenging will be the growing emergence of apolitical insurgencies in which the attempt to seize power will not be based on the call for "self-determination," either reactionary or revolutionary, but driven by the quest for monetary gain by criminal enterprises that seek to secure a region in order to pursue their mercenary objectives. These insurgents may work under the cover of political commitment and tactically ally themselves with political actors of either the left or the right, but their objectives are essentially quite conservative—to have a base of operations from which to conduct their enterprises. In a very real sense they can be viewed as the illicit face of the multinationals who employ their power to indirectly control nominally independent states. These enterprises may be more nefarious, for they will not be bound by the edicts of international law and the requirements of international trade. They may indeed become highly organized "free agents" who will not be reluctant to use extortion and violence in pursuit of their objectives, even while they seek to cloak themselves with legitimacy by coopting or controlling a nominally independent state.

Those who would seek to counter these apolitical insurgencies might have to apply the strategic plans of the multinationals to compete with the new mercenaries. They may also have to form alliances not with other states, but with nonstate actors who have the capabilities to engage in economic competition against these criminal enterprises. In pursuit of their respective objectives, national security, or economic awards, states and corporations might have to form uneasy alliances in large parts of the world where either no one governs or criminal enterprises are asserting themselves as quasi states. The challenges created by the rise of nonstate actors, the increased "privatization of public violence," and a far more ambiguous and broader view of what may constitute a threat to national security will force policy makers to look to alternative views in countering a form of warfare that traditionally placed an emphasis on the primacy of politics, but may now become increasingly apolitical.

In the new insurgent battlefield, the role of psychological warfare will be amplified as a result of the technological innovation which has led to a profound communications revolution. The proliferation of hand-held cameras and low-power television stations, and the impact of the internet and the fax machine may enable small and remote insurgent groups to engage in a form of armed propaganda hitherto undreamt of by the most dedicated and skillful adversaries. The emergence of "virtual insurgencies," where the conflict and the quest for legitimacy may not be be primarily based on actual physical conflict, but on the ability to erode the basis of internal and external support through propaganda and perception management may represent a crucial innovation in the application of information warfare.

CONCLUSION

Confronted with the profound changes in the international political environment and the interaction of those changes with dramatic improvements in communications and weapons technology, those who engage in or counter insurgency will be forced to do battle in a new and often daunting environment. While tactics may stay the same, the strategic objectives and the means to achieve them may differ. As we enter a new millennium, the changing face of insurgency will represent a major challenge to those who must understand and address this form of conflict, which in one sense is very old but in another is at the cutting edge of a new political and technological age.

NOTES

1. For a fine overview of the nature of insurgency, see Bard E. O'Neill, *Insurgency and Terrorism: Inside Modern Revolutionary Warfare* (Washington, D.C.: Brassey's, 1990). For an outstanding study on the Soviet strat-

egy during the Cold War, see Richard H. Shultz, Jr., *The Soviet Union and Revolutionary Strategy: Principles, Practices and Regional Comparisons* (Stanford, Calif.: Stanford University, Hoover Institution Press, 1988).

2. Rupert Emerson, *From Empire to Nation: The Rise to Self Assertion of the Asian and African People* (Cambridge: Harvard University Press, 1960), p. 96.

3. For an insightful discussion of insurgent Islam, see Sean K. Anderson, "Iran: Terrorism and Islamic Fundamentalism," in *Low-Intensity Conflict: Old Threats in a New World*, ed. Edwin G. Corr and Stephen Sloan (Boulder, Colo.: Westview, 1992).

4. Stephen Sloan, "International Terrorism: Conceptual Problems and Implications," *Journal of Thought* 17, no. 2 (Spring 1982).

5. Xavier Raufer, "Gray Areas: A New Security Threat," *Political Warfare* (Spring 1992): 1. See also, Stephen Sloan, "Technology and Terrorism: The Privatizing of Public Violence," *IEEE Technology and Society Magazine* 10, no. 2 (Summer 1991).

6. For a fine discussion of many of the aspects of information warfare, see Matthew G. Devost, Brian K. Houtin, and Neal Allen Pollard, "Information Terrorism: Political Violence in the Information Age," *Terrorism and Political Violence* 9, no. 1 (Spring 1997).

7. As taken from David G. Bradford, "The Shadow Falls: The Gray Area Phenomenon in Today's World."

8. For a discussion of the requirements for countering an insurgency, see Max G. Manwaring, "Toward an Understanding of Insurgency Wars: The Paradigm," in *Uncomfortable Wars: Toward a New Paradigm of Low Intensity Conflict*, ed. Max G. Manwaring (Boulder, Colo.: Westview, 1991).

5

The U.S. Army Experience in Bosnia-Herzegovina: Challenges for Now and the Future

Max G. Manwaring

The experiences of the United States in Bosnia in the late 1990s have raised many questions about the pitfalls and opportunities of intervention in disturbed societies in the ambiguous and less-than-completely understood post–Cold War environment. This article focuses on the events of that time to identify areas where U.S. performance can improve in similar operations in the twenty-first century.

· · ·

Your responsibility is to 2010 down the road. So, you need to look to the grand picture and not just at Bosnia. . . . I will tell you that as we move into the next century, we really need to be aware of the political environment within which we must operate, and how we can best adapt to the complexities of contemporary stability operations.

Plenary panelist comment,
Bosnia-Herzegovina After Action Review Conference,
April 13–17, 1997[1]

Since the end of the Cold War, the international security system has undergone fundamental changes. In place of the relatively orderly and predictable Cold War structure, the new world "disorder" has generated a system in which time-honored concepts of security and the classical military means to achieve them are no longer completely relevant. This is a security environment in which ambiguous nontraditional, intranational, national, transnational, regional, and international "well-being" considerations—as opposed to traditional national territorial, resource, market, and other vital interests—are paramount.

Well-being tends to be defined as political stability. The more than one-hundred armed conflicts that have taken place since the end of the Cold War have virtually all been destabilizing intrastate affairs. Solutions to these more ambiguous challenges tend to involve some type of peace-keeping effort. Thus, the scope and objectives of military missions in this expanded international-security milieu must be broadened to comply with overriding political requirements.

It is within this context that this chapter examines the most salient lessons learned from the independent discussions of two U.S. Army Peacekeeping Institute (USAPKI) hosted conferences entitled Bosnia-Herzegovina After Action Review I and II (BHAAR I and BHAAR II). The primary purpose of the BHAAR process was to examine the first year of the U.S. Army experience in Bosnia to assist the U.S. Army Chief of Staff in his statutory, Joint Chiefs of Staff, and advisory responsibilities. Ancillary purposes were to provide strategic and high-level operational perspective to other senior leaders involved in peace and stability operations, and to enhance future U.S. Army doctrine, organization, professional military education, and leadership development.

The lessons derived from the BHAAR conferences are highly interrelated and focus on (1) the high probability of future multinational and multiorganizational peace operations; (2) the need for an integrated strategic planning process; (3) the need to develop mature service, joint, and coalition peace operations doctrine; and (4) the need to understand and deal with the political complexity of contemporary peace and stability operations.

The consistency of the lessons derived from this and other peace-keeping cases observed by members of the U.S. Army Peacekeeping Institute is impressive. This consistency warrants confidence that these lessons represent the major military dimensions of effective peace efforts. This consistency also warrants confidence that these lessons are more than adequate to initiate the process of rethinking the peace-keeping mission and to begin reshaping doctrine, refining organization, and developing more effective leaders.

THE HIGH PROBABILITY OF FUTURE MULTINATIONAL AND MULTIORGANIZATIONAL PEACE OPERATIONS

The underlying assumption throughout the BHAAR process was that, even though the U.S. Army must prepare for conventional war, there is a high probability that the president and Congress will continue to require military participation in peace and stability operations well into the next century. As a consequence, the army must also prepare to deal with the threats and challenges associated with these kinds of operations.

The threats to the "unstable peace" of the post–Cold War era center on causes and effects of myriad instabilities and destabilizers. They include human starvation, widespread disease, environmental devastation, increasing poverty, lack of socioeconomic and political justice, criminal anarchy, large-scale refugee flows, illegal drug trafficking and organized crime, extreme nationalism, irredentism, militant religious fundamentalism, militant secular reformers, ideologues, demagogues, greedy civil and military bureaucrats, terrorists, insurgents, warlords, ethnic cleansers, and rogue states.

These instabilities and destabilizers are acknowledged in the more than sixty formal threats to international peace and security declared by the United Nations Security Council since 1990. These kinds of threats require responsible international organizations and/or individual powers to aggressively take control of a situation from those who are profiting from chaos, establish law and order, feed and harbor victims, and ensure a secure environment for the establishment of responsible civil authority.

Increasingly, military peace keepers are expected to cooperatively support and protect that civil authority and a subsequent political legitimization process. The intent is to ensure that an internationally supported government does not revert to the unstable status quo ante and reinitiate another threat to the interdependent global community.

In responding to a given stability-threat situation, there may be no identifiable enemy military formations to attack and destroy, no specific territory to take and hold, no generally accepted government with which to work, and no mutually agreed legal niceties to help control the situation. These political ambiguities underlie an era of unconventional conflict in which the definition of "enemy" is elusive, and the use of "power" is diffuse.

These ambiguities intrude on the traditional concept of war and require a new paradigm that addresses the addition of a number of controlling political–economic–psychological–social–moral dimensions to conflict that heretofore have not been given much weight. Michael Howard reminds us that these nontraditional aspects of contemporary conflict must be conducted with considerable skill. "Otherwise, no amount of operational military expertise or technological advantage can possibly help."[2]

Thus, because ambiguous peace and stability operations are likely to be a part of the international security landscape for the foreseeable future, the BHAAR participants were in complete agreement that the primary challenge to the U.S. Army is to educate leaders and planners at all levels concerning the subtle and politically dangerous implications of these types of operations.

THE NEED FOR AN INTEGRATED STRATEGIC PLANNING PROCESS FOR PEACE AND STABILITY OPERATIONS AND COMPLEX HUMANITARIAN EMERGENCIES

The BHAAR dialogue consistently referred to the ubiquitous presence of "ad hoc-ery" in planning, coordinating, and implementing the peace-enforcement mission in Bosnia. It was argued that stovepipe independent planning tends to create "strategic ambiguity." In that connection, it also prevents integrated planning, sows confusion, and requires shortfused "quick fixes" to command and control arrangements, mission limits, supported and supporting logistical and personnel mechanisms, rules of engagement, and status of forces agreements. Moreover, it is obvious that "ad hoc-ery" contributes to the duplication and triplication of effort and adds significantly to the political, monetary, and personnel costs of unintegrated peace and stability missions.

In theory, peace operations achieve strategic clarity, unity of effort, and maximum effectiveness as a result of integrating both horizontal and vertical planning and implementation processes from the outset. That is, integrating horizontal multinational political–military planning and operations with vertical national (e.g., U.S. interagency) political–military planning and operations achieves a synergy toward the achievement of an agreed end state.

In the reality of the Bosnia-Herzegovina experience, early U.S. military coordination during the assessment and plan development phases did not take place with key U.S. civilian organizations, international organizations, coalition partners, or nongovernmental organizations. Planning and implementing procedures broke down in the face of competing national and institutional interests and segregated planning and implementing processes. Moreover, ad hoc reaction to changing conditions and "mission creep" became the norm in the absence of a single overarching political–military campaign plan. As a result, there was no strategic clarity; little, if any, unity of effort; and very limited effectiveness.

General John R. Galvin, USA, (retired) argues that continuous and cooperative planning among and between national and international civilian and military organizations, beginning with a strategic assessment of the situation, can establish a mechanism for developing a common vision for ultimate political success (i.e., strategic clarity). Then, shared goals and objectives, a broad understanding of what must be done or not done or changed, and a common understanding of possibilities and constraints will generate an overarching campaign plan which becomes the basis for developing subordinate plans that will make direct contributions to the achievement of a desired end state. Thus, the roles and missions of the various civilian and military elements evolve deliberately—rather than in response to "mission creep"—as the situation changes to accommodate progress toward the achievement of a mutually agreed-upon political vision.[3]

In this connection, the BHAAR dialogue focused on recommendations regarding the need for the United States to develop leaders, planners, and soldiers capable of functioning more effectively in chaotic and delicate coalition political–military planning and implementing situations. The intent is to integrate U.S. Army deliberate and crisis action planning with more casual multilateral and multiorganizational problem-solving processes. Until such a change of mind-set occurs, strategic clarity and effectiveness of effort will be evasive. In the meantime, the political, financial, and manpower costs of "ad hoc-ery" in a multilateral–coalitional and multiorganizational peace-keeping environment will be high.

THE NEED TO DEVELOP MATURE PEACE AND STABILITY OPERATIONS DOCTRINES

The BHAAR process highlighted the fact that current doctrines are inadequate to meet the requirements of contemporary multilateral–coalitional, multiorganizational, and unilateral political–military (e.g., U.S. interagency) peace and stability operations. In the past, these types of operations tended to be unrealistically viewed as providing military solutions to military problems. Presently, the complex realities of peace and stability operations must be understood as a holistic process that relies on various civilian and military agencies and contingents working together in an integrated fashion to achieve a common political goal.

Proposed doctrinal changes concern the need to recognize the real locus of power (i.e., the civil population) in a given operational area, and the relevant civilian and military resources and time stages needed to plan for and implement a truly successful conclusion to a given peace process. In addition, successful peace and stability operations are highly dependent on a doctrine that ensures the rapid and coordinated response of combat, combat support, and combat-service support forces to both enable and sustain a holistic strategic civil–military effort. The harmonization of doctrines will standardize terms and concepts, ensure general agreement on the underlying philosophy of operations, and provide common frames of reference for the many different tasks required of the various international and national players involved in contemporary stability operations.

At the same time, early coordination—based on similar doctrines—during the assessment and plan-development phases of an operation involving international and national civilian organizations and coalition partners, is essential for establishing mission responsibilities, supported and supporting relationships and limits, and for avoiding ad hoc reactions to military contingencies. This coordination is key to the definition of shared partnership goals (i.e., end states), options (i.e., ways), and realistic capability requirements (i.e., means) inherent in the mission planning and implementing processes. All these integrative efforts in turn ensure that conditions that will allow a host nation to develop or renew its political solvency and legitimacy are established—and that a given mandate for peace will in fact be achieved.

The BHAAR plenary panelists strongly supported the arguments regarding the need for and the urgency to develop mature civil–military doctrines for contemporary peace and security requirements. One panelist asserted that it was necessary to go beyond the mechanical process of creating harmonized doctrine and standardized agreements. Another senior panelist took the argument to its inductive conclusion. He contended that "what we really need to come to grips with, in my opinion, is the broader spectrum of what it is we are about in the future. . . . You just can't look at the mechanics of the thing. You have got to look beyond that. If this army is going to truly be an army capable of fighting two MRCs [Major Regional Contingencies], or whatever the policy is, and still be able to meet national diplomacy requirements, you are going to have to deal with these [doctrinal] issues. Now—not tomorrow, not the next day—now. Now is the time for a change of mind-set."[4]

In sum, the BHAAR process stressed the need for U.S. armed forces and civilian agencies, coalition partners, international organizations (IOs), and nongovernmental organizations to harmonize doctrine and standardize procedures, equipment, and communications. Consensus was that U.S. Army doctrine, training, and leadership development must rise to the challenge of preparing leaders, planners, and soldiers capable of operating cooperatively in complex multilateral and multiorganizational peace and stability operations.

THE NEED TO UNDERSTAND AND DEAL WITH THE POLITICAL COMPLEXITY OF CONTEMPORARY PEACE OPERATIONS

The BHAAR concern with the political complexity of peace and stability operations takes us back to where we began—a contemporary world-security environment that dictates a high probability of politically oriented multinational and multiorganizational peace operations in pursuit of intranational, national, and international stability and well-being.

This security concept takes us beyond traditional peace-keeping responsibilities. It takes us beyond providing some form of humanitarian assistance or refugee assistance in cases of misery and need. It takes us beyond protecting a people from another group of people or from a government. It takes us beyond compelling one or more parties to a conflict to cease human-rights violations and other morally repugnant activities. It takes us beyond repelling simple aggression. The amorphous contemporary peace-keeping task is to create internal conditions within failed or failing states that can lead to peace and stability with justice.

As the U.S. Army experience in Bosnia-Herzegovina demonstrates, these internal conditions are created in a failed or failing state as a result of redefining "enemy" and "power" in predominantly political–sociological–psychological–moral terms. This requires that the "enemy" be carefully discerned and politically isolated from the rest of a given society. This also requires exceptionally prudent use of power. The blunt force of military formations supported by tanks, artillery, and aircraft could be irrelevant or even counterproductive. In that connection, the more subtle use of "soft" power supported by "niche" psychological warfare, careful intelligence work, and surgical precision in removing individual, illegal political actors from within the general populace is imperative.

Once the necessary internal conditions for peace and stability are established, "only sustained, cooperative work to deal with underlying economic, social, cultural, and humanitarian problems can place an enforced peace on durable foundations."[5] Otherwise, it will only be a matter of time before a relapse into instability and conflict occurs. Political considerations and solutions, logically, must be a fundamental part of the peace-keeping process now and in the future.

The BHAAR consensus was that because of the more complex political–strategic environment, peace keepers must be correspondingly more sophisticated. Leaders at all levels must make difficult decisions in ambiguous situations. They must understand the complete political–strategic nature of their tactical and operational actions. They must understand ways by which force can be employed to achieve political, psychological, and military ends. They must understand ways political considerations affect the use of force. They must understand how to communicate and deal with a diversity of peoples and cultures. They must understand and deal with the local and global media. Finally, they must understand how to cooperatively plan and implement interagency, international organization, nongovernmental organization, and coalition military operations. Any denial of any of this is unthinkable.

IMPLICATIONS

Two common denominators that transcend the BHAAR process have immediate implications for the U.S. Army. The first common denominator is the need to philosophically accept that the Cold War is over and learn how to optimize capabilities in an ambiguous political environment that puts the military in a political facilitator role to enhance world stability. This relates specifically to professional military education and leadership-development responsibilities. The second denominator involves the political, coalitional, and multiorganizational partnership requirements that mandate doctrinal and organizational change for strategic clarity and greater effectiveness in contemporary peace and stability operations, which is fundamental to unity-of-effort concerns.

In both the leadership development and unity-of-effort areas of concern, changing the U.S. Army mind-set demands a carefully staffed, phased, and long-term validation, planning, and implementation program. The recommended basic direction for such an effort is outlined as follows.

Professional Military Education and Leadership Development

There are at least four general educational requirements necessary to modify Cold War mind-sets to better deal with complex multiorganizational and multinational peace-keeping operations.

First, the study of the fundamental nature of conflict has always been the philosophical cornerstone for comprehending the essence of conventional war. It is no less relevant to nontraditional warfare. As examples, concepts such as "enemy," "war," and "victory" must be redefined; nontraditional interests centering on "national well-being" must also be carefully defined; and the application of military power and the use of legitimate coalition partners to achieve political ends must be rethought and refined.

Second, cultural awareness, through civilian and military exchange programs and language education and training, prepares leaders for the complexities of contemporary conflict management. U.S. Army personnel must interact collegially and effectively with representatives of U.S. civilian agencies, non-U.S. civilian government agencies, international organizations, nongovernmental organizations, local and global media, and other military organizations.

Third, information can be a force multiplier. At the same time, lack of timely intelligence can be a force minimizer. Waiting for higher or other headquarters to provide timely, accurate, and detailed local intelligence has proven costly in terms of mission achievement and force protection. As a consequence, professional military education must foster the idea that commanders must take responsibility for collecting and managing information to the extent necessary to achieve tactical and operational objectives.

Finally, education and training for contemporary peace and stability operations must prepare military peace-keeping personnel to be effective warfighters. Peace missions have and will continue to put military forces into "harm's way." Political actors in an unstable situation in which peace operations may take place are likely to have at their disposal an awesome array of conventional and unconventional weaponry to use for their own narrow purposes. For many societies, violence is a normal and accepted way of effecting change or maintaining status quo. In either case, peace keepers must—first and foremost—be good, professional soldiers. At the same time, because of the environment in which they must work, peace-keeping soldiers must display great sensitivity, considerable restraint, and iron discipline.

In these terms, then, BHAAR recommendations stress the idea that "we really need to be aware of the political environment within which we must operate, and how we can best adapt to the complexities of contemporary stability operations."[6]

Unity of Effort

The United States is not the only political actor in the world-security arena, and it is not the only player in more specific international peace-keeping operations. A bewildering array of international organizations and nongovernmental organizations, as well as U.S. and other government civilian and military organizations, respond to complex humanitarian and peace-keeping emergencies and state collapse. Moreover, many of these players will have been operating in a given situation long before the military might be called on to stabilize that situation.

When the U.S. military is placed into such an environment, the question arises, "Who is in charge?" The answer is probably, "Don't know; nobody and everybody!" Given such a convoluted organizational situation, it is difficult to make military peace-keeping and stabilizing actions credible or effective. For these actions to be politically and financially cost effective, there must be a clarification of responsibilities and relationships and an accepted mechanism to create and enhance the civil–military harmonization of actions necessary to achieve the desired end state. The creation of that unity of effort to gain ultimate success must be addressed at different levels.

First, at the highest level, the primary peace-keeping parties must be in general agreement with regard to the objectives of a given set of operations and the associated political vision. Nevertheless, although such an agreement is a necessary condition for unity of effort, it is not sufficient. Sufficiency and clarity are achieved by adding appropriate policy implementation and military management structures and mind-set adjustments at two additional levels.

The second level of effort requires an executive-level management structure that can and will ensure continuous cooperative planning and execution of policy among and between the relevant U.S. civilian agencies and that armed forces are established (i.e., vertical planning and operations). That structure must also ensure that all political–military action at the operational and tactical levels directly contributes to the achievement of the strategic political end state.

Third, steps must be taken to ensure clarity, unity, and effectiveness by integrating coalition military, international organizational, and nongovernmental processes with U.S. political–military (i.e., interagency) planning and implementation processes (i.e., horizontal planning and actions). It is clear that the political end state becomes elusive and operations suffer when there is no strategic planning structure that integrates key multinational and multiorganizational civil–military elements of a peace or stability mission. It is also clear that duplication of effort is costly in political, financial, and personnel terms.

At its base, however, unity of effort requires educational as well as mechanical solutions. Despite an adequate organizational architecture, ambiguity and confusion are likely to reign unless the various civilian and military leaders and organizations involved in peace and stability operations can develop the empathy (i.e., mind-set) necessary to work cooperatively. Unity of effort ultimately entails the type of professional military education that leads to effective politics and skillful diplomacy, as well as doctrinal and organizational solutions.

As a consequence, BHAAR recommendations resolutely support the notion that "we [the United States] need to play in a way that synergizes everything we do. It is not enough for us to do it as a nation or as an army alone. We must change our notional mind-set to be part of a synergistic process."[7]

A FINAL THOUGHT ON LESSONS LEARNED FROM THE EXPERIENCE IN BOSNIA-HERZEGOVINA

Within the contemporary global security structure, the United States remains the world's only superpower. No other power currently possesses the attributes needed for effective international and regional leverage—political clout, economic impact, cultural appeal, and military reach. However, the United States cannot do everything alone. Given proper leadership and support, there are those legitimate international partners who can and will assist the United States in creating a more peaceful and stable international security environment. The special status of the United States allows it the opportunity to facilitate positive change. By accepting this leadership challenge, the United States can help replace conflict with cooperation and harvest the hope and fulfill the promise that peace and stability operations offer.

NOTES

1. The first Bosnia-Herzegovina After Action Review (BHAAR I) conference was held at Carlisle Barracks, Pennsylvania, May 19–23, 1996. The second Bosnia-Herzegovina After Action Review (BHAAR II) conference was held at Carlisle Barracks, Pennsylvania, April 13–17, 1997. The BHAAR process is an initiative of the Chief of Staff of the U.S. Army (CSA). BHAAR I centered on lessons learned from the planning, deployment–entry, and initial operations phases of Operation Joint Endeavor (OJE) through D+60. BHAAR II examined lessons from the operations, plans and transition, and redeployment phases of OJE from D+61 through D+365. In both conferences, a strict policy of nonattribution was enforced. More than one hundred 04 (major) to 09 (lieutenant general) military and civilian equivalents participated as conferees and plenary panelists in BHAAR I and BHAAR II, representing over fifty different national and international civil and military organizations. Despite differences in experience and level of activity in Bosnia, the tone and substance of the discussions generated an exceptionally productive consensus. The BHAAR process

provided more than seventy-five recommendations to the CSA that focused on the strategic and high-level operational lessons learned which related to his Title 10, Joint Chiefs of Staff (JCS), and advisory responsibilities. The author was the rapporteur at both conferences.

2. Michael Howard, "The Forgotten Dimensions of Strategy," in *The Causes of War* (London: Temple-Smith, 1981), p. 109.

3. Interview with General John R. Galvin, USA (retired) conducted by Max G. Manwaring, August 6, 1997 in Boston, Massachusetts. The complete interview is included in the Spring 1998 special issue of *Small Wars & Insurgencies* 9, no. 1, later published as *Toward Responsibility in the New World Disorder: Challenges and Lessons of Peace Operations*, ed. Max G. Manwaring and John T. Fiskel (London: Frank Cass, 1998).

4. Nonattribution.

5. Boutros Boutros-Ghali, *An Agenda for Peace: Preventive Diplomacy, Peacemaking and Peacekeeping* (New York: United Nations, 1992), p. 33.

6. Nonattribution.

7. Ibid.

6

U.S. Unconventional Warfare Doctrine, Policies, and Operations: Experiences and Lessons from Central America, 1980–1990

Alfred R. Barr and Caesar D. Sereseres

In the 1980s, several insurgencies raged simultaneously in Central America, an area which came to be seen as the last great regional battleground between the United States and its communist adversaries. Since then, democratic processes seem, however unsteadily, to be taking root in most of the Central American states. Consequently, American policy makers are already forgetting important lessons from that former battleground—lessons which this chapter recalls to our attention.

As we move into a new century, it is appropriate to look back at American military involvement since the end of World War II. Of particular interest, given the expected nature of warfare in the early twenty-first century, should be U.S. interventions into unconventional war environments. In the short-term future, U.S. allies, friendly governments, or "clusters" of population identified by their religion, culture, race, or ethnicity will be subjected to armed threats or actual violence. These conflict situations may or may not directly affect vital U.S. national security interests. However, humanitarian and moral concerns may drive a decision for military intervention to rescue an ally or defenseless populations. Current evidence and trends suggest that there will be more internal wars and the likelihood of more military interventions. The question thus presented in this chapter then is this: What is it that we have learned or should learn from past U.S. experiences in unconventional warfare? This chapter argues that one of the most recent and telling unconventional warfare involvements of the United States is in danger of being lost. The Central American wars of the 1980s deserve close scrutiny and serious analysis.

Throughout the Cold-War era, the utilization of unconventional warfare remained a vague and uncertain thread in American foreign policy. Beginning with U.S. support for the Greek government fighting a civil war in 1946 and the Philippine government fighting the Huk insurgency in the early 1950s, continuing through the 1980s when the United States supported anti-Marxist insurgencies in Angola, Cambodia, Nicaragua, and Afghanistan, unconventional warfare policies and forces played a significant if not determining role in American foreign policy.

Crucial to the implementation of U.S. Cold-War foreign policy was the ability to protect and sustain pro–U.S. regimes throughout the world. In the early decades of the Cold War, it was sufficient merely to be an "anticommunist" government and/or a government confronted by a communist threat—be it a neighboring communist state or a communist-supported insurgency. By the late 1970s and throughout the 1980s, the ability of Washington to support regimes facing a communist threat had to often be tempered if not conditioned by the client's human-rights behavior and democratic credentials.

The last great Cold-War battleground was in Central America from 1980 to 1990. It was here that the ability of the United States to support democratic allies and the democratization process was most tested on the unconventional-warfare battlefield. Central America during this period was the scene of strong insurgencies in Guatemala and El Salvador, two guerrilla-force incursions into Honduras, a Cuban–Soviet allied regime in Nicaragua, and significant political, economic, and military support to clients in the region from Cuban–USSR–Eastern Bloc–Viet Nam allies.

The Central American wars of the 1980s were the last great "regional wars" of the Cold War. The Central American wars also made up the most consistent and longest unconventional war struggle for the United States during the Cold War. No other unconventional war theater directly involved the U.S. military for a longer period. For example, by 1965–1966, Viet Nam had become a conventional war supported by unconventional war programs and forces. The United States lost a central role in the Afghanistan resistance early in the war and relied heavily on Pakistani military and intelligence organizations to manage the covert assistance to fight the war against the Soviet military.

The Central American conflict from beginning to end was unconventional. From the day that a 7th Special Forces Group Green Be-ret team arrived in El Salvador in 1981 to train the first rapid reaction battalion of the Salvadoran armed forces, until March 1990 when the Central Intelligence Agency was required to terminate support for the Nicaraguan Resistance, the U.S. government, including the Department of State, all the military services and intelligence agencies were involved in one of the most complex unconventional warfare battlefields of the Cold War.

Yet, despite the high profile and very public policy debates over the American role in Central America and the significant success of these policies that included a substantial role for U.S. military forces, most of what took place has gone unnoticed or not remembered. Several ironies should be noted. First, neither the military services nor the Central Intelligence Agency as institutions desired involvement in the Central American wars. The conflicts were seen as highly political, "dirty" guerrilla wars that reminded them of Viet Nam. The Reagan administration commitment to El Salvador in 1981 would come some six years after the fall of Saigon and less than ten years after the American military departure from Viet Nam. Memories were sharp, and the pain was still evident.

It was not only the American left and Democratic liberals in Congress that were concerned about Central American military intervention. The Pentagon was even more worried about "another Viet Nam" in El Salvador. The Pentagon senior military leadership clearly understood that military involvement in Central America had little support in Congress and even less support in American public opinion.

Another irony was that despite Pentagon bureaucratic resistance, congressional legislative restrictions and conditions, and strongly negative public opinion polls, the U.S. unconventional war effort across the breadth of the Central American region proved innovative, flexible, and in the end, successful. By 1990 success could be demonstrated in a defeated insurgency in Guatemala, a stalemated war in El Salvador that forced peace negotiations, the electoral ouster of the Sandinista government in Nicaragua, the departure of Cuban, Soviet, and East Bloc military and intelligence personnel and logistical networks from the region, the semblance of stability and democratization in Honduras and Costa Rica, and the removal of General Noriega from power in Panama. The United States came to the assistance of democratic allies found in segments of the governments, armed forces, political parties, and civil society. The end result was the promotion of a regional democratization process that has continued through the late 1990s.

These outcomes were not easily predictable in the period from 1980 to 1982 when it appeared to most people in Washington that Central America was not salvageable without a direct American military intervention. The Central American wars, within an un-conventional warfare environment, clearly demonstrated the ability of the United States to muddle through in providing assistance and support to democratic allies subjected to Cold-War threats of Marxist-led insurgencies, Marxist–Leninist regimes supporting insurgencies, and the policies of Havana, Moscow, and Hanoi to provide global networks of support to insurgencies and self-identified revolutionary governments like that of the Sandinistas.

A further irony is found in the acclaim given the regional and country-specific peace processes that formally ended the Central American wars. High praise is properly given to President Oscar Arias for the Arias Peace Plan (formally known as the Esquipulas II Peace Accords) of August 1987. The United Nations is given significant credit for facilitating the end of the thirty-six-year war in Guatemala. The Guatemalan Peace Accords were signed in December 1996. The United Nations provided good offices to end the twelve-year war in El Salvador. The El Salvador peace agreement was signed in January 1993. The United Nations and the Organization of American States were given credit for disarming and demobilizing the contras in Nicaragua in June 1990. In some circles, the United States was and continues to be vilified as being responsible for the duration, intensity, and outcomes of the Central American wars.

The last and most important irony is the reluctance or inability of the U.S. military establishment to recognize the unconventional warfare operational and political successes in the Cold War's last major battlefield. In a recent study by Susan L. Marquis entitled *Unconventional Warfare: Rebuilding U.S. Special Operations Forces*, no more than one paragraph out of 270 pages of text is devoted to the unconventional warfare experiences and lessons of Central America![1]

The purpose of this chapter is to (1) describe the general evolution of unconventional warfare doctrine, policies, and operations during the Cold War; (2) examine the Central American wars during the 1980 to 1990 period; (3) assess the American unconventional warfare experiences in the Central American region during this period; and (4) identify the lessons of the Central American unconventional warfare theater and comment on the much-debated future of unconventional special-operations forces in the twenty-first century.

RETROSPECTIVE

There was a time when many believed that an unconventional warfare capability was important, and it was the U.S. Army that led the way. Many strategic thinkers in the 1950s felt that the current war-fighting doctrine of massive nuclear retaliation, though cheap, did not offer decision makers the flexibility to respond to crises at lower levels of intensity than direct confrontation with the Soviet Union. Lower-intensity conflicts had already taken place, notably in Korea and the French war in Viet Nam, and wars of national liberation in the Third World were looming.

General Maxwell Taylor led the way in 1959 with his book *The Uncertain Trumpet*. Taylor's book was largely an argument against the doctrine of massive retaliation (and the monopolization of defense resources by the Air Force). Its call for "a flexible response" and the forces to fight in an unconventional environment was made in general terms. General Taylor wrote that "while our massive retaliation strategy may have prevented the Great War—a World War III—it has not maintained the Little Peace."[2] The book had great appeal to strategic thinkers who did not want to look into the nuclear abyss at every crisis, and their number included the new president, John F. Kennedy, who asked Taylor to serve as his military advisor.

There was much comment in the early 1960s on the challenge presented by "national liberation movements" and how to apply unconventional warfare to this emerging problem. There was plenty of experience around and plenty of examples of unconventional wars that had already been fought or were in progress. Partisans had played a role in World War II and immediately after. Some U.S. policy makers had even served in those conflicts. Among them was William Colby, who had been an OSS commando in Europe, and Dean Rusk and Roger Hilsman at the State Department, who had served in the China–Burma–India theater. The communists had come to power in China after fighting as guerrillas in the early stages of their movement and had developed doctrine for fighting "wars of national liberation." The United States had fought Filipino guerrillas early in this century and had provided advice and aid to President Magsaysay in the Huk rebellion after World War II. Sir Robert Thompson had already made a name for himself in the insurgency in Malaya. A Viet Minh guerrilla force victory at Dien Bien Phu had led to an uneasy truce in Viet Nam, a burden the United States increasingly assumed.

In his book, *The Counterinsurgency Era*, Douglas Blaufarb wrote that the era began as early as 1950 and notes that John Kennedy had visited Viet Nam in 1951 and was already forming opinions on how to deal with the situation there and in Algeria. After Kennedy became president, National Security Council aide Walt Rostow delivered a Kennedy-cleared address on guerrilla warfare at Fort Bragg in June 1961. Two months later Roger Hilsman elaborated a counterinsurgency strategy in a speech that later appeared in book form with a forward by the president.[3] In early 1962, President Kennedy signed a National Security Action Memorandum that established a Special Group (Counter Insurgency) which would advise on unconventional threats. The group's membership included Robert Kennedy, Maxwell Taylor, Edward R. Morrow, and Undersecretary of State for Political Affairs Ambassador U. Alexis Johnson.[4]

In July 1962 Ambassador Johnson published a sort of cookbook article on how the United States would apply resources to defeat a war of national liberation. The article outlined the threat and the coordinated response that U.S. foreign affairs agencies should bring to bear. The article closed with a prescient note that warned that the local government was responsible for positive action and that perhaps only radical reforms would be able to "ameliorate the worst causes of discontent and redress inequities." Johnson noted that persuading a government to take remedial measures before it was too late was "always a difficult task and sometimes an impossible one."[5] Perhaps this warning should be the prime "lesson learned" from Viet Nam.

By 1962 unconventional warfare was in vogue, there was much comment about it, and units like the Army Special Forces were highly touted, at least by the White House. The Central Intelligence Agency (CIA) had taken guerrilla warfare to heart and trained insurgents to go into Cuba, Tibet, and elsewhere. The army's Special Forces were to cooperate closely with or be "adopted" by the CIA in Viet Nam where they organized irregular forces to fight the Viet Cong and the North Vietnamese Army (NVA). CIA Operations Director Desmond Fitzgerald announced in December 1965 to the graduating class of the career trainee course that the entire class would go directly into the paramilitary operations course. At the State Department, all the single officers in the spring 1966 class of Foreign Service Officer basic course eventually were assigned to Viet Nam.

Given the amount of expertise and knowledge about counterinsurgency and Viet Nam, it was almost tragic that Robert McNamara chose to cite as one of the reasons for our failure in Viet Nam the charge that we knew little about Viet Nam and the challenge of unconventional warfare. As stated earlier, several senior officials in the Kennedy administration had actually served in the Army in unconventional warfare roles during World War II, and many others like Walt Rostow and Alexis Johnson were thinking and writing about it.

It is more than just ironic that we lost not one, but two wars in Viet Nam. We lost the big war—the conventional war—never having lost a battle to the North Vietnamese Army or main-force Viet

Cong; rather, we tired of it, and the North Vietnamese disengaged to allow our combat forces to go home under the cover of "Vietnamization" and let the political scenario of the peace settlement run its course. And, we lost the political war as well. Although, as pacification czar Robert Komer has written, the overall pacification program was a success by any standard of measurement, we should not have allowed a venal, corrupt, undemocratic, South Vietnamese regime to undermine our efforts to provide political stability in that country. South Viet Nam was a government much like that which Ambassador Johnson had warned about in his 1962 article. Given the resources we were to put into the country and the political stake we assumed, we should not have been the least bit hesitant about forcing the South Vietnamese to accept political reforms we thought necessary in order to enable them to resist the North.

POST–VIET NAM DEBATES AND THE USE OF FORCE DOCTRINE

> While the U.S. military was, for the most part, uninterested at best and suspicious at worst of unconventional warfare prior to the Vietnam war, after the U.S. defeat in Vietnam such warfare was *total* anathema.[6]

The U.S. military, especially the army, did not want to remind itself of its Viet Nam experiences. While there were many "lessons learned" in Viet Nam that addressed such issues as logistics, communications, intelligence, and air–ground tactical operations, the fundamental lessons of counterinsurgency were largely ignored. There were lessons to learn from Viet Nam—too many lessons, and often contradictory.

Richard D. Downie, in a thought-provoking, comprehensive study of the politics and institutional psychology of how the U.S. military learns lessons from previous conflicts, concludes that "the Army clearly recognized deficiencies inherent within its counterinsurgency doctrine, but took no steps to correct those shortcomings." Colonel Downie goes on to explain that the Army in particular sought "lessons," but that "The Army could not achieve consensus on an approach to counterinsurgency—and there was no doctrinal change."[7] However, by the mid-1970s, the most salient "lesson" to be drawn from Viet Nam by the senior military leadership was to avoid involvement in such wars.

The real world of international politics and U.S. foreign policy "crises" would not permit the U.S. military the luxury of picking its own wars. While there was a respite from major U.S. military interventions between 1972 and 1980, the failures and near-failures of Desert One, Grenada, and Lebanon continued to raise public and private discussions about the ability and desire to engage in unconventional conflict. Numerous government studies addressed Viet Nam, future conflict scenarios, and the capabilities of the U.S. military to successfully engage in unconventional war. The feeling was that Viet Nam had (hopefully) been an aberration—but that "the Army did not change its doctrinal approach for the counter-insurgency assistance effort in El Salvador from Vietnam War era concepts. . . . The Army did not learn from its counterinsurgency experience in Vietnam."[8]

The Weinberger–Powell Doctrines: The Roadblock to Unconventional War Interventions

What began to etch the U.S. military's (especially the army's) negative feelings about unconventional warfare into the policy that must be dealt with today was the November 1984 presentation of what was known at the time as the Weinberger Doctrine. For all the notoriety the Weinberger Doctrine has acquired as the keystone of post–Viet Nam policy on the use of military force, as a document, the defense secretary's speech was nuanced and reasonable compared to what it became when it was selectively quoted and tailored, to finally become what is now known as the "Powell Doctrine." Although the Powell Doctrine always went beyond what Weinberger wrote, and began to erode when the Soviet Union collapsed, it remains unfortunately part of our political language on the use of force. And for Powell himself, it meant that he would be among the most reluctant to come to the decision to commit U.S. forces to the Gulf War, and it led him to make the highly criticized recommendation to end the war after only one-hundred hours.

A close reading of the Weinberger speech reveals that it left plenty of room for early intervention in a crisis. Weinberger wrote as follows:

• "We must be prepared, at any moment, to meet threats ranging in intensity from isolated terrorist acts, to guerrilla action, to full scale military confrontation."
• We must consider "the consequences of failing to deter conflict at the lowest level possible."
• "Because we face a spectrum of threats . . . choosing the appropriate level of our response is difficult. Flexible response does not mean just any response is appropriate."
• "As we are a major power . . . we must be prepared to deal with a range of possibilities, a spectrum of crises, from local insurgency to global con-

flict. We prefer to limit any conflict in its early stages, to contain and control it."

- "We should know precisely how our forces can accomplish those clearly defined objectives. And we should have and send the forces needed to do just that."

- "We must also be farsighted enough to sense when immediate and strong reactions to small events can prevent lion-like responses that may be required later. We must never forget those isolationists . . . who [ignored Danzig and the Rhineland]."

- "Yet no one should interpret what I am saying here today as an abdication of America's responsibilities—either to its own citizens or to its allies. Nor should these remarks be misread as a signal that this country . . . is unwilling to commit forces to combat overseas."[9]

Although Weinberger's statement said many of the right things, Secretary of State George Shultz read the mood at the Pentagon and the meaning behind the words. He knew of the army's stubborn reluctance to commit forces to low-intensity conflicts was deeply felt. Shultz wrote about his exasperation, saying the Weinberger Doctrine had turned into a "battle royal between Cap and me." Shultz called the doctrine "a complete abdication of leadership."[10]

It is worth noting some of the differences between Weinberger and Powell in some of what Weinberger called his "tests" for the use of force. The selective and oversimplified version of the Weinberger Doctrine known as the Powell Doctrine was set in concrete following the Gulf War and the prestige the army (and Powell) won in its astounding victory. The Powell Doctrine remains part of our current language on the use of force; but it went well beyond what Weinberger wrote.

What became in the Powell Doctrine "overwhelming force" had been in the Weinberger tests a commitment to a wholehearted effort with the clear intention of winning. But Weinberger was also clear that "if the particular situation requires only limited force to win our objectives, then we should not hesitate to commit forces sized appropriately." By January 1993, in President Bush's address at West Point, this test had become, can the application of force "be limited in scope and time?" The reference to the commitment of U.S. forces only for "vital interests" in the Powell Doctrine was "vital national interests and those of our allies" in the Weinberger speech. The word "vital" was dropped from the Bush speech at West Point.

Another point dropped from the West Point speech was the Weinberger–Powell reference to the necessity to have "the support of the American people and their elected representatives in Congress" before the U.S. commits combat forces abroad.This test erodes presidential leadership in foreign affairs, as Shultz pointed out, and would reduce the executive branch to waiting for the public opinion polls to reflect some glimmer of interest in a foreign disaster waiting to happen.

The weight of the Powell Doctrine remains especially useful to those who would stonewall foreign policy initiatives by using the oversimplistic but prestigious doctrine to ask the impossible and the irrelevant of policy makers. General Powell himself took on all comers, including Margaret Thatcher, in late 1992 when trying to keep the United States from committing forces to Bosnia. After standing by for years while the Serbs committed genocide, we searched our souls to find a U.S. "vital interest." Once we finally decided to go into Bosnia, we insisted on formulating an "exit strategy" which gave us a twelve-month deployment—which was known to be nonsense. The term "exit strategy," which has so plagued any discussion on U.S. policy in Bosnia, does not appear at all in the 1984 Weinberger speech.

Even General Hugh Shelton ran into the remains of the Powell Doctrine during his Senate hearings on his nomination to be chairman of the Joint Chiefs of Staff, as he was badgered about the "exit strategy" for Bosnia. The Senators wanted to know when the troops would come home. The smart answer would have been something along the line of deferring to the secretary of state or the president; yet, it is still assumed that foreign policy questions involving the military can be answered by the generals.

A criticism of Pentagon foot-dragging in Bosnia with respect to the Powell Doctrine came from an unexpected source. Once the United States had made a commitment to go to Bosnia, the interagency negotiations on the responsibilities for the Implementation Force began. The State Department favored an aggressive role for IFOR, but the Pentagon negotiated for restraint. The draft annex on IFOR reflected the Pentagon's position. During the negotiations in Dayton, former Assistant Secretary of Defense Richard Perle entered the negotiations as a consultant for the Bosnians. After reading the annex that dealt with the duties of IFOR, he called the annex "a pathetic evasion of responsibility by the Pentagon."[11]

The downside to the Powell Doctrine, besides nibbling at the constitutional question of civilian control of the military, has several components. If the United States is believed to use force and commit troops only *in extremis*, then credibility and deterrence is lost. Some adversaries may tailor their mischief-making to remain below a threshold of U.S. commitment, causing considerable damage before a U.S. response is initiated; this in turn makes a belated response more difficult and costly. Ironically, the doctrine's support of the use of overwhelming force is a return to the 1950s theme of massive retaliation and inflexibility, which the army as an institution then opposed.

Politically, the Weinberger–Powell Doctrine has been used as an argument to stonewall intervention and the limited use of force options available to the foreign-policy community. Logically, the opponents of intervention see special-operations forces as "symbols of intervention" and thus paint them with the same brush. There is a tendency to place greater budgetary, manpower, and capability limits on the "white" or overt side of special-operation forces, and less on the "dark" or covert side of forces involved in direct action missions, such as JSOC/Delta, Rangers, and the army's special operations Aviation Regiment.

Yet, most commentators agree with what James Woolsey said when he was director of the Central Intelligence Agency: Although the United States had slain the Soviet dragon, there were still lots of snakes in the jungle. If it is true that the U.S. Army now only wants to "do deserts," and not jungles or mountains, how do we deal with the snakes of the world when an armored corps is inappropriate?

In their book on the reforms that rebuilt the U.S. Army in the 1980s, Dunnigan and Macedonia wrote in 1993 that two of the three threats to be faced in the 1990s will be unconventional: guerrillas and terrorists. They add that the army is unenthusiastic about dealing with either threat.[12] President Clinton and former National Security Advisor Tony Lake have sought to bring more flexibility to the use of force in foreign policy, and Secretary Albright has strongly signaled she will be an activist. To General Powell's considerable consternation, she has asked, of what use is our superb military if we cannot or will not use it?

The Reagan Doctrine: Favoring the Use of Limited Force

According to Reagan administration policy maker Peter Rodman, what became known as the Reagan Doctrine was an idea that evolved over time. The name was coined by columnist Charles Krauthammer writing for *Time* in the spring of 1985. National Security Advisor Bud McFarlane said that "not one nano-second" went into analysis or planning for the doctrine, which gave systematic support to guerrilla forces fighting communist dictatorships in the Third World. As Krauthammer defined the doctrine, it was "overt and unashamed American support for anti-communist revolution." Krauthammer had called attention to a vague and little noticed passage from Reagan's State of the Union address in February 1985: "[We] must not break faith with those who are risking their lives—

on every continent, from Afghanistan to Nicaragua—to defy Soviet-supported aggression and to secure rights which have been ours since birth."[13]

Rodman outlines the intellectual development of the doctrine and notes an early contribution by Elliott Abrams, then assistant secretary of state for humanitarian affairs. In a 1981 memo, Abrams argued that our struggle with the Soviets was a moral one and that our credibility depended on our being committed to democracy in response to rightist regimes as well as leftist. Secretary of State Haig spoke of a "democratic revolution" in a Berlin speech in September 1981, and Reagan in his famous June 1982 Westminter speech called attention to the growing crisis of totalitarianism and the inevitable triumph of democracy. March 1983 saw the "evil empire" speech, and in June 1984 in Dublin, Reagan said that the people of Nicaragua and El Salvador had the right to resist Communism. In January 1985, CIA Director Casey claimed "the tide had changed," since the 1980s marked the decade in which freedom fighters were resisting communist regimes. A March 1986 essay by the president noted the phenomenon of armed resistance to Communism, and stated that "we must not fail to respond to it."[14]

Yet, in spite of the fact that "we must not fail to respond," not everybody was convinced of how to go about responding. Secretary of State Shultz, as part of his "battle royal" on the use of force with Weinberger, weighed in strongly in a February 1985 speech in San Francisco. Shultz called for U.S. support of democratic revolution in Nicaragua and elsewhere and called attention to dissident movements in Eastern Europe. He noted Nicaragua was on the front line, and said "those who would cut off these freedom fighters from the rest of the democratic world are, in effect, consigning Nicaragua to the endless darkness of communist tyranny." Angelo Codevilla, a conservative intelligence specialist, warned that Reagan's policy was being undermined within the administration. He noted bureaucratic infighting within the State Department and the CIA and also within the Department of Defense, where some civilians were champions of the policy, but the uniformed military was much more cautious.[15]

The uniformed military responded to the Central American crisis in different ways. In El Salvador, the Southern Command led a small advisory effort that was limited to fifty-five "trainers" by Congress. Guatemala, because of its human rights problems, did not receive substantial U.S. military assistance. As for the contras, the military wanted to have as little to do with them as possible, but the Pentagon did go along with an ambitious Southcom plan to pressure the Sandinistas and aid the Salvadorans from bases in Honduras.

ORGANIZING FOR LOW-INTENSITY CONFLICT

The 1987 National Security Decision Directive (NSDD) on low-intensity conflict was the result of a concern that our failure to liberate the Iran hostages (which ended in Desert One), the many shortcomings and coordination difficulties in the Grenada operation, and the difficulties in mounting a comprehensive security-assistance program for our Central American allies all represented an organizational or doctrinal problem.

President Reagan signed a national security study directive in October 1986 to look at how a more concerted effort could be directed to low-intensity conflict (LIC) challenges. The army's Training and Doctrine Command had just finished an LIC project of its own and published a two-volume final report in August that outlined a program of reforms needed for the United States to operate effectively in the low-intensity arena. Part of the impetus to write a national strategy for low-intensity conflict had come from the Congress, which in its appropriation for that year called for the establishment within the National Security Council a coordinating body for LIC and mandated a new assistant secretary of defense for special operations and low-intensity conflict (SO/LIC). A National Security Decision Directive on Low-Intensity Conflict was signed by the president in June 1987.

The Pentagon was slow to react to the congressional call for a separate SO/LIC command and assistant secretary. At a March 25, 1987 hearing before the Senate Armed Services Committee, Noel Koch, a former deputy assistant secretary of defense and director of the office for special operations planning charged that "the Department of Defense has done everything possible to circumvent the will of the Congress." Much of the Pentagon's delay in creating the command, he charged, was due to the lack of leadership by Secretary of Defense Weinberger. "With all due respect to John Lehman," Koch said, "the Pentagon doesn't need 600 ships, it needs a rudder."[16]

Legislative Reforms: Building Unconventional Warfare Capabilities against the Will of the Pentagon

The conflictive lessons of Viet Nam, the desire on the part of the military services to avoid politically risky unconventional conflicts, the poor performance of the military in Desert One (some of which was replicated in the failure of numerous special operations missions in the Grenada intervention), and particularly the resistance of the senior military leadership in the Pentagon, finally drove concerned congressional leaders and staff to begin a process of legislating military reform. The explicit objective would be to build and support a U.S. special operations and unconventional warfare organization with the proper resources, authority, and authorized missions to carry out American foreign policy.

The desire for such changes had been discussed for years since the Desert One failure. One significant step taken was the preparation and publication of the Senate Committee on Armed Services report entitled *Defense Reorganization: The Need for Change*. Released October 1985, the report and its recommendations became the basis for the Goldwater–Nichols Department of Defense Reorganization Act of 1986. The Goldwater–Nichols reform legislation cited the lack of U.S. military capabilities to engage unconventional (low-intensity conflict) war threats; the lack of coordination within the U.S. government—including the military services; and the need for consistent resources within a recognized organizational setting.[17]

The Defense Reorganization Act of 1986 was reinforced by the Cohen–Nunn amendment which called for the creation of a U.S. special operations command. The amendment, strongly and publicly opposed by the Pentagon military and civilian leadership, became law in November 1986. The law created the building blocks for a unified special operations command by establishing the following: (1) an assistant secretary of defense for special operations and low-intensity conflict; (2) a unified command for special operations forces; (3) a major force program that would integrate all special operations requirements into one budget; (4) the creation of special operations commands in all unified commands; and (5) the creation of a board for low-intensity conflict to be located within the National Security Council. Additional legislation, dealing with budget proposals and reviews, command authority, reporting compliance, and congressional oversight, from 1986 to 1988 was passed by Congress, in spite of continued resistance from Pentagon leadership.[18]

Thus, during the mid-1980s, two major, but ironically unlinked, struggles were taking place in unconventional warfare. One was the bureaucratic fight in Washington over the creation—against the will of the Pentagon—of a special operations command and an assistant secretary of defense for special operations. The second struggle was taking place on the Central American battlefield. The first began with the failure of Desert One—the hostage-rescue operation in Iran. It was later described as a failed special operation that reflected serious organizational and equipment flaws in the U.S. military's unconventional warfare capabilities.

The second major unconventional warfare struggle began with the failed "general offensive" of the Salvadoran guerrillas in January 1981. Both struggles would carry through the decade and spill over into the 1990s. However, the unconventional battleground of Central America would not play a role in the public and private debates over the establishment of a centrally coordinated, separately budgeted, and politically supported special operations command. At the time, it was the only obvious point of "real world" reference and justification for the need to upgrade and support special operations forces for the purpose of carrying out U.S. foreign policy objectives in unconventional war environments.

CENTRAL AMERICA AND UNCONVENTIONAL WARFARE POLICY

The Central American region consists of seven countries: Guatemala, Belize, Honduras, El Salvador, Nicaragua, Costa Rica, and Panama. These countries have a total population of some thirty million. Central America has had a long history of regional wars dating back to the nineteenth century. What made the regional wars of the 1980s distinctive was the internationalization of the conflicts and actors. The two main Cold-War adversaries, the United States and the Soviet Union, were supported by a cast of governments and nonstate actors alike.

In support of the United States were the British in Belize and off the Caribbean coast, the Koreans, Chileans, Argentines, Taiwanese, Israelis, and South Africans. Allied with the Soviets were the Cubans, members of the Eastern Bloc (especially the East Germans), Viet Nam, and the PLO. Weapons came from throughout the world, including mainland China. The international wings of the political parties in the United States, Latin America, and Europe also became involved. Human rights groups of all political persuasions joined the battle. Guerrilla front groups proliferated throughout the Central American region, the United States, and Europe. By the late 1980s, the United States and the Soviet Union–Eastern Bloc had committed over $5 billion to their Cold-War struggle in the region.

Before 1980, Central America had witnessed a guerrilla war in Guatemala (1962–1970) that had ended in defeat for the insurgents; a successful insurgency (1962–1979) by the Sandinistas in Nicaragua; a growing but low-profile insurgency that began in El Salvador in the mid-1970s; a new insurgency in Guatemala that began in 1972; and the establishment of a military populist regime under General Omar Torrijos in Panama.

By 1990, the Panama Defense Forces were militarily defeated and demobilized by a direct U.S. military intervention; a guerrilla

insurgency was defeated in Guatemala but not brought to the negotiating table; a stalemate on the battlefield existed in El Salvador; and a peasant insurgency supported by the United States forced
the Sandinistas into an unexpected electoral defeat. The costs of
the Central American wars between 1980 and 1990 were significant: over $6 billion just for the United States alone to fight the
wars and sustain the economies of the region; hundreds of thousands killed; thousands disappeared; several million internally displaced refugees; hundreds of thousands of Guatemalans,
Salvadorans, Hondurans, and Nicaraguans fleeing legally and ille-
gally to the United States; and severely damaged economies that
would take years to repair.

In the 1980s, the battlefield actors were not always easily identifiable. Nevertheless, one can say the following: In 1981, a 35-thousand-
man Guatemalan army, supported by more than 200 thousand
members of the civil defense forces, faced some 8 thousand to 12
thousand National Revolutionary Unity of Guatemala (URNG)
guerrillas. In El Salvador the armed forces and police of 50 thousand, supported by a small number of civil defense forces, engaged
12 thousand Farabundo Marti (FMLN) guerrilla fighters. And in
Nicaragua, the Sandinista army, state security forces, militias, and
reserves numbering more than 100 thousand faced a contra force
of 20 thousand. A critical event that provided the geopolitical setting for the Central American wars was the military defeat of the
Somoza National Guard in July 1979. It was the Sandinista victory, the first revolutionary guerrilla success since Fidel Castro
took power in Cuba in 1959, that lent a decisive Cold-War tone to
the wars of the 1980s.[19]

With the Sandinista military victory as backdrop and inspiration, the FMLN guerrillas launched their "general offensive" in
January 1981, less than two weeks before the inauguration of President Reagan. It is this failed guerrilla offensive and the direct support links between the FMLN and the Sandinista government in
Managua (revealed and documented after the offensive) that resulted in the United States having a military presence in Central
America for ten years. The FMLN carried out a second failed offensive against the capital in November 1989. By 1989 and 1990, the
logic of the battlefield had driven all parties to the recognition that
negotiated agreements were the only way to bring about a lasting
peace in the Central American region.

The peace processes came by way of the battlefield. It took a major
U.S. military buildup and presence in the region to assure that (1)
Marxist guerrillas would not win on the battlefield; (2) assistance
from Cuba, the USSR–Eastern Bloc, and Viet Nam would not give

an advantage to the Sandinista government or guerrilla insurgencies over their opponents; and (3) there was a coercive dimension to U.S. diplomatic and political endeavors in the region.

"Preparing the battlefield," as General Paul Gorman often stated, in support of an unconventional war (or a potential conventional U.S. military intervention) took three long years to accomplish. Building up Southern Command Headquarters at Quarry Heights, Panama and other component military services in areas in Panama took several years. Establishing National Security Agency communications-intercept sites, CIA facilities and networks, and aerial and seaborne intelligence platforms took time, money, and arguing for scarce resources within the intelligence community of Central America.

By 1985, the combination of unconventional and conventional forces and operations had penetrated virtually every nook and cranny of the Central American region. The explicit objectives were to first isolate the battlefields from external support and secondly support the local security forces to isolate and defeat the guerrillas. In the case of Nicaragua, U.S. unconventional forces had multiple missions: (1) interdict the logistical supply networks between Nicaragua and El Salvador; (2) support the contra insurgency through training, logistics, and planning; (3) prepare special operations contingency plans in support of a direct U.S. military intervention; and (4) create the necessary military infrastructure to defend Honduras against a military attack by Nicaragua.

Thus, by the mid-1980s, Navy Seals, Air Force AC-130 gunships, Army intelligence collection aircraft, Army Special Forces, and CIA paramilitary specialists were operating in, around, and over the Central American region. Special intelligence collection units were deployed in the field. Elements of the 82nd Airborne, the 75th Ranger Regiment, and the 7th Special Forces Group engaged in day-and-night drops in the Mocoron region of Honduras near the Nicaraguan border. Seals were deployed in the Gulf of Fonseca and Special Forces training and reconnaissance detachments operated along border regions of Central America.

By 1987, U.S. unconventional forces were the critical component in the U.S. military presence in the region. All services provided unconventional-warfare specialists. They were involved in all aspects of war: advising, training, logistics, intelligence, planning and operations, special operations, civic action, psychological operations, counterterrorism, civil defense, long-range patrolling, and humanitarian assistance. These forces kept the fiscal costs of the American military involved in Central America at acceptable levels. The several billions of dollars spent over the decade can be compared to the $500 million bill to deploy conventional forces to Haiti for six months! Politically, the unconventional forces kept the American presence at a much lower profile and acted as an effective shield to the conventional force option of direct military intervention.

The unconventional forces and operations helped in a concrete way to shape the conflict environment for U.S. foreign policy endeavors in the region. Without these forces, and with a reliance almost exclusively on conventional forces, operations, and doctrines would have not only been expensive but unworkable, given the political climate in the United States and the nature of the Central American combatants.

Honduras: Building an Unconventional–Conventional War Infrastructure—"Preparing the Battlefield"

> I'm going to cut the top off of Tiger Island.
> —General Paul Gorman, June 1985

Honduras became the hub of the military's efforts to confront Communism in Central America. General Paul Gorman, the new commander of the Southern Command, led the way. In a June 1985 luncheon meeting at the Ambassador's residence in Tegucigalpa, he outlined how he would bring to Honduras various military units for exercises, intelligence gathering, and military construction through training. Already underway in Honduras were the previously negotiated permanent improvements to Palmerola airfield and plans to construct a Regional Military Training Center (RMTC) on the north coast to accelerate training for the Salvadoran armed forces.

General Gorman's review of Tiger Island referred to only one of the several intelligence efforts he launched from Honduras. Tiger island was located in the Gulf of Fonseca, and it was thought to be a major transit point for arms shipments from Nicaragua to Salvador. Gorman did indeed cut a piece off the top of the island for a radar station to monitor the gulf and a communications-intercept site. From Palmerola, the United States flew several kinds of reconnaissance platforms against the FMLN and the Sandinistas.

The United States established a joint task force at Palmerola to support a constant program of military exercises. The exercises brought all kinds of U.S. military units to Honduras to train and for the Honduran army to train with. The U.S. units included construction, armor, medical civic action, and airborne forces. In the waters off Central America, several carriers visited to train and show force, as did the battleship *Iowa*. The Regional Military Training Center, staffed by the Special Forces, processed thousands of

Salvadorans, and an equal number of Hondurans. The demands on the Special Forces's Spanish-speakers was so heavy that at some points it was difficult to staff the center. Eventually, almost all of the Central American nations participated at the RMTC by sending students or faculty. All this activity attracted visitors—3 thousand in one year including congressmen, both supportive and suspicious, who found out you could "do" Honduras on a weekend, and military and civilians from Washington. Also visiting were additional concerned citizens from the United States who generally were opposed to the U.S. policy in Central America and required usually contentious briefings from the embassy.

The cooperation of the government of Honduras gained it substantial military and economic assistance and assurances of U.S. support in the event of a Sandinista attack. The facilities of the joint task force at Palmerola were eventually turned into a regional antinarcotics center, and Honduras became a natural site for one of the installations of the Caribbean Basin Radar Network.

Counterinsurgency in El Salvador and Guatemala

The wars in Guatemala and El Salvador provided two distinct contexts for counterinsurgency. In Guatemala, after the "Captains' coup" of March 23, 1982, the military assumed direct responsibility for both the administration of government and the administration of the war effort. The Guatemalan army and their civilian allies developed a strategy of "going it alone." In the case of El Salvador, the armed forces had a strong and determined partner in their war against the FMLN guerrillas—the U.S. government and military. While the United States provided economic, financial, and military support valued at over $3 billion, U.S. assistance for the Guatemalan effort to defeat the URNG guerrillas was estimated to be in the millions of dollars. The irony was that the Guatemalan army developed a highly successful counterinsurgency campaign with scarce resources, while the Salvadoran armed forces never were able to seriously damage the guerrilla infrastructure and war fighting capabilities despite American support and assistance.[20]

Between 1982 and 1985, the Guatemalan army engaged in countrywide operations based on a total mobilization strategy. The government was reorganized to fight the war and provide basic services to populations in the areas of conflict. The army was reorganized into large task forces that stayed in the field for years in specific areas where guerrillas concentrated their forces. And the Guatemalan army made the controversial decision to arm and train several hundred thousand farmers—mostly Indians in the northern highlands. It worked, and the guerrillas were largely destroyed as an effective military force by 1995. It was done with minimal U.S. support, international isolation, and few national resources. The key to the success was taking the war to the small villages and staying to secure a government presence. To use the Chinese and Vietnamese term, the Guatemalan military and civilian architects of the counterinsurgency turned the conflict into a "people's war."

In El Salvador, American presence and assistance was essential in determining that the Salvadoran army would not lose on the battlefield. However, U.S. support was not sufficient to ensure victory, early negotiations, or a more successful and less punitive peace treaty in 1992. Despite enormous resources from Washington, the FMLN guerrillas staged their "final offensive" in January 1981 with approximately 6 thousand to 8 thousand combatants. When the FMLN launched their "offensive" against San Salvador in November 1989, the estimated number of guerrillas was between 8 thousand and 10 thousand. Government and population mobilization was not a key to the counterinsurgency strategy in El Salvador. The complete burden of fighting the war rested with the army—the government, the private sector, and most of the population were bystanders.

Without U.S. presence and assistance, the Guatemalan army militarily defeated the guerrillas. However, it would not be until almost ten years later that a final peace treaty was signed to end a thirty-six-year internal war. In El Salvador, U.S. assistance and policy produced a stalemated war that ended in a peace agreement which decidedly weakened the armed forces as an institution and created a relatively weak, independent civilian police force. Today, El Salvador has one of the highest violent crime rates in the Western Hemisphere in the absence of effective, viable security organizations.

The wars themselves were complex, bloody, and prolonged. They were internationalized, and hundreds of global actors (state and nonstate) became party to the Central American conflicts. The Reagan administration strategy was simple and direct: "save" El Salvador from a communist victory, punish (primarily with the contras) the Sandinistas for supporting guerrilla wars in El Salvador and Guatemala, and hope that the Guatemalan army on its own could avoid defeat. It is often forgotten that in 1980 and 1981, the URNG guerrillas had mobilized and armed some 10 thousand combatants, and controlled the northern highlands from the Mexican border to within a thirty-minute drive from the capital, Guatemala City. The URNG in Guatemala and the FMLN in El Salvador started out almost on equal terms in 1981; however, the Guatemalan guerrillas were far closer to a military victory than their colleagues in El Salvador. Thus, the counterinsurgency success of the

Guatemalan army has to be seen as even more remarkable in the context of minimal resources, international isolation, and American distancing.

U.S. strategy was fortunate in the Central American region. It was an unconventional environment from 1980 to 1990 in which the United States was reluctant to engage. The Guatemalan army did it without the United States; the El Salvador army—with substantial American material and political support—fought the war on its own with marginal civilian participation on the battlefield; and the contras fought an orthodox peasants' war with modern Cold-War military technology. The Nicaraguan Resistance, a largely peasant army with traditional peasant values, successfully carried out their campaign of "punishing" the Sandinistas. And, surprisingly, their presence and survivability for two years after the U.S. Congress cut off all lethal assistance led to early elections in Nicaragua and an even more surprising political defeat for the FSLN government at the polls. All three wars were linked, not just in terms of Washington's regional strategy, but also in operational terms throughout the 1980s.

Supporting Insurgency: The Nicaraguan Resistance

It has been written that the contra program went to the CIA because Weinberger's Defense Department would not "touch it with a fork," and CIA's Casey "would have killed for it." Much of what was secret about the "secret war" was exposed by a *Newsweek* article in November 1982. George Shultz wrote that both bureaucracies were uncomfortable with the program because it was only nominally secret, and some thought was given in 1983 to going public with the program and transferring it to the Defense Department. However, Defense resisted because the policy and the program were controversial, and like the CIA, it feared congressional wrath.[21]

One of the secretary's comments on the Middle East also applies to the contra program. Shultz observed that "Cap Weinberger and the Pentagon were extremely wary and reluctant to use the formidable resources lodged in the Department of Defense. The CIA and Bill Casey were as independent as a hog on ice and could be as confident as they were wrong."[22]

The source of the controversy is obvious, and the truth about the controversy is ironic. The congressional Democrats supported the Sandinistas because they had thrown out the Somoza dictatorship and because they did not want to see the United States bullying a small country in Central America in trying to make its own revolution succeed.

More important, public support for the contras was soft and the president was seen by the congressional democrats as vulnerable on the issue. By the time of his downfall, Somoza had alienated almost all of Nicaragua's elite, and acting together, they brought him down. Because the Sandinistas had made sacrifices and were organized and armed, they were able to take over the leadership from the front that formed the first post-Somoza government. The governing Sandinista directorate was made up of the sons and daughters of Nicaragua's elite. They were educated at private secondary schools in Europe and the United States—including Phillips Exeter.

The contras, on the other hand, were charged with being little more than the remnants of Somoza's defeated National Guard. Some guardsmen played important roles in the contra program (such as serving as the organizational links to American assistance) and less to the contra movement inside Nicaragua. These guardsmen despised the Sandinistas and were ready and willing to train and fight with the peasant base that would become the army of the Nicaraguan Resistance. The overall numbers of contra fighters dictate that the defeated National Guard and the contra army were two different things. The National Guard was normally an army–police force of 5 thousand to 6 thousand, which expanded to about 9 thousand during the war with the Sandinistas. Had even one in ten joined the contras, their number would have been less than a thousand.

At the end of the war, the Organization of American States and the United Nations demobilized over 22 thousand contra fighters.[23] Hence, the National Guard was numerically a minor part of the contra army, and one researcher puts their participation at most at about 700. The same researcher notes that while fighting Somoza, the Sandinistas never had a firm foothold in Nicaragua's rural areas. One Sandinista officer told him they were merely a "rejected graft" among the peasants.[24]

A sociological study of the contras and their families done by a contractor for the U.S. Agency for International Development in 1988 revealed that the army was overwhelmingly of peasant (*campesino* or *indio*) origin, overwhelmingly Catholic, uneducated, and poor. These *campesinos* recognized early on that the Sandinistas were betraying their interests, and many who had fought with the Sandinistas formed the core of a group called the *milpas* which began the rural rebellion in Nicaragua against the Sandinistas even before the formation of the contras in Honduras. Soon after the demobilization of the contras in June 1990, Sandinista *comandante* Luis Carrion (a graduate of Phillips Exeter) admitted in a long interview in *Barricada* that it was Sandinista rural policies that had driven the campesinos into revolt and created the contras.

The controversial contra program was actually a series of programs with one fiscal-year funding—some with military aid, some without. Continuity and momentum suffered as a result. The programs began with a presidential finding signed in November 1981 by President Reagan for a covert paramilitary operation inside Nicaragua. Between 1982 and 1990, the United States provided approximately $200 million in military and nonlethal support for contra operations. The program probably also suffered from being run by the CIA. By the 1980s their capacity for unconventional warfare had been gutted. One casualty was the political side of waging a guerrilla war. The contra *comandantes* needed political training, which would have been practically a matter of doctrine had the U.S. Army been training them.

The poorly educated *campesino comandantes* (who made up about 80% of the contra field commanders) needed to be able to better articulate in positive terms the political aims of the contras for recruitment and motivation of their troops and supporters in order to establish the foundations for a future political movement. The former guardsmen—the "educated elite" of the contra commanders—could have used some help in being recast politically to lead a peasant rebellion towards a new Nicaragua. Postdemobilization attempts to form a contra political movement met with very limited success—the contra supporters were about one-third of Nicaragua's electorate, but elected only one of their former leaders to the National Assembly.

The CIA did establish a political directorate to lead the contras in their various iterations, but it became largely a public-relations exercise. The Miami-based directorate was split along ego lines and did not function as a leadership. A talented support staff was immobilized by the fractious directorate. The directorate meant nothing to the *campesino* army: their trip to the mountains to introduce themselves to the army leaders as their "political leadership" fell flat on its face.

At the end of the war, a State–CIA split developed as the State Department attempted to push more power and decision making to the resistance army leaders. The CIA had already quashed two attempts by resistance army leaders to reform their own leadership and move away from National Guard influence. Department of State officials felt that the Miami Directorate had become a farce, especially from the point of view of public relations, and that the people doing the fighting and the dying deserved to be recognized in their own right. In terms of public relations, they showed a new face of the contras—courageous, honest men and women of rural stock who were fighting to regain what the Sandinista regime had taken from them: land, independence, and dignity.

When the military program for the contras ended in February 1988, the CIA quickly lost interest. The agency sought to close down the Miami operation and turn its support entirely to those politicians in the directorate who were going back to Nicaragua to participate in the election campaign. The State felt that the resistance army still could have used some political support from Miami staffers, but was unable to forestall the closing of the Miami offices.

CIA military operations were dependent on military officers detailed to the contra operations base. In 1986 and 1987, the formal, organized training of the contras was carried out by U.S. Special Forces, not CIA paramilitary officers. Several military officers played key roles in supporting and training the contras for military operations. The contra strike into the Las Minas area of Nicaragua in December 1987 was their greatest military success—it involved over 7 thousand combatants. For some Sandinistas, this operation confirmed that the Nicaraguan Resistance was in fact a political–military force that threatened their ability to govern the country. At their base in the mountains on the Honduran border, the contra commanders had planned this large and complicated operation under the supervision and guidance of American advisors.

CENTRAL AMERICAN LESSONS AND THE FUTURE OF UNCONVENTIONAL WARFARE IN U.S. FOREIGN POLICY

Central America was the last Cold-War battlefield for the United States. It was a ten-year-long unconventional war environment. And, with the possible exception of President Reagan and a scattering of political appointees and career officials, there was little genuine enthusiasm for an operational involvement in the region's conflicts throughout the administration.

By the mid-1990s, in the aftermath of the Persian Gulf War, this ten-year unconventional war had been forgotten and buried. Yet, some $10 billion was expended in military operations, intelligence platforms, and direct military, economic, and financial assistance. A unified command, the United States Southern Command, headquartered at Quarry Heights, Panama, went from "sleepy command" to the only command involved operationally in a series of regional wars. The number of joint staff positions almost doubled, the 193rd Infantry Brigade was built up, additional aircraft were deployed to Howard Air Force Base, and Southern Command established Pamerola Airbase in Honduras—designated Joint Task Force Bravo. Every Special Operations unit in the U.S. military establishment deployed personnel into the region: Army Special

Forces, Army Rangers, Delta, Navy SEALS, U.S. Air Force AC-130 gunships, and U.S. Marines. Their presence was low profile and not large in numbers. Nevertheless, they helped to shape the nature of the wars and their outcomes.

The CIA established the Central American Taskforce (CATF) to coordinate all intelligence, paramilitary, and covert operations in the region. The Defense Department created the Central American Joint Intelligence Team (CAJIT) to coordinate all-source information on the region and to develop "target packages" for friendly forces in the region. This was indeed a monumental effort that would take years to establish in the region, in Panama, and in Washington, D.C.[25]

This effort was directed at only one goal: save Central America from Communism. Just as these wars were coming to an end in Central America, the Soviet Union was coming to an end as a global power and unified federation of republics. The Berlin Wall came down in 1989, and the USSR as it was known during the Cold War came to a dramatic close by 1991. The Cold War would also fade into history with the collapse of the Soviet Union and the ensuing Persian Gulf War. In the midst of all this drama in global politics, the events in Central America became but a vague memory for some, and a nightmare for others, but amnesia set in for those in senior diplomatic, intelligence, and military positions.

Given the events of the period of 1989 through 1992, it is somewhat easy to understand how history prevented Central America from being center stage during the Cold War. However, the region could not be ignored given the numbers: seven countries, 28 million inhabitants, a combined gross domestic product of $25 billion, 40 thousand armed guerrillas involved in four countries, 200 thousand active duty military personnel, and 400 thousand police and paramilitary–self-defense forces. It was also estimated that more than 150 thousand people died in these wars, thousands more were made to disappear, and several million became internally displaced or became refugees throughout the region, Mexico, the United States, and Canada. In the end, the Guatemalan guerrillas were defeated militarily, the Salvador guerrillas created a military stalemate on the battlefield that led to negotiations, and the contras succeeded in creating economic and fiscal chaos that led to an electoral defeat for the Sandinistas.

Despite the involvement dictated from the presidency, U.S. diplomatic, military, and intelligence officials saw with some disdain all that embodied Central America: unpopular regimes in power, human-rights abuses, unpopular policies at home, messy wars, an emphasis if not a reliance on U.S. special operations personnel, covert operations, and the heavy hand of the CIA. For many within the U.S. government, Central America had all the trappings of Viet Nam, that is, a political and military disaster constantly criticized by Congress, the public, and the media.

Senior officials could argue throughout the 1980s that U.S. security interests in Central America were peripheral to its "global interests" in Europe, the USSR, China, and the Middle East. The political risks were high, and the security payoff, minimal. If these same military and civilian officials could cast aside Viet Nam as a very bad "aberration" in warfare, then it would be much simpler to cast aside Central America, even though victorious, as an aberration in warfare. Central America, ironically, was not seen by the critics as part of the big picture in the waning decade of the Cold War.

Despite the disdain for and distancing from the Central American experience, there are lessons that should be examined for possible relevance to future unconventional war involvement. Clear lessons do emerge from America's involvement in Central America.[26] Listed are five primary lessons that require further examination for future unconventional warfare contingencies:

1. U.S. military and CIA paramilitary personnel, doctrines, and support systems can adapt to unconventional war environments, given sufficient time and resources.

2. The U.S. government remains its own worst enemy. The bureaucratic costs of coordination and cooperation are too high. Despite Viet Nam (or perhaps because of Viet Nam), the learning curve and the periodic need to reinvent the wheel of unconventional warfare has dragged on for years.

3. U.S. intelligence platforms, analysis, and real-time intelligence support can buy time and space for an ally on the battlefield, but can in no way guarantee victory.

4. No amount of U.S. resources, advice, operational support, leverage, and presence can sufficiently change the culture of a combat organization it is supporting (military establishment or guerrilla organization); the United States can only hope to change behavior on the battlefield sufficient to secure victory for or prevent defeat of the ally.

5. The poorest area of unconventional warfare performance by U.S. military, CIA, and State Department programs and personnel is in political warfare and psychological operations.

U.S. government, and especially U.S. military, responses to unconventional war environments suggest that little has been drawn from our own Central American experiences. Organizing ourselves and "preparing the battlefield" remain the major challenge for the United States in unconventional-warfare policy. Clearly this is the highest priority lesson to draw from both Viet Nam and Central

America. It appears, however, that future U.S. involvement in internal wars will continue to demonstrate this political, policy, and organizational shortcoming in managing our unconventional-warfare operations.

EPILOGUE

The interest of the average American in foreign affairs has never been strong. It may have been Senator Fulbright who commented that if you asked an American for a political opinion about a subject that touched his life, generally you would get a reasonable and thoughtful answer. But foreign affairs, he said, was usually not one of those subjects. Fortunately, the average American recognized the threat the Cold War represented and was willing to make the sacrifices to fight it. When the wall came down, and victory was declared, Americans reverted to a historical theme: Bring the boys home, and then let's get on with our lives.

It is not as easy to disengage from warfare today as it was before in our history, though the urge to do so remains. President Bush made a brief attempt after the Cold War to retain the public's interest in foreign affairs with a concept he called the "New World Order," which called for new ways of working with other countries and the United Nations to deter aggression. The message was a bit vague, and the public did not respond. President Clinton and his top foreign affairs aides gave speeches over several months outlining his second administration's policy of engagement and multilateralism. When they finished, newspaper editors bemoaned the impression that the White House had no foreign policy. Voters looked for a peace dividend even in foreign aid.

National opinion polls consistently determine that Americans believe that the U.S. government gives away ten percent of their tax dollars in aid. Their preferred level of assistance would be three percent. Average annual international assistance and programs make up about one percent of the total federal budget. Aid "wasn't playing in Peoria" anymore. (The quip is doubly ironic for Peoria because it is headquarters for Caterpillar and had been receiving millions over many years in foreign aid funding for overseas delivery of its excellent earth moving equipment!) Another illustrative phenomenon of a new type of isolationism was the attack on the United Nations, which surfaced with venom during the 1996 presidential campaign.

Americans now are also less likely to want to read about foreign affairs. Responding to the lack of reader interest, three leading news magazines halved their coverage of foreign news between 1985 and

1995. The editor of *Foreign Affairs* noted that Americans were following the example of their elected leaders: "The media, to a great extent takes its lead from public officials as to whether foreign policy is worthy of coverage. And we have a virtual blackout in both parties." The editor at *U.S. News* said there would be an inevitable decline in foreign bureau presence, and a *Newsweek* editor said that the ties that bind the international community would be economics and business, science and technology, and culture and lifestyle. "You can't just kind of wave your magic wand and pretend that the striped-pants diplomat's news is as interesting as it was during the Cold War because it plainly isn't."[27]

A poll released in October 1997 revealed that the U.S. public was no more isolationist, but also no more satisfied with the state of world affairs than it had been four years earlier. The poll also revealed that opinion leaders were almost twice as optimistic about U.S. foreign policy as the public at large.[28]

Yet, recent polling has also shown that Americans remain "concerned and even idealistic about the world's problems."[29] Two polls found that Americans want to cooperate multilaterally to solve world problems and that they hold the United Nations in high regard. They are also increasingly aware of how foreign crises can affect their own lives. A *New York Times* editorial concluded that Americans care more about the world than they are given credit for and that the test of leadership remains to demonstrate the connection of foreign problems to their own lives. The editorial also points out a serious flaw in the Weinberger–Powell Doctrine. Leaders cannot wait for the citizenry to become aware that something that has happened abroad has affected their lives or outraged their sensibilities to act in crises situations. Leadership must be out in front of public opinion, mobilizing the citizenry to support those actions taken to deter serious problems before they become unmanageable. Leadership also requires that the forces necessary be maintained for the flexible responses required for deterrence.

What if unconventional warfare had not fallen on hard times after Viet Nam? What if there had been clear lines of authority and doctrine in special operations to plan and execute the rescue of our hostages in Iran? Would there have been a disaster at Desert I? Would the Grenada operation have gone off with better interservice coordination?

And in Central America, what if we had not had to accede to a fifty-five-man limit on advisors in El Salvador? Perhaps with U.S. advisors accompanying Salvadoran army units, the massacre at El Mazote would not have happened, nor the killing of the Jesuits (nor the killing of the three nuns). With American public opinion not constantly outraged by the actions of the Salvadoran army, would more involvement by the U.S. Army have been possible? The Salvadoran guerrillas fought the army to a draw, despite close to a billion dollars in direct and indirect U.S. military assistance and intelligence operations support. How was it possible that after Viet Nam, the U.S. government and the U.S. Army associated itself with a military "stalemate?"

What if the U.S. military had been primarily responsible for the training of the contras? The contras were able to remain a thorn in the side of the Sandinistas despite the on-again, off-again U.S. assistance. In the end, the contra success was based on sheer determination and self-sacrifice. Their training and objectives were tailored for quick military results on the battlefield. But, when the war was over, the contras fell apart. They had not become a cohesive movement that would translate into political power. They had not been trained to see that guerrilla war is political war. When the 22 thousand resistance combatants disarmed and demobilized, they possessed minimal political skills.

In the future, to do better, Americans need to accept the political and moral realities that frame an intervention with unconventional forces. To do better in aiding those who have fallen victim to the political tragedy of tribalism, minority status, or failing states, we need to be confident that we are "the last best hope of the earth."[30] We have defined ourselves in this role over and over for two hundred years, despite our traditional reluctance to intervene in world affairs.

We must accept who we are, and we must accept that the prevention of suffering and persecution is part of our political and moral psyche and tradition and that it rightly influences foreign policy. In the words of General Powell, "We must lead."[31] We should try to act in coalition, and we should encourage other actors. But for the foreseeable future, our leadership is vital. We have the moral resources, and often we alone have the material resources. In Central America, even hesitant, reluctant, and small interventions proved enough to defeat or stalemate our political opponents.

We must maintain the forces necessary for timely interventions in the future that might prevent human suffering in the short term, and a larger political and military challenge in the long term. As Weinberger noted in his 1984 document, a small-force European intervention to challenge Hitler in the Rhineland "could perhaps have prevented the Holocaust." The word "intervention" is neither a bad word, nor a bad concept, and it could save us from repeating painful history. It is a necessary element of U.S. foreign policy in order to overcome what has become the internal contradiction in the Weinberger–Powell Doctrine: If the United States wishes to prevent small problems from becoming large problems, and if it wishes to lead, then it must be prepared to intervene—even if the purpose lies beyond the bounds of traditionally defined national interests.

NOTES

1. See Susan L. Marquis, *Unconventional Warfare: Rebuilding U.S. Special Operations Forces* (Washington, D.C.: Brookings Institution Press, 1998). The sole acknowledgment to Central America is found on page 265 in the following passage: "Army special operators, particularly Special Forces, found relevance in the challenges of increasing tension and American interest in Central America. In El Salvador, Special Forces were deployed to Central America in small numbers to act as trainers and advisers to government forces."

2. Maxwell Taylor, *The Uncertain Trumpet* (New York: Harper & Brothers, 1959).

3. See Douglas Blaufarb, *The Counterinsurgency Era: U.S. Doctrine and Performance, 1950 to the Present* (New York: The Free Press, 1977), pp. 53–60.

4. In 1987, when preparing the approval memorandum for the secretary of state for the National Security Decision Directive (NSDD) on Low Intensity Conflict, one of the authors, who had been the State Department representative on the LIC Working Group, noted that the 1987 LIC NSDD recommended the establishment of a Low-Intensity Conflict (LIC) board. This LIC board would have a charter similar to that assigned to the Special Group (Counter Insurgency) some twenty-five years earlier.

5. See U. Alexis Johnson, "Internal Defense and the Foreign Service," *Foreign Service Journal* 39 (July 1962): 20–23.

6. Ernest Evans, "Salvador's Lessons for Future U.S. Interventions," *World Affairs* 160, no. 1 (Summer 1997): 43.

7. Richard D. Downie, *Learning from Conflict: The U.S. Military in Vietnam, El Salvador, and the Drug War* (Westport, Conn.: Praeger, 1998), p. 6.

8. Downie, *Learning from Conflict*, p. 163. The study by Colonel Downie represents an extraordinary analysis of the obstacles to learning and introducing doctrinal and institutional change into the U.S. military establishment. Despite the trauma of Viet Nam and the changing nature of the international environment concerning the proliferation of internal wars, little had changed in counterinsurgency doctrine and organization by the time the Reagan administration committed Special Forces advisors to El Salvador ten years later.

9. Caspar Weinberger, *The Uses of Military Power*, news release no. 609–84, Office of the Assistant Secretary of Defense (Public Affairs), The Pentagon, Washington, D.C., November 28, 1984.

10. See George P. Shultz, *Turmoil and Triumph* (New York: Charles Scribner's Sons, 1993), p. 650.

11. See Richard Holbrooke, *To End a War* (New York: Random House, 1998), p. 284.

12. James F. Dunnigan and Raymond M. Macedonia, *Getting it Right* (New York: Wm. Morrow and Company, 1993), pp. 242–243.

13. See Peter W. Rodman, *More Precious Than Peace: The Cold War Struggle for the Third World* (New York: Charles Scribner's Sons, 1994).

14. Ibid., pp. 271, 280.

15. Ibid., p. 285.

16. Noel Koch, *Defense News*, Washington, D.C., April 13, 1987.

17. For a detailed description of the evolution and politics of the legislation and the building of U.S. special operations capabilities, see Susan L. Marquis, *Unconventional Warfare*; and John M. Collins, *Special Operations Forces: An Assessment* (Washington, D.C.: National Defense University Press, 1994).

18. See John Collins, *Special Operations Forces*, for details on the structure and capabilities of special operations forces in all the military services. He also provides background information on the effort of Congress to impose the needed changes on the Pentagon, pp. 9–22.

19. For a general overview of events in the Central America region and Washington's response during the 1980s, see Roy Gutman, *Banana Diplomacy: The Making of American Policy in Nicaragua, 1981–1987* (New York: Simon & Schuster, 1988); Cynthia J. Arnson, *Crossroads: Congress, the President, and Central America, 1976–1993*, 2d ed. (University Park: Pennsylvania State University Press, 1993); and Robert Kagan, *Twilight Struggle: American Power and Nicaragua, 1977–1990* (New York: The Free Press, 1996).

20. For comparisons of the two counterinsurgency wars, see the following: Benjamin C. Schwarz, *American Counterinsurgency Doctrine and El Salvador: The Frustrations of Reform and the Illusions of Nation Building* (Santa Monica, Calif: RAND, 1991); A. J. Bacevich, James Hallums, Richard White, and Thomas Young, *American Military Policy in Small Wars: The Case of El Salvador* (Washington, D.C.: Institute for Foreign Policy Analysis, Pergamon-Brassey's International Defense Publishers, 1988); Caesar D. Sereseres, "The Guatemalan Legacy: Radical Challengers and Military Politics," in *Report on Guatemala, SAIS Papers in International Affairs*, no. 7 (Washington, D.C.: Johns Hopkins University, 1985); and Caesar D. Sereseres, "The Highlands War in Guatemala," in *Latin American Insurgencies*, ed. Georges Fauriol (Washington, D.C.: National Defense University Press, 1985).

21. Shultz, *Turmoil and Triumph*, p. 289.

22. Ibid., p. 84.

23. For an assessment of the contra demobilization and the role of the Organizations of American States, see Caesar D. Sereseres, "The Regional Peacekeeping Role of the Organization of American States: Nicaragua 1990–1993," in *Managing Global Chaos*, ed. Chester Crocker and Fen Oster Hampson (Washington, D.C.: U.S. Institute of Peace Press, 1996).

24. For a detailed analysis of the political and sociological roots of the Nicaraguan Resistance, including the role played by former members of the National Guard, see Timothy C. Brown, *Commandos of the Comarcas: Origins of Nicaragua's "Contra War"* (Ph.D. diss., New Mexico State Uni-

versity, 1998), p. 146. Brown concludes that the numerical high for former guardsmen in the resistance was 437—about 3 percent of the total force.

25. For a brief overview of U.S. programs and resource allocations to fight the wars in the region, see *Central America: Impact of U.S. Assistance in the 1980s*, report to the Chairman, Committee on Foreign Relations, U.S. Senate (Washington, D.C.: U.S. General Accounting Office, July 1989).

26. For a background to lessons learned, see Caesar D. Sereseres, "Lessons from Central America's Revolutionary Wars, 1972–1984," in *The Lessons of Recent Wars in the Third World*, ed. Robert E. Harkavy and Stephanie G. Neuman (Lexington, Mass.: Lexington Books, D. C. Heath and Company, 1985).

27. See Robin Pogebin, "Foreign Coverage Less Prominent in News Magazines," *The New York Times*, September 23, 1996.

28. This analysis is provided in "Foreign Affairs Still Unpopular on Main Street," *The New York Times*, October 10, 1997.

29. Editorial, "Idealism, Past and Present," *The New York Times*, January 4, 1998.

30. Colin L. Powell, "U.S. Forces: Challenges Ahead," *Foreign Affairs* 71, no. 5 (Winter 1992–1993): 33.

31. Ibid.

Defeating Shining Path: Strategic Lessons for the Future

Enrique Obando

The Shining Path of Peru is one of the most notorious insurgent movements of the century. Many believe that it provided the pattern of insurgencies to come. This chapter identifies fundamental lessons to be learned from the protracted conflict against the Shining Path—lessons that should provide interesting reading for U.S. policy makers.

In 1980 the Communist Party of Peru, a Maoist group called Shining Path by the press, began a violent struggle against the Peruvian government. Subversion was initially confined to the Andean department of Ayacucho. By 1984 it had spread to one-third of the Peruvian territory, and by 1990 its presence was apparent throughout most of the country. From the beginning it was clear that this was not the traditional Latin American guerilla conflict. In contrast to the 1960s revolutionary movement, Shining Path used terrorism on a vast scale as its most important tactic and engaged in using narcotic trafficking as a way to obtain money for the insurgency. By 1992 the Peruvian government was on the verge of collapse. However, that same year Abimael Guzman, Shining Path's almost mythical leader, was captured, which marked the beginning of the end for his party. By 1995 subversion was under control in Peru after fifteen years of internal war and more than 30 thousand deaths. All wars have their lessons, and subversive wars are no exception. This is not to say that we should prepare ourselves to fight a future war, believing that it will be just like the one that has ended. But to forget the lessons we have learned is to condemn ourselves to repeating the same mistakes. The purpose of this chapter is neither to narrate a history of the Shining Path's subversion, nor the way in which the Peruvian government dealt with it; but rather, to extract strategic lessons from this struggle. Therefore, the reader will not be fatigued with an extended account of facts and data that cover more than eighteen years and the periods of three presidential administrations, from 1980 to the present.[1] Instead, the only facts that will be mentioned are those having a direct relevance in explaining the lessons that can be learned from that protracted war. Thus, each of these lessons will be enunciated, explaining the facts from which they are extracted.

LESSON 1: MANY OF THE STRATEGIES TO FIGHT SUBVERSION WERE KNOWN AND FORGOTTEN BY THE PERUVIAN ARMED FORCES AND HAD TO BE PAINSTAKINGLY RELEARNED

When subversion began in Ayacucho in 1980, the response of the Peruvian government was to refuse to accept that it had an insurgency on its hands. This was exactly the same reaction of the administration of Fernando Belaunde fifteen years earlier in 1965, when insurgency erupted in the Peruvian highlands. The unwillingness to recognize the problem in the 1960s made it difficult to eradicate when it was finally acknowledged. The armed forces had to struggle for eight months to defeat a group of intellectuals entrenched in the mountainous jungles. In 1980 the government repeated its mistake and the period of rejection of reality was even longer. When the government finally recognized the problem, the subversion was deeply entrenched, and its eradication took more than fifteen years. The first lesson—to recognize subversion as soon as it happens and act swiftly, and not to negate its reality for political reasons—was forgotten. A quick response by the government could have crushed the insurgency at its beginnings and could have prevented years of bitter warfare.

Another forgotten lesson from the 1960s was the necessity of winning the support of the people. Civic action was the way the army tried to win the people in 1965, but they knew that more had to be done. As a consequence of the 1965 insurgency, the idea of having the people on its side came to be so important for the Peruvian armed forces that three years later in 1968, they engaged in a coup to implement an ambitious plan of structural changes in the country. The idea was to redistribute wealth in favor of the poorest sectors of Peruvian society. However, by 1980 that effort had failed, and the new civilian government implemented a neoliberal economic policy. This made sense from a purely economic point of view, but huge sectors of Peruvian society were socially and economically hurt. When subversion erupted, the Belaunde government was going through an economic crisis. Instead of giving economic support to the areas affected by subversion, it opted for the cheapest solution: military repression, with all the complications that military operations among a civilian population bring. The result was the alienation of the population in those areas and the growth of Shining Path.

A third forgotten lesson from the 1960s was that the experience of other countries' antisubversive operations is of the greatest help. In the 1960s Peruvian military officers looked at the French experience in Algeria and the American experience in the pre–Viet Nam era. Those experiences were useful to create antiinsurgency commandos, both in the army and the police. An antiinsurgency doctrine was also developed based on the French doctrine of *guerre revolutionnaire*. This was useful in defeating a small insurgency of intellectuals with no popular support. It would not be enough to deal with Shining Path, which initially had popular support in the Ayacucho region and used not only guerilla tactics but terrorism as well. This time neither the government nor the armed forces examined foreign experiences in antiterrorist strategies. They persisted with their old tactics of the 1960s, which not only proved unsuccessful but also resulted in human-rights violations. The accusations of violation of human rights that came from external sources such as Amnesty International and foreign governments, ironically, locked the government and armed forces into their timeworn tactics. They were unwilling to seek advice from countries that were openly criticizing the Peruvian human-rights record. Had they looked outside, they would have discovered that

- Since 1960, the British had developed an antiinsurgency doctrine to deal precisely with the type of subversion Peru was suffering, based on their Malayan experience.
- By 1980, the year Shining Path began its operations, a huge bibliography on terrorism already existed.

These developments were absolutely ignored in Peru. Only after ten years, and then thanks to the efforts of some civilians, did the Peruvian government begin to adopt effective strategies modeled on the British and Italian experiences. The core ideas were then understood. Subversive war is not only a military war, but a political war for the hearts and minds of the people. Whoever wins the support of the people wins the war. If the revolutionary, according to Mao's dictum, moves among the people like a fish in the water, it makes no sense to exhaust oneself trying to catch every fish in the pond; it is easier to simply drain the pond. Without the people's support, the subversives will not be able to survive. Tactics like a repentance law could be put to use with great success. The Peruvian government granted pardon or a less extreme penalty to subversives willing to surrender and cooperate with the authorities. Intelligence became the center of the antisubversive strategy. In 1992, as a result of the reforms implemented by the Fujimori government, Abimael Guzman was captured. For such a centralized and authoritarian party as Shining Path, this was the beginning of the end. By 1995, the once powerful subversion was under control.

LESSON 2: THE CAUSE OF SUBVERSION IS NOT SIMPLY POVERTY, BUT ALSO THE FRUSTRATED EXPECTATIONS OF CERTAIN SECTORS OF SOCIETY

Since the 1920s, when social mobilization began in Peru, the idea that poverty was the cause of social upheaval was at the core of revolutionary and antirevolutionary thinking. That was the view of the American Popular Revolutionary Alliance (APRA) in its initial revolutionary years in the 1930s and 1940s. That was also precisely the idea of the military government of General Juan Velasco Alvarado (1968–1975) which tried to avoid a communist revolution by promoting social change. It is also still the view of many Peruvian intellectuals, politicians, and soldiers, and the Catholic Church as well. Reality, however, is more complex. From an analysis of the membership of Shining Path, something that social scientists had already known for some time is discovered: Revolutionaries do not come from the poorest strata of society, but usually from a relatively better educated middle class.[2] In the case of Shining Path, even though it initiated its subversive operations in the countryside and had some peasants among its cadres, the majority of their members were not of peasant extraction, but from the provincial, urban, educated middle class.[3] The great majority of its leadership also came from that stratum. Poverty seems to be an element that can contribute to the upsurge of subversive movements, but it is neither the principal ingredient nor the detonator. The frustration of certain sectors of the middle or even upper classes is a better explanation as a cause for subversion. In the case of Shining Path, it is important to link the foundation of this party with the process of loss of status of the provincial upper and middle classes in Ayacucho. This is a process that took about forty years, in which the once powerful and proud upper and middle classes ceased to be a part of the national elite. A generation later, many of the sons of the former Ayacucho elite were in Shining Path. When an elite loses power, we can expect the formation of a counterelite. Some of its members will try to regain the power they lost by changing the rules of a game that keeps them on the losing side.

Social frustration, a more plausible explanation for subversion, has two modes. In the first mode, when the elite loses its former prerogatives, some of its members begin looking for a change in the status quo. In the second mode, the sons of the lower classes obtain a university education and as a result expect consequent improvement in their level of life and status. Yet the predominant economic social structure prevents them from achieving this goal. Within this social group are the "educated marginals." Education in this case is one of the major variables to consider when examining subversion.

The government of an underdeveloped country has to match two variables: employment and education. If employment grows more rapidly than education, development will be halted because of a lack of qualified workers or professionals. But if education outpaces employment, and this continues for a considerable period of time, the frustration and discontent of the "educated marginals" could cause the onset of subversion. As long as the social pressure for economic success does not cease to work, the "educated marginals" will fall into anomie, a situation in society in which social pressure works upside down. Instead of pressing the individual to respect social norms, social pressure works to push him into disobedience of the norms. The competition for success becomes more important than the norms. Some sectors as a result go into delinquency to achieve that success, while others will try to evade reality through all kinds of esoteric means. Still others will try to change by violent means the society that condemns them to marginality. This last group will initiate subversion, and some of them will resort to terrorism.

That was the situation with Shining Path. In the 1950s and 1960s, the Peruvian governments made a priority of education. Education was one of the most important ways to achieve upward mobility. The sons of peasants could and did become professionals and achieve economic and social success. However, this was frustrated by the economic crisis of 1975—a crisis that in some ways is still going on. The economy stagnated, and education outpaced development, resulting in all the problems of social frustration that this causes. The new, educated class expected an income and a social status that society was unable to provide. Many of them were not even able to finish their university degrees. Many of those who did could not find jobs, and those who did were not adequately paid. They could not achieve their economic goals by following the rules. Since the social pressure of the members of their own class, a class that had succeeded just one generation ago, continued to push them to attain a higher economic and social status, anomie was the result, and the norm breaking that comes with it. Some members of this new class reverted to common delinquency as a way of satisfying their economic needs. Most of those who got jobs in the government or in private enterprise were implicated in white-collar corruption. Others went into narcotic trafficking. Still others tried to solve their problems by running away from reality, converting to new oriental religions, Protestantism, or to a Peruvian sect that followed the Old Testament. Emigration was the response of others. Finally, there were those who decided to change reality through subversion and terrorism.

Clearly, a government in a developing country should be especially careful to match the growth of the economy with the growth of education. To prepare people for nonexistent positions creates a climate that induces the growth of subversion. The problem is not poverty alone, but people expecting something they cannot achieve. Poor people will not revolt if they respond to their poverty as the normal way of things and have no higher expectations. Education creates expectations for a better way of life. When these expectations go unmet, frustation results, and it is this frustration—the possibility of hope for a better life—that generates subversion. This does not mean that we should condemn people to ignorance. On the contrary: To achieve development, education is central. But we must be aware of the risks we are incurring if we do not do things correctly. We have to be careful not to divorce education from economic growth, because the consequences can be devastating.

LESSON 3: BESIDES SOCIAL CAUSES, THERE ARE PSYCHOLOGICAL CAUSES FOR WHY PEOPLE GO INTO SUBVERSION

What should these psychological causes mean to us? It should make it clear that even if social problems are resolved, there is always the possibility of terrorism, because some terrorists act out of individual psychological reasons that have nothing to do with ideology or social environment. During the Cold War, some analysts considered that insurgency was the result of the diffusion of communist ideas. That was only partly true. The problem is not the ideology, but why people accept it.

There is a tendency for individuals with certain psychological characteristics to enter into socially destructive activities, no matter what the ideology. In the absence of an ideology like Marxism, people can accept the most bizarre ideological concoctions. The ideology of Shining Path was precisely one of these. People became terrorists not because they believed a particular doctrine; rather, they believed that doctrine because it offered them the possibility of exercising violence. They will embrace any doctrine that permits them to do violence. They are action-oriented, aggressive people.[4]

Peruvian orthodox Marxists were surprised at the strange ideological blend of Shining Path, which called itself Marxist, Leninist, Maoist, and Stalinist all at the same time, mixing terms that were supposed to exclude each other. The acceptance of such an unsophisticated version of Marxism finds its explanation in the lack of sophistication of Peruvian provincial intellectuals. However, for some people ideological coherence is not that important. These people were looking for any justification that acknowledged their need for fanatical action.

Clearly, not all terrorists join these activities for psychological reasons. Nor does a comparative study reveal a particular psychological type, a particular personality constellation, or a uniform terrorist mind. But although diverse personalities are attracted to the path of terrorism, an examination of memoirs, court records, and interviews suggests that people with certain personality traits and tendencies are drawn disproportionately to terrorist careers.[5] We can find an extremely high frequency of the psychological mechanisms of externalization and splitting in the population of terrorists, which contributes significantly to the uniformity of their rhetorical style and their special psychologic. The cause seems to be a particular type of psychological damage during childhood, which produces narcissistic wounds. Individuals with a damaged self-concept have never fully integrated the good and bad parts of the self. These parts are split into "me" and "not me." The individual idealizes his grandiose self and splits out and projects onto others all the hated and devalued weakness within. He looks outward for the source of difficulties. He needs an outside enemy to blame.

For some people political violence is not instrumental but an end in itself. As they strike out against the establishment, they are really striking against the enemy within.[6] This means that we are always going to have some kind of violence in society, because its occurrence is not entirely related to social conditions. In some cases that violence could be transformed into political violence, even in the absence of social or political causes. Thus, terrorism could happen at any time without any discernable cause, except for the psychological one.

LESSON 4: FUTURE TERRORISM IN PERU WILL TRY TO MANIPULATE EXISTING MYTHS OR WILL TRY TO CREATE THEIR OWN

José Carlos Mariategui is the most important theoretician of the Peruvian Marxists, named as the founding father by almost all Peruvian leftist parties. Shining Path is no exception. However, Guzman emphasized issues in Mariategui's writings that were mostly ignored by other groups or that were considered to be altered by changes in Peruvian society since Mariategui's time. One of these ignored themes was the issue of myth. For Mariategui, revolution should become imprinted in the people's minds as a myth. Myth in his view was more powerful than reason in making people fight for a cause, because it is based in the unconscious. In this he makes an important departure from orthodox Marxism. He makes a theoretical defense of myth as a revolutionary tool unquestionably influenced by Georges Sorel, who had used the term "myth" in the same was as Mariategui.[7] Guzman took Mariategui's idea and constructed the myth of Shining Path and of President Gonzalo. Shining Path made an early attempt to manipulate mythical symbols to get into the unconscious of the people. Guzman called himself *Puka Inti* (the red sun) an allusion to the Incas' sun god and to the legend that tells that Tupac Amaru, an eighteenth-century Indian rebel, asked the *altomisayoc* (the Indian high priest) what he should do to win the war against the Spaniards. The high priest answered, "You should make the sun shine bright. But if you do not succeed in doing so it will take 200 years before the sun will shine in this land again." That was May 1780. In May 1980, two-hundred years later, Shining Path began its armed struggle in what was supposed to be the fulfillment of this prophecy, with Guzman as a red (communist) sun that began to shine over the Inca landscape after two-hundred years.

However, reality was very different. Guzman and the leaders of Shining Path were not Indians, but urban Andean professionals of mixed blood. Guzman decided that after winning the revolutionary war, Shining Path would eradicate Quechua, the Indian language, because it was necessary to unite the people under one language, which would be Spanish. The same fate awaited all folk customs.

Guzman tried to manipulate mythical symbols for practical reasons in order to win the support of the population. However, being a Maoist, he was highly influenced by Chinese iconography.[8] Guzman therefore chose the wrong set of symbols—that is, Chinese symbols—or, in the best of cases, Western urban symbols, as in the case of the black dog symbol. When Shining Path began its armed struggle in 1980, they hung dead black dogs from lampposts as symbols of Teng Diao Ping (a traitor to the Chinese Revolution in Guzman's view) and the Peruvian bourgeoisie. In China the dog is not a pet but an animal to be eaten and mistreated. In the Western tradition, there is ambivalence. The dog can be a pet but also a symbol of indignity ("You are a dog" used to be an insult; "to be treated like a dog" describes a denigrating treatment). In both traditions the color black is a sinister symbol. So then the killing of black dogs was intended to symbolize the killing of evil. However, in the Andean world, the dog, especially the black dog, has a very powerful and positive symbolic value. It is the equivalent of Cerberus in Greek and Roman mythologies—the dog that guards the entrance to the underworld. Black dogs in Andean symbolism help the souls of the dead enter the other world. Nobody in the Andean tradition will mistreat a black dog unless he wants to run the risk of not being able to enter the world of the dead, left as a wandering spirit. Shining Path's use of symbols was a clear demonstration of the ignorance of Andean traditions. Even though the members had a close relationship with the Ayacucho peasantry, a Shining Path former member once confessed, "The ideology blinded us"—they were not able to see the peasant world except through Marxist lenses.[9]

Having been unable, out of ignorance, to use Andean symbols effectively, Guzman worked to create myths for the party and himself. For ten years the existence of Guzman was a real mystery. Nobody knew for sure if he really was the head of Shining Path or not. There were rumors that he had died years before and that another leader was in charge, or that the party had collegiate direction. But from time to time somebody would arise to say he had seen him. Others would say that he was out of the country. He was everywhere and nowhere. And the security forces were not able to tell where he was or if he really existed. He was considered a great tactician by the security forces and the greatest Marxist theoretician alive by his own forces. Shining Path spoke of him as being the fourth sword of Marxism, considering him a great contributor to Marxist theory at the level of Marx, Lenin, and Mao. Gonzalo had become a myth, and contributing to the myth was the cult to the personality of Guzman. This was the case with Mao and Lenin as well, but the cult of personality came after victory. In Guzman's case this was done before achieving victory.

The ideology became a myth as well. The party had the truth, but what that truth exactly was, no one bothered to explain. It was not necessary. Its force came precisely from its vagueness. "Gonzalo's thought" was some kind of esoteric knowledge that was only revealed to the initiated, and to be initiated meant to go into the party and fight. Shining Path's militants could not question Guzman's ideas because they became dogma. His sayings were studied in a way a child learns the catechism: by repeating phrases or writing hundreds of times the same "inspired" sentence. Militants would obey his order blindly, even knowing they were going to die, as was the case when an uprising broke up in the prisons to embarrass Alan Garcia's government in the middle of an international meeting of the world's Social Democratic parties in 1986. They could have surrendered before the security forces attacked, but had orders not to do so, and so all those members participating died.

The party was part of the myth as well. Nobody knows how many militants it had. Even the security forces estimated 30 thousand cadres and 100 thousand supporters. The party was seen as a perfect invincible machine. Nobody knew for sure who was a member of Shining Path. The party let it be known that all structures of government and society were infiltrated. On occasion security forces would discover that the personal advisor of a minister, the son of a general, an engineer in the electricity company in Lima, or a member of Peruvian high society were cadres of Shining Path. Even in the armed forces and police buildings, graffiti praising President Gonzalo and the people's war were found inside. The party was everywhere—it had a thousand eyes, and it knew everything. This created a sense of terror in society and of powerfulness in Shining Path militants that was enhanced by huge electrical blackouts of the principal cities of the country, especially Lima. With chronometrical precision, lights went off at midnight on New Year's Eve or on Guzman's birthday, and terrorist attacks followed. The myth of an all-powerful party led to armed strikes, in which Shining Path paralyzed several cities, including Lima several times, calling for a strike that everybody obeyed out of fear of retaliation by a party that could see all and knew all. The selective killings of some of the few people who dared to work (taxi drivers or bus drivers) was enough to inspire terror in a population of seven million in Lima. In Guzman's words, "When the party becomes a myth it cannot be destroyed."

Shining Path and its myth were finally destroyed by the Peruvian security forces, but not until after more than fifteen years of struggle. The idea of using myth as a political weapon is one of the most dangerous legacies of Peruvian terrorism. Sendero failed in the use of the Andean symbolic codes, because it did not know those codes and tried to supplant them either with Chinese or its own revolutionary symbols. On the other hand, the idea of the party as a myth depended on the party's successes. When the security forces captured the high command of Shining Path, the myth of its invincibility ended. The people in Shining Path did not know the rules of symbolic and mythic logic. However, if the party had managed to use to its benefit the real myths existing in society or to generate a new myth, not even defeat would have affected it. Myth becomes *stronger* in defeat because it is the only hope that is left for a people who want to believe in something. In the future, if someone knows how to use the Andean symbolic codes or to use the rules of symbolic logic to generate a new myth, he could manage to generate an ethnic, religious, or nationalistic uprising in the Andes. The power of this new instrument, discovered by Shining Path, is so great because it is based on the unconscious. We should not doubt that a future terrorist movement would use it, and we should prepare to deal with it.

LESSON 5: WE NOW KNOW WHAT WORKS AND WHAT DOES NOT IN COUNTERINSURGENCY

In the first years of struggle against Shining Path, the government considered the insurgency as a military problem and gave the military the mission of destroying it. The military used state terror against subversive terror. If the subversives used terror to control the population, the state used terror to press the population into obedience. The result was the opposite of the government's hopes. The human-rights violations that resulted, far from controlling the situation, helped the subversives to grow instead. Also, the government did not give the necessary political support to its armed forces to win the war. We now know that subversion is not a problem that can be dealt with by military means alone. It is a war that has a military side to it, but is basically political in nature. It has to be fought not only by the armed forces but also by the government as a whole. The government has to win the support of the people by demonstrating real interest in their problems and making it clear that the people who support the government will receive economic assistance. Justice is a central issue in this struggle. The government has to appear just and efficient. More important, the government has to respect the law. To break its own laws makes the government unpredictable and alienates the population.

Subversive forces know that they cannot defeat the security forces militarily. What they can do is take away from them the will to fight. If the subversives have the support of the population, the security forces will never manage to destroy the insurgents. This will generate desperation and will result in more human-rights violations, which will increase the number of people sympathizing with the subversives or going directly to its cadres. The more the population supports the insurgents, the less will the security forces have to continue the struggle. Who has the people on its side will win. This is war for the hearts and minds of the people.

The idea of hearts and minds worked very well in Malaya when the British fought a Maoist insurgency from 1948 to 1960. It also worked very well in the Philippines when President Ramon Magsaysay fought the Huk guerillas in the 1950s. It lost its prestige when it did not work in Viet Nam. The idea of strategic hamlets suggested by Sir Robert Thompson, one of the strategists of Malaya, was a right idea wrongly executed. The South Vietnamese authorities made a mess of this idea because of corruption and an attempt to speed up the project by giving priority to increasing the quantity of hamlets rather than improving the quality of them. However, the idea did work in Peru in the form of the *rondas campesinas* (peasant patrols). The peasants were armed to fight against the Shining Path with the support of the army. To do this, it became very clear that good civil–military relations with the population were of highest importance. The soldiers have to be picked for their toughness but also for their capacity to have good relations with the population.

LESSON 6: THE JUDICIARY SYSTEM IS AN IMPORTANT TOOL TO WIN AN ANTISUBVERSIVE WAR

All the efforts of the police or the armed forces to capture subversives will be of no avail if the judiciary system is not working adequately to send those subversives to prison. In the Peruvian case the law was too soft on terrorism. In addition judges were terrorized by Shining Path into letting the subversives free. The result was extrajudiciary executions by the armed forces and police, who knew that to send a prisoner to the judge was to guarantee his release. But new laws severely punished subversion and protected judges from terrorism. Military judges were also called to hear the most important cases because they were less prone to blackmail by the terrorists. However, in spite of these efforts many innocent people still were sent to prison.

The problem of an incompetent judiciary is more complex than it appears at first glance. If the judiciary is an independent power from the executive, it cannot be reorganized by it. On the other hand, if the judiciary is corrupted, it will be very difficult for it to reorganize itself. In the Peruvian case things were even more complex because the Peruvian Congress was opposed to the antisubversive strategy of the executive branch. In the middle of this struggle between powers, Shining Path grew. The result was that the executive branch closed Congress and overrode the judiciary in an effort to achieve an antisubversive strategy. This makes clear the need for good civil–military relations, whereby the Congress, through the National Defense Committee, should be informed of what the strategy and the purpose of the war is. If the armed forces commit errors in the fight against subversion, those errors should be acknowledged and whoever is responsible should be punished. The policy of protecting men that have committed atrocities or not recognizing human-rights violations when they happen only created mistrust and an unnecessary battle between Congress and the executive branch, which in turn helped the subversives. It is necessary to protect these judges from subversive terror.

LESSON 7: SHINING PATH USED NARCOTICS TRAFFIC TO OBTAIN MONEY FOR THE REVOLUTION. ANY OTHER SUBVERSIVE MOVEMENT IN THE AREA WILL DO THE SAME

This is now almost standard around the world, from Colombia to Chechnya. It will continue to be practiced even more because the states that used to support revolution no longer exist, like the Soviet Union, or no longer support this type of activity, like Cuba or China. We have, however, the exception of the rogue states. We know now that Iraq's Saddam Hussein financed some Latin American extremist, left-wing parties in the late 1970s. However, for extremist groups, narcotics traffic is an easy way of obtaining cash without giving away political independence. The reason why Shining Path went into an alliance with the narcotics traffickers was because its international ally, Maoist China, suffered an important political change with the arrival of Teng Diao Ping to power. China found itself open to capitalism and not interested in supporting Maoist subversion around the world. So Shining Path went to narcotics trafficking, as did the MRTA, another Peruvian subversive group, and the FARC in Colombia; and the list goes on.

The alliance of subversion with narcotics traffic depends on the well being of narcotics trafficking. There is a possibility that in the long run this traffic will be stopped, not by any policy the United States or any Latin American government can muster, but because of a rule of substitution for natural raw materials with synthetic alternatives. Every raw material that Latin America has exported to the developed world has in the long run been substituted by synthetic alternatives. Guano, a natural fertilizer, was substituted with synthetic fertilizers. Rubber was replaced by synthetic rubber. Copper is now being made with new optic fibers. Coca is just another raw material that in the long run will end up being replaced by a synthetic drug that can be produced and commercialized in the developed world. In some ways, drug substitution for synthetic alternatives is already taking place. Drugs like cocaine and opium are being replaced in the illegal U.S. market by methamphetamines. This is by far the most prevalent synthetic controlled substance clandestinely manufactured in the United States. Methamphetamine is cheaper than cocaine in many illegal markets. Long associated with motorcycle gangs that supplied users in western states, this drug has spread eastward.[10] The worst of these is crack, which can be manufactured at home and requires little overhead to produce. Ephedrine, an over-the-counter cold medication, can be combined with a shopping list of chemicals easily obtained from stores and industrial supply companies (common drain cleaners figure in some formulas) and cooked in a kitchen sink from recipes downloaded from the Internet. This drug is known as the poor man's cocaine. Crack is too cheap, too available, and too addictive. It is the American drug warrior's nightmare come true.[11]

This can change the picture of easy money from narcotics trafficking in underdeveloped countries. However, if narcotics trafficking remains lucrative, then it is clear that any subversive group will turn to narcotics trafficking to finance its operations.

LESSON 8: A STRATEGY OF PURE TERRORISM CAN EVENTUALLY DESTABILIZE A COUNTRY AND CREATE CONDITIONS FOR A SUBVERSIVE TAKEOVER

In Peru, it almost worked. When Shining Path lost the support of the peasantry, it looked for a short cut to victory. Instead of employing a strategy of slowly winning the support of the population by patient political work in the root organizations of the workers and peasantry, they decided to rely on pure terrorism. The idea was to bomb all the malls and commercial districts in Lima and create fear in the entrepreneurial community, in order to force it to abandon fiscal support of the country and government. That would have broken the banking system, resulting in the loss of the savings of the city's population. The result would have amounted to hunger, desperation, looting, and military action to control the looting (which was already taking place in some districts by August 1992), and eventually, the inescapable situation of troops firing on the crowds. This could have broken an army composed of conscripts with no pay at all and led by officers who earned between $200 and

$400 a month. This did not happen because of the capture of Abimael Guzman at the precise moment when Shining Path was ready to launch an all-out offensive against Lima. But a strategy of this type can destabilize a country where the banking system is small, as in Peru, and where institutions are not solid. It can also create enough chaos to generate conditions for a subversive takeover.

This is a dangerous gamble for the subversives. To launch a terrorist operation of such size, they would have to suffer heavy casualties and risk the capture of the high command, which is precisely what happened in Peru. This is the subversive equivalent of a war of attrition. Who will last longer? Who will crumble first? For countries with a weak economy, this kind of strategy can be crippling, but in countries with a strong economy, this kind of strategy will not work.

LESSON 9: FOREIGN INTERVENTION IS PRECISELY WHAT THE SUBVERSIVES ARE LOOKING FOR

The strategy of pure terrorism on a large scale looks for two possible results: Either the economic system collapses, or an international intervention takes place to prevent this from happening. This last move is precisely what the terrorists are expecting. Foreign intervention would allow them to call for a war of liberation against foreign occupation. The situation is even better for the subversives if the foreign troops are ethnically and culturally different from the population, as was the case with the Americans in Viet Nam or the Russians in Afghanistan.

However, in the Peruvian case, intervention never materialized. We know that the United States is reluctant to intervene in low-intensity operations in Third World countries after the terrible experience of Viet Nam. Knowing this, future subversives will probably not remain local but will go global, attacking U.S. targets in U.S. territory, in an attempt to push the United States into fighting an antiguerrilla and antiterrorist war on the subversives' terrain. If a well-organized terrorist group cannot be controlled in its country of origin and keeps attacking U.S. targets in U.S. territory, the temptation for intervention will be great. But this is a temptation the United States should reject because it will mean fighting a war in the very conditions chosen by the enemy. The only strategy available in this case is to support the government that is fighting a terrorist group in every possible way except direct intervention. This is true not only for the United States but for any other country that feels tempted to send troops to another country to fight against a local terrorist or subversive movement.

LESSON 10: THE UNITED STATES CAN BE AT
TIMES A MOST UNRELIABLE ALLY

Some countries have learned this the hard way. Peru discovered that despite all the anticommunist propaganda during the Cold War, when it was confronted with a major threat during the years of Shining Path, the United States made it very clear that it would not help the Peruvian government. What U.S. help existed was for antinarcotics operations, and the United States also made it very clear that the helicopters used for these operations could not be used for counterinsurgency. In the worst moments of the war against Shining Path, when the country was fighting for its survival, what Peru received instead of help was criticism for human-rights violations. Those criticisms were unfortunately true, but as it became apparent in the early 1990s, in the event of a terrorist takeover, human-rights violations by Shining Path would vastly exceed those committed by the government. Peru ended up fighting and winning its antisubversive war alone.

Help did go to Peru for antinarcotics operations. But even in the antinarcotics war, the help from the United States was erratic. In 1991 the United States signed an antinarcotics agreement with Peru, in which great importance was given to alternative development. However the United States only promised $94.9 million in economic support, of which $34.9 million was for military assistance. This was not an impressive amount to fight a mafia that moves more than $79 billion a year. The U.S. government's point of view, however, was that this was a first step; if it proved successful, more help would become available in the future. However, Congress had other ideas and cut the money for military assistance because of human-rights violations by the Peruvian security forces and because of suspicion that those forces were actually collaborating with narcotics traffickers. Of the support to alternative development only $29.4 million was budgeted for that year. In 1992 the situation worsened, and in the San Antonio summit, the Bush administration changed policies from one of support of alternative development back to one of repression of narcotics traffickers. On this occasion the U.S. government budgeted only $11 million as support for the Peruvian antinarcotics effort. This was the result of a change of policy by the U.S. Congress, then dominated by the Democrats, who thought that the Bush antinarcotics policies had achieved nothing of importance and decided to cut funds. This caused a problem for the Peruvian government, which had promised thousands of coca-growing peasants financial help to change coca production to legal alternative crops with the support of U.S.

money. As this support did not materialize, the Peruvian government had to leave the coca-growing peasants on their own, frustrating an important effort to change illegal crops for legal ones.

But these were not the only problems. As part of the 1991 agreement, the United States deployed two radar systems in Peru to help the Peruvian Air Force interdiction effort of narcotics-traffic aircraft. As a result of the closing of the Peruvian Congress by President Fujimori, the systems were withdrawn. They were sent back a year later, after Fujimori had held a new election for Congress, only to withdrawn again in May 1994 because someone at the Pentagon discovered after three years that it was illegal to support the shooting down of civilian airplanes, even though they were being used to smuggle drugs. The radar systems were sent back to Peru in December, only to be withdrawn for yet a third time because of the Ecuadorian–Peruvian conflict of January and February 1995. By April 1995 they were back again.[12] These radar detection systems were of Korean War vintage and were inoperable more often than not. The same was the case of the helicopters which in the first months of 1995 were not operable.[13] Finally these problems were overcome, and U.S. help to Peruvian antinarcotics efforts increased substantially. But the continuous change in policy that characterized the U.S. position from 1991 to 1995 left the impression that this could happen again any time, and that the United States can be, at times, a most unreliable ally.

Incoherent international policy can also be the result of the number of different actors taking part in the decision-making process of U.S. foreign and defense policies, an interagency process in which nobody is in charge and decision making may be an inordinately long process. Bureaucratism and micromanagement seem to be the present rule in Washington. The fragmentation and dispersion of power and authority prevented the United States from becoming a garrison state during the Cold War.[14] On the other hand, "the U.S. open and transparent system makes it easier for America's negotiating partners to monitor U.S. compliance with commitments."[15] However, this is of little help for any foreign chancellery when an international agreement with the United States is left in limbo by a failure on the part of Congress to honor the executive branch's decision or by a bureaucratic miscoordination within the executive branch.

CONCLUSION

After reviewing the lessons of the Shining Path insurgency, I return to our first lesson—the most important of all, and one which will apply always to any country: Remember what has been so painstakingly learned about low-intensity conflict and terrorism. The post–Cold War world will not be a world deprived of insurgencies and terrorism. On the contrary, the international arena seems ready for conflict in many countries around the world. These conflicts will be of a different kind—a more complex kind—because they will include ethnic and religious elements. We should not expect the new conflicts to follow the lines of the old, but it will be a serious blunder to forget the old lessons, because many of them could still be applicable to the new situations.

NOTES

1. For a history of the Shining Path subversion, see Gustavo Gorritti, *Sendero: Historia de la guerra milenaria en el Peru* (Lima: Editorial APOYO, 1990); Geronimo Inca, *El ABC de Sendero Luminoso y del MRTA* (Lima: Grupo Editorial Geronimo Inca, 1994); Carlos Tapia, *Las fuerzas armadas y Sendero luminoso: Dos estrategias y un final* (Lima: IEP, 1997); Cynthia McClintock, *Revolutionary Movements in Latin America: El Salvador's FMLN and Peru's Shining Path* (Washington, D.C.: USIP, 1998); David Scott Palmer, "The Revolutionary Terrorism of Peru's Shining Path," in *Terrorism in Context*, ed. Martha Crenshaw (State College: Pennsylvania State University Press, 1995).

2. Eric Wolf, *Peasant Wars of the Twentieth Century* (New York: Harper and Row, 1969).

3. Dennis Chavez de Paz, *Juventud y terrorismo: Caracteristicas sociales de los condenados por terrorismo y otros delitos* (Lima: IEP, 1989).

4. Jerrold Post, "Terrorist Psycho-Logic: Behavior as a Product of Psychological Forces," in *Origins of Terrorism: Psychologies, Ideologies, Theologies, States of Mind*, ed. Walter Reich (Cambridge, Mass.: Woodrow Wilson International Center for Scholars, 1990).

5. Post, "Terrorist Psycho-Logic," p. 27.

6. Ibid., p. 26.

7. Martin A. Miller, "The Intellectual Origins of Modern Terrorism in Europe", in *Terrorism in Context*, ed. Martha Crenshaw (State College: Pennsylvania State University Press, 1995), p. 54.

8. This will be apparent by looking at Shining Path's drawings and pictures made in the Chinese Maoist style, with no originality or Peruvian influence whatsoever.

9. Interview in Lima on February 2, 1985 with a former Shining Path member who asked for anonymity.

10. Office of National Drug Control Policy (ONDCP), *The National Drug Control Strategy: A Ten Year Plan, 1998–2007* (Washington, D.C., 1998).

11. *Time*, June 22, 1998, pp. 24–32.

12. *El Comercio*, April 15, 1995.

13. There were ten helicopters of Viet Nam War vintage. *El Comercio*, May 2, 1995.

14. Aaron Friedberg, "Why Didn't the United States Become a Garrison State?" *International Security* 16 (Spring 1992).

15. Michael Mastanduno, "The United States Political System and International Leadership: A 'Decidedly Inferior Form of Government'?" in *American Foreign Policy: Theoretical Essays*, ed. John Ikenberry (New York: HarperCollins, 1996), p. 343.

8

The United States, Japan, and the Defense of Democratic States in the Western Pacific

Peter J. Woolley

The armed forces of Japan, while considerable in size and equipment, have not engaged in combat since 1945. Thus, the ability of the country to support U.S. or UN aims in the Pacific and other areas, or even to defend itself effectively, is subject to speculation. Even the willingness of the Japanese government to deploy quite limited units outside the home islands has been problematical, but, as this chapter suggests, significant changes may be occurring.

INTRODUCTION

A Crisis Develops

On day one there was a Bosnian Serb uprising that threatened NATO ground troops and tens of thousands of Croat and Muslim Bosnians. On day two there was an attempted coup d'etat in Indonesia, followed by the immediate threat of civil war in that country, and the announcement that the straits and seas of the Indonesian archipelago were an exclusion zone, closed to all international shipping. On day three a surly government in Ukraine was threatening nuclear blackmail. On successive days the crisis worsened in both Europe and Asia. At least, this is how the scenario unfolded recently in strategic games played out at a United States war college.

The brightest and best officers, ones who would be considered some day for flag rank, played parts as the American president, the secretaries of state and defense, and as other members of the National Security Council. Their task was to assess, decide, and respond to crisis heaped upon crisis.

Other players in the strategic game were invited from universities, the State Department, and other federal departments and agencies. These guests played the parts of foreign governments, the NATO secretary general, and of various officers of the United Nations.[1]

With turmoil in Indonesia developing first into civil war and then into a confrontation with Malaysia and Singapore, the Japanese government was frantic. Japan sent urgent dispatches to the U.S. government asking, then demanding, what the United States planned to do. The Asian situation and Japan's concerns were ignored as the American government, overwhelmed by events and unfamiliar with politics on the Pacific Rim, concentrated its efforts on the more familiar territory of NATO and the European theater. Not until the Japanese government sent a *demarche*, threatening to act alone in the waters of the southwest Pacific, did the United States hastily respond and insist on taking the lead in protecting shipping, defending international passages, and mediating the conflict.

Debriefing

The Americans in this strategic scenario were not merely overwhelmed by the number of crises to which they had to respond. They were overwhelmed by the complexity of dealing with upheaval in a region where there is no functional equivalent of NATO, with its integrated command structure supported by countries whose people and governments have long identified themselves closely with U.S. global interests. Intelligent and well-educated officers were daunted also by the prospect of cooperating with Japan—still seen by some as a rival rather than an ally—and they were shocked by the possibility that Japan might usurp U.S. leadership in the Pacific. After ignoring the Japanese government for some time, they shouldered Japan out of the way completely. In short, the American players treated Japan as a very junior and annoying partner.

The scenario played out at that war college, in that year, and with those players may not have been realistic. However, though it was merely an exercise in analysis and policy making, pieces of the scenario might be credible. Those American decision makers may never be the ones to handle such crises. The Japanese players were not really Japanese and perhaps took a perverse pride in tweaking, on behalf of Japan, the nose of the American giant. Nonetheless, we can make use of the scenario to offer some basic reminders and to proffer some assertions.

The Pacific Rim is host to a number of countries that fall somewhere on the spectrum of democracy—or somewhere at least beyond the complete absence of democracy (e.g., Republic of South Korea [ROK], Taiwan, Hong Kong, Thailand, Malaysia, Singapore, and Indonesia). Some of these countries will face internal and external threats to their stability, their development of democratic practices, and their commercial or diplomatic relations with the United States. When crises occur, the United States should take the lead in organizing a coherent policy of diplomatic, economic, or military interventions in the region. At such times, the United States will both ask help of other Asian nations (where it can find help) as well as be asked by Asian nations for help. Among those Asian–Pacific nations, Japan is the most powerful, the most democratic, the most stable, and the one whose interests seem to coincide most nearly with those of the United States.

JAPANESE AND AMERICAN INTERESTS COINCIDE

In the United States at least, it is not commonplace to assert that Japanese and American interests coincide to a great degree. Many well-informed and attentive members of government and the general public are more likely to view Japan as an actual, or potential, rival to U.S. economic power, rather than as a country whose economic prosperity is intimately linked in positive ways to that of the United States.[2] Even many of those who are well aware of Japan's importance as an economic partner see it as a country that must be sternly tutored on the subject of trade and firmly kept on the straight-and-narrow path of democracy and liberal economics. Still others point an accusing finger at Japan as a free rider in security affairs, linking Japan's post-war prosperity to the American security umbrella. And even many who trouble to know something about Japan's security arrangements and Self-Defense Forces undervalue those forces, seeing them either as a token contribution to the alliance or as a stealthy and clever vehicle for technology transfer. It is much less common to see the many fundamental similarities between the United States and Japan; to see the enormously important cooperation that has come from an enduring and mutually beneficial political alliance; and to remark upon the many changes that Japanese foreign policy has undergone through half a century of democracy and prosperity. But it is this latter view that strategists might better use in their predictions of, and prescriptions for, destabilizing antidemocratic movements in Asia and elsewhere around the world.

Indeed, Japan is, in essential ways, like the United States: a wealthy, democratic country dependent on stable international trade for its industry, commerce, and wealth. Japan has a substantial military establishment: Its military expenditure, measured in U.S. dollars, ranks fourth in the world—and in fact ranks second among industrialized countries.[3] It is true that Japan's public is extremely wary of international entanglements but, as recent developments have shown, under clearly defined circumstances and limits, Japan is willing to do its part in fostering political stability around the globe. In this way the skepticism embedded in Japanese public opinion when it comes to foreign relations is not dissimilar from that of many American editorial writers, perennially cautious about America's role and commitments abroad.

It should hardly be surprising that Japan is among the most supportive of U.S. interests in the Pacific and that the Japanese Self-Defense Forces (JSDF) are the greatest complement to the U.S. force structure in the Pacific theater. Scenarios of instability, disrupted international commerce, and imperilled democratic development are of grave concern to a Japanese regime that accounts for 18 percent of the world's GDP and has done much in the past three decades to aid the economic and political development of Pacific Rim countries as well as to cooperate with U.S. defense planning.

Also like the United States, Japan is wrapped in the comforting embrace of the sea and is thereby insulated (though not isolated) from the rest of the world. Yet quite unlike the United States, Japan has well-armed neighbors and potential trouble spots are nearby: The distance from Japan's western shore to the Korean peninsula is fewer than a hundred miles and the important Siberian city of Vladivostok is only four-hundred miles from Japan's northern island of Hokkaido. Thus, while the United States may see upheaval in Asia as something far in the distance, and perhaps far in the future, the Asian world looks very different to those seated on the Pacific Ocean's western rim.

While a prosperous America of the 1990s expressed, at least officially, a certain optimism in the new world order, the spread of democracy, and the ultimate triumph of liberal market practices, Japan's outlook was cautious, the economy was mired in stagnation, and analysts fretted over the rapidity of change in East Asia. And while the United States in the post–Cold War decade sought an elusive peace "dividend" by cutting back on defense expenditures, Japan largely resisted any real reductions in defense spending and claimed that political uncertainties on the Pacific Rim demanded continued vigilance.[4] Japan's annual white paper on defense repeatedly explained, "The situation around Japan is complicated . . . unstable . . . and fluid."⁵ What did Japan's foreign policy analysts see?

Despite the final dissolution of the Soviet Union in 1991—or perhaps because of that dissolution—Japan's geopolitical concerns became more complex, not less. The list of potential problems was long. The new Russian Republic was, even after several elections, unstable and verging on chaotic. The Chinese government seemed stable for the short term but, as events in Tienanmen Square showed, China was not immune to domestic disorder. Moreover, China had begun to pursue a number of territorial disputes with neighbors. Anxious concern with developments in China increased in the 1990s—not despite the opening of Chinese markets but, in fact, because the opening of trade and commerce made China's domestic situation less predictable, bringing both dissent and corruption to the surface of Chinese politics. For these reasons, Japanese foreign-policy analysts feared the consequences for Japan (and Korea and Taiwan) of upheaval in China—including a monumental refugee crisis, the loss of hard-won and expensive investments in Chinese industries, environmental contamination by China's worsening air and water pollutants or from ill-maintained nuclear reactors, or a chauvinistic grab for long-disputed territory.⁶

At the same time, North Korea's surreal saga of famine, internal power struggles, and threats of war against the South suggested other unhappy scenarios for Japan and the United States. North Korea's nuclear weapons program, its wretched economy, and its militaristic regime quickly became a recipe for international disaster. Conflict on the Korean peninsula remained one of the chief concerns for Japan, as it did sporadically for the United States. Indeed, Japan's defense white papers continued to assert that the "Korean Peninsula is inseparably related with Japan geographically and historically, hence the maintenance of peace and stability on the Korean peninsula is of vital importance to the peace and stability of East Asia as a whole, including Japan."⁷

Elsewhere on the Pacific Rim, dozens of territorial disputes lurked behind the rosy facade of rapid economic development. Among these disputes were conflicting claims in the Kurile Islands, the inheritance of the new Russian Republic, still occupied by a Russian Army division, and still a continuing source of irritation between the Japanese and Russian governments. Japan perennially insisted that the Russian Republic abide by the 1855 Treaty of Commerce, Navigation and Delimitation in which the islands south of Uruppu belonged to Japan: Etoforu, Kunashiri, Shikotan, and the Habomai islets.

Another perhaps more dangerous argument continued over the Senkaku Islands of the East China Sea. These tiny islets, occupied

by Japan but just two-hundred miles from Taiwan, were claimed
also by China and Taiwan. However insignificant the mass of these
islands may have been, the international Law of the Sea, with its
exclusive economic zones, made even the smallest islet important—
especially if oil or mineral deposits were to be discovered beneath
the ocean floor.[8] Events of the post–Cold War decade showed that
continuing interest in the islands combined with national chauvin-
ism might destabilize the area. In 1990, for example, Japanese ul-
tranationalists installed a lighthouse on Uotsuri to underscore their
enthusiasm for Japan's territorial stake. A few months later, Japan's
Maritime Safety Agency intercepted two Taiwanese vessels intend-
ing to land on one of the islands and stage a protest. Official statements from China, Taiwan, and Japan followed, all unequivocally
reasserting their claim to the islands.[9] A replay of the incidents
occured in 1996 as Japanese nationalists again constructed a lighthouse on one of the islands, and again, Taiwanese fishermen protested, sending a hundred boats to the area.[10] Again in May and
June of 1997, the protests continued and Japan's Maritime Safety
Agency was fending off fishing vessels. Japan, for its part, could
not have tolerated Taiwan's claim to the islands; to have done so
would have strengthened China's claim, and exacerbated the Sino–
Japanese dispute.[11]

Further from Japan but still of great concern were the actual
and potential problems (including the threat of religious and ethnic rebellion) of Indonesia, Thailand, Cambodia, and the Philippines. In this region of substantial Japanese business activity were
not only new records of production, trade, and profits but also ominous signs of instability. Despite their UN–supervised elections,
Cambodian factions were yet armed to the teeth. And in 1997
Cambodia's communist faction proved that skepticism was war-
ranted as it suceeded in a coup d'etat against the Royalist faction—
just as it seemed the Khmer Rouge was disintegrating.

Thailand with its prospering economy was subject to the cross-
winds of traditionalism and the demands of a growing, educated
middle class. In 1992 an elected but shaky parliament took over
the reigns of government from a military junta but was harried by
constant protests over land reform, corruption, and a gyrating cur-
rency. Adding to the Thai government's problems were armed Muslim separatists in the southern provinces of Narathiwat and Betong,
as well as disputes with the ugly government in Myanmar and continuing problems with refugees from Cambodia. Meanwhile, Indonesia, undergoing explosive population growth, complex ethnic and
religious tensions, and rapid economic development was another
crisis waiting to happen and regularly resorted to violence to sub-

due protesters. Eventually the venerable Suharto regime collapsed. Likewise, the future of the Philippines, with its many tongues and peoples as well as economic classes and economic disparities, could not be viewed with equanimity.

Even as Japan had been reluctant to become directly involved in territorial disputes, domestic upheavals, or inter-Asian conflicts, it was nonetheless anxious to play some role in support of both the United States and the international community it leads. Given Japan's substantial economic interest around the world, the Japanese government has been obliged, as the United States has been by its self-interest, to be concerned with matters a long way from its shores. The U.S. economy is the largest in the world; Japan's is perhaps the second largest. The United States is richly endowed with natural resources; Japan is not. Japan is consequently the world's number-one importer of twenty different categories of primary goods, including iron ore, coal, and unmilled cereals. Japan's vaunted economic power is in large measure the product of a stable international order. Like those of the United States, Japan's investments, income, influence, supply of raw materials, domestic luxuries, and even inexpensive labor depend a great deal on stability abroad. Hence Japan, like the United States, has come to actively encourage and reinforce the international order.

Skeptics remain. Is Japan capable of supporting and complementing U.S. defense interests? If so, to what degree? Even if Japan is capable, is the government not too timid and too much restrained by domestic politics, to be willing to assist the United States? And are other Asian countries willing to contemplate receiving more than just Japan's economic assistance? Such questions will linger, but it is well worth considering how to view Japan as a valuable ally in Pacific security affairs rather than as an annoying rival—a rival, for example, for market share in the internationalized automobile industry. Japan has been coming to recognize, just as the United States has done, that threats to democratic countries anywhere may be threats to all democracies; that political instability in developing countries is a threat to the international community at large; and that terrorism, insurgency, and revolution are more often the tools of tyrants than of democrats.

COINCIDENTAL POLICY AND ACTIONS

That Japan's interests coincide with those of the United States in the Pacific can be shown in part by surveying some of Japan's fundamental foreign and defense policies. Despite the many casual observers who find in every Japanese policy dispute, in each hesitation and every dilemma, ample reason to criticize Japan's security policies as inadequate to the task, there is much evidence to the contrary. Overseas economic assistance, facilities for U.S. armed forces, participation in UN peace-keeping operations, the JSDF's force structure, and sea-lane defense are well established policies and actions indicative of Japan's important role as a supporter of U.S. interests.

Overseas Development Assistance

Japan has a substantial program of overseas economic assistance, especially for countries of the Pacific Rim. Japan's assistance, by several measures, not only exceeds economic aid given by the United States but is the greatest amount given by any country of the world.[12] Moreover, that assistance has increased steadily over a decade, while American foreign aid has been under congressional attack, reduced, and channeled to a smaller number of recipients. Japan has responded positively over the years to the U.S. request that Japan increase its financial support for developing countries.

Japan's aid is not strictly humanitarian, nor is it merely an economic tool. Rather, it is a strategic gesture made to foster both economic and political stability. It should not come as a surprise that Japan directs most of its aid to Asia and to the most strategically sensitive countries. More than 65 percent of Japan's aid is extended to counties of the Pacific Rim, with Indonesia and China receiving the greatest amounts. Japan now sees foreign aid, as does the United States, as a political and diplomatic tool—as a preventative measure against threats to political instability in countries of special concern. As far back as 1991 (not coincidentally the last year of Soviet rivalry), Japanese policies began to link aid directly to the broad goals of democratization and environmental protection and to the better defined goals of reducing weapons exports and liberalizing both internal and external trade rules.[13]

In recent years, Japan's economic power has been put to use in trade embargoes led by the United States. Japan's cut-offs of both trade and economic assistance in support of U.S. or UN political and security goals only add to the power of U.S. leadership in the post–Cold War era, and for this important support, Japan is scarcely recognized.

Facilitating U.S. Forces

Japan's hospitality to U.S. armed forces is unusual even among American allies. While many apparently canny observers believe that U.S. armed forces in Japan serve the purpose of restraining Japan and making other Asian countries more comfortable with the rehabilitation of Japan's armed forces, in fact, both the United States and Japan reap many benefits from their cooperation on Japanese territory.

The United States stations troops, military aircraft, and naval vessels in Japan, whose missions are directed at the same regions and trouble spots which concern the Japanese government, such as the Korean peninsula. The Japanese government bears much of the cost of the American bases, including paying for Japanese employees working for U.S. armed forces and the cost of all utilities such as water and heat. Japan's financial support of the U.S. military amounts to the equivalent of $6 billion (or 625 billion yen) per year. Japanese governments have been supportive of the U.S. bases even when domestic interest groups have been severely critical of U.S. military facilities, the noise and pollution they produce, and the precious land they occupy. The United States would certainly not serve its strategic interests better, nor save any money, by stationing its armed forces elsewhere.

CONTRIBUTIONS TO UN PEACE-KEEPING OPERATIONS

Another way in which Japan has demonstrated its support of international order has been its participation in UN peace-keeping operations. Once unthinkable, Japan has used this vehicle to deploy armed forces, however small, at great distances from Japanese shores. Albeit after heated debate, Japan's Diet passed the "Law Concerning Cooperation for United Nations Peace-keeping Operations and Other Operations" in 1992, legislation that was successfully renewed in 1995. Japan now allows its JSDF to participate in UN peace-keeping activities under strict conditions. Any given dispatch of JSDF personnel must have prior approval by the Diet, the discretion of JSDF personnel is limited in any given operation by laws unique to each operation, and the entire cabinet, not just the prime minister, must approve of operational plans. So far, these regulatory restrictions have neither inhibited the development of new missions nor Japan's expanding participation in UN operations. To the contrary, the careful consideration received by each mission has not merely minimized the risk but ensured the public's support for such operations.

American public support for military operations abroad waxes or wanes with the public's perception of success of the mission.[14] Few objections, for example, were raised in 1992 when President Bush deployed soldiers to Somalia to ensure that food be delivered to hundreds of thousands of starving people. Months later, a fruitless

manhunt for a clan leader, said to be an incorrigible culprit in Somali politics, resulted in the deaths of eighteen American soldiers
and humiliating television footage. American public opinion turned
and the U.S. troops were withdrawn. By contrast, other episodes of
U.S. intervention have maintained the American public's support
so long as the mission met expectations by minimizing casualties
and fulfilling publicly announced goals. Likewise, what has been
seen in Japan in the 1990s is a series of qualified successes in UN
peace-keeping operations that actually increased public support of
JSDF deployments. A poll in 1989 showed that less than one-quarter
of the public wanted the JSDF to participate in UN peace keeping,
but 72 percent would approve of the JSDF deployment abroad to
help with disaster relief. Two years later, in 1990 and 1991, a majority of Japan's public opposed the general notion of cooperating in the allied war effort against Iraq, but the public was evenly
split over the more specific questions of whether to send JSDF planes
to help evacuate refugees and to send physicians or technicians to
help in noncombat areas.[15] Shortly after the passage of the peace-
keeping bill in 1992, public opinion showed about one-third were in
favor, one-third were opposed, and one-third were undecided. After the deployment of JSDF engineers to Cambodia and the successful election there, 55 percent of the public approved of the
legislation.[16]

While some critics continue to see Japan's peace-keeping legislation as limiting and of little help, others see it as an important
evolutionary step in Japan's foreign policy. Surely, the mere passage of the bill was a significant departure from past policy. And
the passage of the bill was not just for show. It was immediately
followed up by the deployment of 600 SDF troops and 75 civilian
police to Cambodia where the United Nations was monitoring a
cease-fire and preparing for elections. It is true that most of the
JSDF troops were engineers, not soldiers, and thus many observers were not satisfied. But the test of political will came in May
1993 when a Japanese police officer was killed in Cambodia and
four others injured in an ambush. In Japan, the event was front-
page news, yet the government resisted impassioned pleas to withdraw the Japanese contingent. The foreign minister declared that
Japan could not be "the first to say goodbye and leave Cambodia
just because there is some fighting in some areas."[17] Thus, however
many difficulties there were with peace-keeping participation, Japan is on a new course that includes sending uniformed and armed
troops abroad. Since 1992 Japan has sent SDF units to Mozambique,
Zaire, Rwanda, and the Golan Heights—and all this in the midst of
a vast electoral realignment that at times brought to power parties

which in previous eras opposed the existence of the JSDF altogether. Japan also continues to pay 14 percent of the expenses for all UN peace-keeping operations.

Limits remain on Japan's participation in UN operations. But one of the most important limits is not a consequence of Japanese culture or history, as many would believe, but of American experiences in intervention: Japan is not willing to approve proposals that allow the United Nations or the United States to change the nature of the mission in midcourse (as was done in Somalia). Otherwise, the careful nurturing of public support would be in vain were the JSDF or the Japanese government to be involved in the failure of a mission never clearly presented to the legislature or the public.

Airlift, Civil Defense, and Minesweeping

As the Japanese government and public become used to their active participation in troubled areas abroad and as the self-defense forces gain experience, one can expect that Japan's involvements will multiply and that the JSDF's range of activities will expand. Indeed, this has already been the case. The JSDF has both the equipment and the necessary training to perform a variety of important missions. The Air Self-Defense Force (JASDF), for example, has more than fifteen C-130 transports. These were used to airlift personnel and supplies to refugee camps in Zaire and Rwanda and can likewise be used to deal with refugee crises in Asia.[18] More C-130 transports will be acquired, and the air force will continue drawing up contingency plans which require their use.[19]

Though the Ground Self-Defense Forces (JGSDF) were in the early 1990s behind the other services in preparing for their deployment abroad, they have caught up and in fact have deployed forces abroad, even if mainly engineers. Though commentators continue to reiterate that Japan is unlikely to send armed troops to hostile areas, the position of JGSDF has changed remarkably through the decade. Troops carrying sidearms have been sent to areas where little hostility was anticipated, such as Mozambique, and noncombat troops have been sent to areas where some risk was anticipated, such as Cambodia. One of the peculiar features of the JGSDF is that it has long practiced disaster-relief operations in Japan, and this training gives the JGSDF an obvious role to play in many UN missions.

Meanwhile, the Maritime Self-Defense Force (JMSDF), the most cosmopolitan of Japan's armed forces and the one with the most operational experience abroad, boasts an expertise in clearing seaborne mines. The JMSDF has more than forty of the most modern mine warfare ships and far outstrips the U.S. Navy in this specialty, both in numbers of ships and experience. In fact, the JMSDF experience reaches back to post–World War II days when they cleared mines from their own territorial waters: It includes minesweeping in Korean waters on behalf of the Americans during the Korean conflict and, more recently, minesweeping in the Persian Gulf following the war in 1991.[20]

Unfortunately, American defense specialists have given little attention to the practice of clearing seaborne mines—whether done by the U.S. Navy or the JMSDF. The U.S. Navy has had no need to clear mines from American territorial waters since 1942, and mine countermeasures simultaneously became a career dead end for officers and a low budget priority.[21] Despite the intensive use of minesweepers in the Persian Gulf, mine countermeasures in the U.S. Navy are still an obscure specialty, fighting losing budget battles. One cannot help but wonder when will be the next time the United States asks for Japanese help, specifically in the form of minesweepers. The question of where may be easier to answer—anywhere from the Senkaku Islands to the Straits of Malacca.

Meanwhile, Japan continues to develop another important security role in the western Pacific: sea-lane defense.

Sea-Lane Defense

During the Cold War, the strength of Japan's economy and the desire of the United States to have its defense burden shared more evenly among allies combined to convince the Japanese government to take up the defense of sea lanes up to one-thousand miles south and southeast of Japan. The commitment was first made in 1981, though was obscured by bickering between the American and Japanese governments, not only about the particulars of sharing the burdens of defense, but about U.S.–Japanese trade in general and Japan's domestic market practices. Thus, it went largely unnoticed through the 1980s that Japan was rapidly acquiring the ability to fulfill its commitment to sea-lane defense and by the end of the decade had done so.[22] The JMSDF had embarked upon an extensive upgrade program for its long-range maritime reconnaissance aircraft, which included acquiring forty P3Cs and a new class of destroyers with guided missiles. The JMSDF also added Harpoon and Sea Sparrow missile systems and close-in weapons systems to existing destroyers and frigates. As early as 1983, the JMSDF and U.S. Navy had begun joint exercises for the mock defense of Pacific trade routes.

The end of the Cold War enhanced and amplified Japan's naval position rather than diminished it, and naval forces in the Pacific changed remarkably in the 1990s.[23] Most significant among those changes was the deterioration of Russia's Pacific Fleet: in poor condition, much of it unseaworthy, and some of it underwater. By some reports Russian sailors were underfed, and ships were not fully crewed. Desertion and corruption were rampant. Even fuel was in short supply. The result was that months passed without new deployments.

Some analysts then preferred to point to growth in China's navy and the examination of China's maritime ambitions became a new industry for navy-watchers.[24] Nonetheless, a careful reading of the literature on China's naval developments showed the common thread to be China's *potential*, rather than any *actual*, maritime threat. The actual size and condition of the Chinese navy changed little from year to year and was far from being first rate. China's five nuclear-powered attack submarines were only barely serviceable. Its obsolescent diesel submarines were no match for the high-technology, antisubmarine warfare capacity of the JMSDF. And the ability of China's naval crews was limited by rare and brief deployments. Ships of China's new *Luhu* and *Jiangwei* class carried modern armaments, but most of China's frigates and destroyers were not equipped with either area-missile defense systems or strong antisubmarine defenses. One analyst concluded that China is "in short, one of the weakest of the great powers and the least qualified to fill any so-called vacuum in Asia."[25]

Certainly the U.S. Navy was counted the most competent, reliable, and powerful naval force in the Pacific, and the United States was best qualified to fill any so-called vacuum in Asia. But the United States in the 1990s was concerned as much with balanced budgeting as it was with Asian power relations and consequently was preoccupied with downsizing its armed forces. The United States reduced its naval presence in the western Pacific (and is likely to continue to do so). Further, U.S. naval forces assigned to the Pacific were, as always, also assigned to the Indian Ocean and to the Persian Gulf. At any given time, barring extraordinary efforts, only about one-third of the U.S. Pacific fleet was available for operations in the western Pacific Ocean.

At the same time the JSDF's naval forces were, and continue to be, of high quality, and the peculiar political shifts of the 1990s resulted in Japan's active-duty principle surface combatants outnumbering those of either Russia or China. The JMSDF increased its fleet in both relative and absolute terms and continues to purchase the most technologically advanced systems. In general, the JMSDF of the 1990s was far more competent than the U.S. public perception of it. The U.S. commander of the Pacific Fleet even in 1991 claimed

Japan has the capability to defend itself against all but perhaps a resurgent Soviet Union. They have invested a lot of money to build a very capable self-defense force. . . . We operate with the Japanese Navy a lot, they are good. We have a mutual defense arrangement with Japan, but they really have the capability to defend themselves.[26]

And although the Japanese constitution and public opinion still limit the deployment of Japanese armed forces, those limits are not as strict as they once were and are growing more liberal virtually every year. Japan's commitment to sea-lane defense should be viewed as a great help to a United States that finds its defense commitments in the post–Cold War era hardly diminished, while the forces at its disposal are diminished. A thousand miles of Japanese sea-lane defense allows the United States, if it will allow itself, to uphold commitments elsewhere. And a thousand miles is a long way: From Osaka to Chi-lung, Taiwan is almost exactly a thousand miles; from Yokohama to Shanghai is only 1,040 miles; and from the JMSDF base in Maizuru to Vladivostok is fewer than five-hundred miles.

LIMITS OF JAPAN IN ASIA

Still one might ask whether Asian nations, even those that might be besieged by rebellion, will ever be willing to receive more than just economic assistance from Japan. Generations of people with first- or second-hand memories of the Pacific War are still alive and in government. For this reason alone, Japan cannot take the place of the United States in fostering stability in the Asian Pacific Rim. There were Asian protests even when Japan deployed mine-sweepers to the far-away Persian Gulf. Singapore's president was most uncomplimentary, likening the American support of Japan's defense capabilities to giving liquored candies to an alcoholic.[27] China too disapproved of the mine-clearing mission, claiming—correctly—it was "a dangerous first step in sending troops overseas."[28] But many other countries did give their public approval. By the time Japan passed legislation allowing the JSDF to deploy abroad and participate in UN peace-keeping operations, protests had died away.

Japan's public has followed a similar pattern. Objections are put forward when policy changes are proposed, such as the peace-keeping legislation or the Persian Gulf minesweeping mission. But the proposal goes forward. The operations are well defined, and the protests diminish. The Japanese public is skeptical of foreign entanglements and certainly not used to them, but also is willing to support both the United States and the United Nations.[29] In this way, Japan's public is not altogether dissimilar from other publics (including that of the United States) that shy away from open-ended commitments, runaway costs, and the possibility of casualties.[30] For these reasons, Japan will maintain definite limits to its peacetime military involvements: It cannot be required to coordinate with U.S. troops if those troops are actively enforcing the peace, and it will not approve of proposals that allow the United States or the United Nations to change the nature of a mission in midcourse, as was done in Somalia and Bosnia. In short, Japan can play a well-defined role following the leadership of the United States and acting within the boundaries of the U.S. Japan Security Treaty and United Nations mandates.

For most people, the boundaries that limit Japan's participation in defense affairs more easily come to mind than the actual and potential roles Japan can fulfill in a partnership with the United States and United Nations. But Japan already does, and will do, more for Western defense than many realize. As we have already seen, the JSDF can participate in sea-lane defense, mineclearing, humanitarian assitance, and peace-keeping operations. If one finds this list lacking, it might be compared to the American military doctrine on MOOTW or "military operations other than war."[31]

The Pentagon's trendy ancronym MOOTW essentially covers every military operation other than "large-scale, sustained combat."[32] According to the official literature, there are sixteen categories of MOOTW, ranging alphabetically from arms control efforts to "support to insurgency."[33] Cynic and critic alike might ask what types of MOOTW Japan might be prepared to undertake. The answer may be surprising. Of the sixteen MOOTW, Japan has already participated in ten: arms control, combatting terrorism, counterdrug operations, humanitarian assistance, military support to civil authorties, nation assistance, peace operations, protection of shipping, recovery operations, and show of force. Of the six remaining MOOTW, Japan is capable of, and given the correct international circumstances likely to undertake, four more: enforcement of sanctions, enforcing exclusion zones, ensuring freedom of navigation and overflight, and noncombatant evacuation operations. Only two MOOTW are beyond Japan's political possibilities in the absence of some wrenching change in the domestic and international system: strikes and raids and direct support to insurgencies.

Of course, the Pentagon's variations on MOOTW tend to be broadly and even loosely defined. In part, this broad categorizing is why we can say that Japan has already performed at least ten such variants. But in part too, Japan's government and Defense Agency are more engaged and more versatile than they are often given credit for. It remains, in part, a diplomatic and defense-planning task for the United States to see that Japan's limitations are also appreciated.

CONCLUSION

One thing that has distinguished the United States from other great powers past and present has been its cultivation of reliable and strong allies. Following World War II, the United States deliberately fostered the political and economic well being of both friends and former enemies, including Japan. Subsequently, the commitment and reliability of those allies was an indispensable element of the successful struggle against the nations of the Soviet bloc. It should be no less axiomatic after the Cold War for the United States to make the most of its position and interest by continuing to cultivate and make use of those allies. To some degree the United States has recognized this. In recent years, for example, the United States acted within the framework of NATO first to enforce the arms embargo against the countries of the former Yugoslavia, and then again to put ground troops in Bosnia in an attempt to enforce the peace accords. The United States did so because its European allies shared the fundamental interests of the United States. So does Japan.

The *strongest* American allies have been, like the United States, industrialized, secular, democratic states committed to the free exchange of goods and ideas, to the stability of the international order, and to warding off the claims and threats of illiberal ideologies. As the United States faces continued threats to the domestic stability of friendly governments, including threats of ethnic or religious rebellions around the globe, it must continue to make good use of its allies, or it will forego an important source of political, economic, and military support.

Japan is willing to aid the United States; public statements year after year make this clear. Japan is also *capable* of aiding the United States; the expanding missions and first-rate equipment of Japan's armed forces demonstrate this capability. Other Asian nations, undoubtedly wary of Japan, nonetheless receive economic development assistance, carry on a large volume of trade with Japan, and have made only the faintest protests as Japan's roles in Pacific defense and in UN peace-keeping operations have grown. Those who prophesy that the twenty-first century will be the Pacific century might also advise that it be the century of American–Japanese cooperation.

NOTES

1. The author played his part as a member of the Japanese government.

2. The past decade produced a spate of books and articles about the Japanese threat that are too numerous to list here. Representative of the thesis in defense matters was George Friedman and Meredith Lebard, *The Coming War with Japan* (New York: St. Martin's Press, 1991). About Japan's political relations with the United States was Pat Choate, *Agents of Influence: How Japan's Lobbyists in the United States Manipulate America's Political and Economic System* (New York: Knopf, 1990). Explaining that "Japanese power is actually a carefully structured hierarchy, and the capstone is . . . the little-understood and low-profile Ministry of Finance" was Eamonn Fingleton, "Japan's Invisible Leviathan," *Foreign Affairs* 74 (March–April 1995): 69–85. In economics and business, there was a veritable cascade of books explaining Japanese success, usually in cultural terms. Among these was Ronald Dore, *Taking Japan Seriously* (Stanford, Calif.: Stanford University Press, 1987), in which the author explained that "the main distinctive characteristics" of Japan included the following: "The Japanese work hard," "The Japanese are well educated," and "The Japanese work cooperatively in large corporations."

3. Defense expenditures are notoriously difficult to compare because, among other reasons, soft currencies such as China's, unstable currencies such as Russia's, or overvalued hard currencies such as Japan's, produce misleading real dollar conversions. In addition, purchasing power differs wildly from one country to another and, in Japan's case, prices for domestically produced goods and services are sometimes two to three times world-market prices. Nonetheless, Japan's military expenditures are far greater than most people realize. See *World Military Expenditures and Arms Transfers* (Washington, D.C.: U.S. Arms Control and Disarmament Agency, annual).

4. Between 1984 and 1994 Japan's military expenditures increased in constant dollars by more than 30 percent. By 1995 the Japanese Diet did agree on a series of defense cuts, but those cuts were more a result of budget pressures in the midst of a chronic economic recession rather than the result of a new, bottom-up interpretation of defense needs. Further, it was debatable whether those cuts had any significant meaning in terms of readiness, training, or even the size of the Self Defense Forces. The so-called "ceiling," or maximum number, for members of the Ground Self-Defense Forces (GSDF) was cut drastically, from 185 thousand to 145 thousand. But, in fact, the GSDF had never recruited nor employed its maximum number of troops. At the time of the "reduction," the GSDF had just under 150 thousand troops. Thus, a 21-percent reduction in the ceiling meant a 3-percent cut in personnel. Likewise, the navy was to reduce its force by an escort division, a few destroyers, and some antisubmarine

aircraft. But those that would be retired were old or obsolete. The air force was similarly directed to eliminate an F-4 fighter squadron.

5. See *Defense of Japan*, translated by Japan Times Ltd. (Tokyo: Defense Agency, annual), where chapters 1 and 2 offer an assessment of the international military situation.

6. For a summary of similar and differing views see Se Hee Yoo, "Sino–Japanese Relations in a Changing East Asia," in *Japan's Foreign Policy After the Cold War: Coping with Change*, ed. Gerald Curtis (Armonk, N.Y.: M. E. Sharpe, 1993), pp. 303–322. See notes that "many Japanese scholars consider China to be the country most threatening to Japan."

7. Ibid., ch. 2, sec. 5.

8. On Japan's territorial disputes in the East China Sea, see K. T. Chao, "East China Sea: Boundary Problems Relating to the Tiao-yu-ta'i Islands," *Chinese Yearbook of International Law and Affairs* 2 (1982): 45–97; and in the same volume Ying-Jeou Ma, "The East Asian Seabed Controversy Revisited: Relevance (or Irrelevance) of the Tiao-yu-ta'i (Senkaku) Islands Territorial Dispute," pp. 1–44. See also Tao Cheng, "The Sino–Japanese Dispute over the Tiao-yu-ta'i (Senkaku) Islands and the Law of Territorial Acquisition," *Virginia Journal of International Law* 14: 221–266.

9. "Japan Reverses Course in Senkaku Islands Dispute," *Japan Times*, Weekly International Edition, 5–11 November 1990, p. 3.

10. *Japan Weekly*, 31 July 1996, p. 2.

11. It was actually over these islands, part of the Ryukyu archipelago, that modern Japan first put its Westernized military to the test in 1872. Retaliating for the murders of several Japanese mariners in the Ryukyu Islands, the Meiji government attacked the island of Formosa, an important Chinese dependency, and by this punitive force won an indemnity from the Chinese government.

12. Among Japan's top ten aid recipients have been China, Indonesia, Philippines, Thailand, Malaysia, and Korea. See Robert Orr, *The Emergence of Japan's Foreign Aid Power* (New York: Columbia University Press, 1990); Alan Rix, "Japan's Foreign Aid Policy: A Capacity for Leadership," *Pacific Affairs* 62, no. 4 (Winter 1990): 461–475; and Shafiqul Islam, ed., *Yen for Development: Japanese Foreign Aid and the Politics of Burden-Sharing* (New York: Council on Foreign Relations Press, 1991).

13. Japan's 1991 "White Paper on Overseas Development Assistance" for the first time tied development aid to political values. See Takashi Kitazume, "Tokyo to Link Aid More Closely to Politics," *Japan Times*, Weekly International Edition, 14–20 October 1991; Yoichi Funabashi, "Japan and the New World Order," *Foreign Affairs* 70, no. 5 (Winter 1991–92): 66 ff.; "New Aid Policy Emphasizes Markets, Demilitarization, Democracy and Environment," *Weekly Japan Digest*, 6 July 1992, p. 14.

14. See, for example, John D. Issacs, "The Domestic Context: American Politics and U.N. Peacekeeping," in *UN Peacekeeping: Japanese and American Perspectives*, ed. Selig S. Harrison and Masashi Nishihara (Washington, D.C.: Carnegie Institute, 1995), pp. 73–88.

15. See Prime Minister's Office, "Public Opinion Survey on Japan's Peace and Security" (August 1989), p. 12; Davis B. Bobrow, "Japan in the World:

Opinion from Defeat to Success," *Journal of Conflict Resolution* 33, no. 4 (Tokyo: Prime Minister's Office, December 1989): 571–604; and Peter J. Woolley, "Low-Level Military Threats and the Future of Japan's Armed Forces," *Conflict Quarterly* 12, no. 4 (Fall 1993): 55–73. For the view of business leaders in Japan during the Gulf War, see "Industry's View of the War," *Economic Eye* 12, no. 2 (Summer 1991): 17.

16. Akihiko Tanaka, "The Domestic Context: Japanese Politics and U.N. Peacekeeping," in *UN Peacekeeping: Japanese and American Perspectives*, ed. Selig S. Harrison and Masashi Nishihara (Washington, D.C.: Carnegie Institute, 1995), p. 98.

17. "Renewed Fighting Revives PKO Debate," *Japan Times*, Weekly International Edition, 22–28 February 1993, p. 1; and "Government Reassesses PKO Mission in Cambodia," *Japan Times*, Weekly International Edition, 17–23 May 1993, p. 1; "Peacekeeping Role Doubts Raised," *Japan Times*, Weekly International Edition, 24–30 May 1993, p. 1. Some critics have taken pleasure in pointing out that after one Japanese policeman was killed in the spring of 1993, twenty other "peace keepers" fled their posts. These fleeing peace keepers were civilian policemen, however, and not members of the JSDF. Kenneth Pyle, *The Japanese Question* (Washington, D.C.: AEI Press, 1996), pp. 154–155.

18. The C-130 carries only ninety-two people, and the range of these planes is 2,300 miles. For their mission to Mozambique the planes had to refuel at least four times, but the 2,300-mile range gives them significant possibilities on the Asian Rim.

19. As the Japanese government sought a policy response to pressure from the United States during the Persian Gulf War, the JASDF drew up contingency plans to help ferry refugees out of Jordan. The government in the end did not approve the JASDF plans, partly because the C-130 transports were not enough in number and could not carry enough passengers. See Peter J. Woolley, "Japan's 1991 Minesweeping Decision: An Organizational Response," *Asian Survey* 36, no. 8 (August 1996): 815.

20. The first postwar dispatch of Japanese warships actually took place in 1950 before the establishment of either the Defense Agency or the JMSDF. Japanese minesweepers were coopted by U.S. forces operating against North Korea. See James Auer, *The Postwar Rearmament of Japanese Maritime Forces, 1945–1971* (New York: Praeger, 1973), pp. 64–68.

21. See Tamara Moser Melia, *Damn the Torpedos: A Short History of U.S. Naval Mine Countermeasures, 1777– 1991* (Washington, D.C.: Navy Historical Center, 1991); and John F. Tarpey, "Minestruck Navy Forgets Its History," *Proceedings* 114 (February 1988): 44–47.

22. Such developments went unnoticed or were undervalued: See, for example, Thomas B. Modly, "The Rhetoric and Realities of Japan's 1,000-Mile Sea-Lane Defense Policy," *Naval War College Review* 38, no. 1 (January–February 1985): 25–36; Michael Ganley, "Japanese Goal to Protect Sea Lanes: More Rhetoric than Reality?" *Armed Forces Journal International* 123, no. 2 (September 1985): 104, 107; Kataoka Tetsuya, "Japan's Defense Non-Buildup: What Went Wrong?" *International Journal of World Peace* 2 (April–June 1985): 10–29. But one study did conclude that with only mar-

ginal improvements Japan would be ready to defend its sea lanes against the Soviet Union, even without relying on the United States. See Daniel I. Gallagher, *Sea Lane Defense: Japanese Capabilities and Imperatives* (master's thesis, Naval Postgraduate School, December 1987).

23. See Peggy Falkenheim Meyer, "Russia's Post–Cold War Security Policy in Northeast Asia," *Pacific Viewpoint* 35, no. 1 (May 1994): 495–512; Benjamin S. Lambeth, "Russia's Wounded Military," *Foreign Affairs* 74 (March–April 1995): 86–98; Douglas Ross, "Maritime Security in the North Pacific during the 1990s," in *Maritime Security and Conflict Resolution at Sea in the Post Cold War Era*, ed. Peter T. Haydon and Ann L. Griffiths (Halifax, Nova Scotia: Centre for Foreign Policy Studies, Dalhousie University, 1994), pp. 79–86.

24. After the dissolution of the Soviet Union, articles quickly proliferated about China's military plans, such as You Ji and You Xu, "In Search of Blue Water Power: The PLA Navy's Maritime Strategy in the 1990s," *Pacific Review* 4, no. 2 (1991): 137–149; Andrew Mack and Desmond Ball, "The Military Build-Up in Asia–Pacific," *Pacific Review* 5, no. 3 (1992): 197–208; "China Moves to Fill Naval Vacuum," *Defense News*, 26 April–2 May 1993, p. 18; John B. Haseman, "Military Developments in the South China Sea Basin," *Military Review* 73 (February 1993): 55–63; Michael T. Klare, "The Next Great Arms Race," *Foreign Affairs* 72 (Summer 1993): 136–152; Nickolas D. Kristof, "The Rise of China," *Foreign Affairs* 72 (November–December 1993): 59–74; Denny Roy, "Hegemon on the Horizon? China's Threat to East Asian Security," *Military Review* 74 (May 1994): 28–32; Stephen L. Ryan, "The PLA Navy's Search for a Blue Water Capability," *Asian Defense Journal* (May 1994): 28–32; David Shambough, "Growing Strong: China's Challenge to Asian Security," *Survival* 36 (Summer 1994): 43–59.

25. Gary Clintworth, "Greater China and Regional Security," *Australian Journal of International Affairs* 48, no. 2 (November 1994): 211–229. But see also Andrew J. Nathan and Robert S. Ross, *The Great Wall and the Empty Fortress: China's Search for Security* (New York: W. W. Norton, 1997); Michael G. Gallagher, "China's Illusory Threat to the South China Sea," *International Security* 36 (Summer 1994): 169–194; and Solomon M. Karmel, "The Chinese Military's Hunt for Profits," *Foreign Policy* 107 (Summer 1997): 102–113.

26. "A Pacific Presence: Interview with Adm. Robert J. Kelly, CINCPACFLT," *Seapower* 34, no. 12 (December 1991): 12.

27. Asked if Japan had changed since World War II, Prime Minister of Singapore Lee Kuan Yew said it had not. See "Lee on Japan's Deployment in Gulf, U.S. Bases," Foreign Broadcast Information Service (FBIS), Daily Report, East Asia *(DR/EAS)*, 8 November 1990, p. 34.

28. "Xinhua on Japan's SDF Deployment to Gulf," FBIS, *Daily Report, China (DR/CHI)*, 23 April 1991, p. 5. See also "Roundup on Japan's Troop Dispatch," FBIS *(DR/CHI)*, 24 April 1991, pp. 4–5; and "Li Peng Discusses Minesweepers," FBIS *(DR/CHI)*, 24 April 1991, p. 13.

29. For one development of this theme, see Peter J. Woolley and Mark S. Woolley, "The Kata of Japan's Naval Forces," *Naval War College Review*

49, no. 2 (Spring 1996): 59–69. But, for example, in September 1990, just after the Gulf crisis began, polls showed about 40 percent of Japan's public opposed any use of the JSDF abroad. By 1992, a national poll showed only 20 percent in outright opposition to using the JSDF abroad under any circumstances and 68 percent actually approving the use of the JSDF for peace keeping. See "Yomiuri Polls Find 68% Approval of Using Troops for Peacekeeping," *Daily Japan Digest*, 6 May 1992, p. 2.

30. Joseph Keddell has argued that in Japan, as elsewhere, "public opinion tends to follow the course of events, rather than to determine specific outcomes." Joseph P. Keddell, Jr., *The Politics of Defense in Japan: Managing Internal and External Pressures* (Armonk, N.Y.: M. E. Sharpe, 1993), p. 4.

31. See Department of Defense, *Joint Doctrine for Military Operations Other Than War* (Joint Pub 3-07), 16 June 1995.

32. According to the *Joint Doctrine* in note 31, p. vii, MOOTW "can be applied to complement any combination of the other instruments of national power. To understand MOOTW, it is useful to understand how they differ from operations in war. Although MOOTW and war may often seem similar in action, MOOTW focus on deterring war and promoting peace while war encompasses large-scale, sustained combat operations to achieve national objectives or to protect national interests."

33. Ibid., pp. iii–1 ff.

9

State and Armed Forces in Russia: Toward an African Scenario

Stephen Blank

Only a few years ago, predictions were widespread that out of the debris of the Soviet collapse would emerge a democratic Russia. Unfortunately, with its experiment in democracy hardly begun, the Russian state is beset by multiple crises. It appears to be losing the ability to protect itself from either internal or external challenges. This chapter, which compares the situation in Russia to that of Africa, presents a prospect that is bleak and disquieting.

By all accounts both the Russian state and its armed forces are currently confronting a major crisis. Indeed, the state's crisis appears with particular sharpness in the military sector and its multiple armed forces. The military crisis is among the greatest symptoms of the threat of a general state collapse, because it reflects a continuing failure in state building as well as specific military causes. This crisis must be seen in both its historical and comparative contexts. To understand the nature of the threats of state disintegration, we must also understand both the military and state roots of the current crises. Russia remains a state made and unmade by war, including the Cold War. Russia's historical efforts to sustain the kind of army and state that its government deemed necessary for playing a great power role have resulted in periods of state crises and of state building. This connection between the state and the military continues today.

State disintegration in Russia occurs when the erosion or collapse of the army's capability to defend Russian interests conjoins
with a general and progressive decline in its ability to govern and
provide the economic, material basis for attaining those interests.
This long-standing pattern reappeared in the period of 1975 to 1991,
as the crisis of the Soviet system began under Brezhnev and accelerated out of control under Gorbachev. But while the crisis of the
state and its armed forces has evolved, it has not abated—quite the
contrary. As recent developments show, Russia's economic future,
at least through 1998, has not improved, falling victim to the Asian
economic crisis that began in 1997. Nor should one believe that
firing the cabinet and finding "honest men" or reformers could save
the situation. President Boris Yeltsin's firing of his cabinet in March
1997 or of his military leadership between May and November 1997
are merely more examples of his endless and perhaps desperate,
tsarist ministerial leapfrog, not a bold initiative.

Ultimately the Soviet Union collapsed because its defenders in
1991 either refused to or could not ably deploy force in its defense.
Thus they reconfirmed the connection between military viability
and state power. Yeltsin's regime survived in 1993 because he ultimately was ready to use force and found the forces he needed. But
a year later he found that the forces he commanded could not defend Russia's integrity, a situation that has worsened since
Chechnya. Today local governments in the Maritime Province and
Dagestan are forming their own militaries or Cossack forces, either because of their opposition to Moscow or because Moscow cannot protect Dagestan. And Ingushetia, Dagestan's neighbor, will
follow suit if Dagestan succeeds, thereby attenuating the state's
monopoly of legitimate force and integrity still further. Yeltsin, after the 1994 Chechnya invasion revealed its futility, confirmed that
the main obstacle to military reforms intended to overcome the
defects revealed in Chechnya was "the lack of an integral mechanism for making decisions in the sphere of ensuring military security."[1] In other words, the military crisis derives from the
fundamental distortion of the state that Yeltsin fostered. The nature of his government is the crisis, not merely failed policies. Indeed, in the military as well as economic sphere, failed policies are
direct outcomes of the deeper political failure to build viable and
effective governing organs.

Chechnya, like other wars in Russian history such as the Russo-
Japanese War of 1904 to 1905 or the Crimean War of 1853 to 1856,
illustrated that in any future wars of this kind, Moscow will become
the war's center of gravity. Protracted wars at the periphery put the
survival of the government in power at risk. Indeed, defeat in Chechnya

has contributed mightily to the unraveling of Russia's integrity and state power. Hence the manifestations of military crisis resemble those that afflict state governance as a whole and are directly traceable to Yeltsin's policy preferences and their consequences.

Yeltsin has decisively failed to overcome the crisis of government or fulfill the two primary tasks of the state that Russian history poses: building an effective state and armed forces. Russia remains a state ruled either by autocracy or despotic oligarchy, and democratization is not in sight, despite the importance of elections. Deputy Prime Minister Boris Nemtsov recently articulated this position, stating that Yeltsin rules like a tsar, that Russia needs such authority at the center or it will fall apart, and that the present constitution resembles that of 1905.[2]

Yeltsin's habitual answer to this and other crises will only aggravate it further. Like earlier tsars, he has announced that he will assume ever more personal responsibility and try to find so-called honest and capable men, reforming bureaucrats, and fire the "bad" or "weak" ministers. Since there is no sign that any of these bureaucrats will accept accountability to anyone except Yeltsin, chances are he will rule by decree, subvert legal institution building still further, and attempt to construct the dictatorship of the state that Deputy Premier Anatoly Chubais has extolled.[3] Yeltsin's personalism aggravates the state's crisis and lack of institutional roots, making it impossible to form an effective state. Therefore Yeltsin and his system remain the single greatest obstacle to the stability and democracy of the Russian state, the two primary tasks of Russian state building.

It should be noted these tasks do not include the instauration of capitalism. Only ideologues or those who disregard Russian history can assume that the primary task of Russian government is creating a flourishing capitalist economy, or even that what we have now is capitalism. The state, as Yeltsin admitted, still interferes far too much and creates favorites and deals, as it is taken over by private interests. As Anders Aslund has recently observed, the Russian state (like many other predatory Third World states) apparently exists for the sole purpose of expropriating the national economy by endless rent-seeking.[4] Inasmuch as this is the historical pattern of Russian autocracy, as well as Communism, the recurrence of this historical pattern, along with that of late autocracy as Nemtsov noted, is not surprising.

A self-starting market, not to mention something approaching the ideal of a self-regulating market, does not yet exist in Russia. And the efforts to impose government order will ultimately militate against that development. Russia's state remains the demiurge of Russia's historical process, even when it has to divest itself of power to create economic viability; an effective but limited state is the precondition for economic reform and prosperity. Consequently any pathologies of statehood afflict every area of governance, including the armed forces.

The challenge of state building is, of course, not confined only to Russia today. It is a ubiquitous challenge for states at all times, and Russia's state and military failure resembles those of African and many other Third World states. Russia's state-building challenge resembles that of the Third World (and also of Peter the Great): to build a state amidst the hurricane of internal and external forces that erode the capacity of backward governments to govern effectively. And as part of that challenge, large police forces are created to stand by the formal army because threats to continued rule are as much internal as external, if not more so.[5] What Michael Bratton observes about African armies can easily be applied to both Russia's armed forces and its state.

However, the development of military institutions in Africa has taken distinctive neopatrimonial forms. African armies rarely resembled an idealized bureaucracy, molded into organizational force by professional training, nationalistic sentiments and shared esprit de corps. Instead, these institutions were riven by political factionalism based on the personal ambition of would-be leaders among the officer corps and on ethnic solidarities within the ranks. Because African armies "incorporate tensions characteristic of civilian elite society as a whole," their interventions in politics constantly reflected the ambitions of particular leaders and factions. Certainly none of the armies under review acted as a unified force. For example, the Nigerian army was splintered into "cabals and cliques"—Most distinctively, the behavior of military actors, including forays into transition politics, was propelled by struggles over coveted offices, rents, and grafts.[6]

These actions invariably bred internal tensions within and among militaries and reflected military leaders' strong predisposition against transferring power over the government or the armed forces to civilians, a trend uniformly perceived as signifying a loss of power by the top brass.[7] Inasmuch as this trend seems to be widespread in transition governments, the interpenetration of these military trends with the same kinds of phenomena in government denotes a broader and more universal crisis in state-building. Thus, while pundits pronounce the end of the state, Russia, true to its centuries-long struggle to become a power of the first rank from a backward position, once again must build a state. Only this time, it is failing.

Even if one accepts the claims that the economy is turning around, it remains clear that both today's crises and state policies inhibit economic growth and recovery. The government cannot promote economic recovery and growth. It cannot even collect taxes. Worse, neither the government nor the many armed forces can effectively defend Russia's territorial integrity or often their own organizational integrity and self-interest. Nor does anyone want to test whether they can defend the government against an internal threat. In all domains the state's capabilities are far beneath the demands it has placed upon itself, not to speak of those placed on it by society, including the armed forces. Although since 1985 we have supposedly witnessed a transitional period, the transition has become the status quo and cannot consolidate itself into a stable form that can enjoy popular legitimacy or real capability. Consequently every aspect of defense policy must be transformed for the army, Russian democracy, and even the state as such to survive. Defense reform, to be meaningful and lasting, entails a comprehensive reform of the state. Meanwhile, multiple possibilities or scenarios for military and state breakdown exist. And without reform, they will probably materialize sooner rather than later.

THE ENVIRONMENT OF RUSSIAN DEFENSE POLICY

Russia has undergone five years of ceaseless institutional experimentation leading to the creation of more bureaucrats today than in 1991. Yet, even so, it remains paradoxically undergoverned, much like mid-nineteenth century Russia.[8] As Sergei Rogov, director of the USA and Canada Institute, observes,

One could say that the state in Russia has attempted to suppress the state, but the specific organs of the state have separated themselves in broad terms and started living their own lives, while ignoring the needs that the overall society expects the state to fulfill. Each agency is doing whatever is useful to itself. Rather than deregulating the economy and society, it seems that the state itself has been "deregulated."[9]

In other words, the state and its multiple militaries have been privatized. Private interests have fused with the state and are using it solely to advance their private, sectoral, or clan interests.[10] Indeed, without private financial support from the Mayor of Moscow, Yuri Liuzhkov, or from American financier George Soros, among others, whole sectors of the armed forces and of the state would have collapsed by now, by the government's own admission.[11] In February 1997 Rodionov begged the private banks to bail out the armed forces. Instead he was told to pay the ministry's bills (which the government had made impossible because it sequestered the money, and the MOD habitually overspent its allowances) and stop expropriating contractors![12] Both the absence of effective civil–military controls and public sources of state finance are acknowledged as hallmarks of a failing state.[13]

The crisis of the civil–military relationship goes a long way in telling us the nature of this particular state. As defined by Jeffrey Simon of the National Defense University, there are four main attributes of effective, democratic, civilian control of the armed forces.

A Clear Division of Authority between the President and the Government (Prime Minister and Defense–Interior Minister) in Constitutions or through Public Law

Questions of who commands and controls the military, makes peacetime promotions, holds emergency powers in crisis, and makes the transition to a state of war must be firmly spelled out in a legally binding document that renders the executive accountable to the law, the legislature, and in cases of struggle between them, either to the independent judiciary, or the electorate.

Parliamentary Oversight of the Military through Control of the Defense Budget

Legislative control over the use of the armed forces in war or peace must be formalized and clear. Relevant ministries must give parliamentary majorities and minorities full and transparent information on budgets and policies and allow for unfettered consultation and open debate between those parties. The latter also need adequate staff agencies and expertise to conduct an effective liaison with the armed forces and police. And all these rules should also apply to oversight of the intelligence agencies.

Peacetime Oversight of General Staffs and Military Commanders through Civilian-Led Defense Ministries

Defense ministries should prepare the defense budget, manage access to intelligence, get involved in strategic planning, and force structure development, promotions, and issues of arms procurements and deployments. This should be done by regularly constituted and accountable institutions, not secret ones, and their processes should therefore be transparent. To accomplish these tasks, defense ministries need legitimate civilian leaders, not just suddenly retired generals, as is now the case in Russia. Defense ministries and all armed forces should be depoliticized, that is, taken

out of all political parties, and not become centers of partisan political activity. Finally, civilian defense ministers must prevent the
General Staff from coopting the ministry and obstructing its supervision of defense policy.

Restoration of Military Prestige, Trustworthiness, and Accountability for the Armed Forces to Be Effective

There must be a legal code defining and limiting the relationships between superior and inferior officers and soldiers and limiting the armed forces' role in national politics. Also, the rights to disobey
illegal orders must be protected, and military funding must suffice to
defend the state and provide for serving the needs of the people.[14]

None of this exists in Russia. Instead, virtually the exact opposite situation prevails, a regression to authoritarian or quasi-
authoritarian structures and policies. For example, the Federal
Security Service (FSB) and the army share or constitute a single
secret service. Almost one-third of army officers are FSB informants,
often recruited because they seek some defense against their supe-
riors' untrammeled arbitrary rule.[15] As the exposé of this relationship observed,

The special departments of the intelligence service recall the NKVD (Ministry of Interior) of the Stalinist period in their unfettered, decisive, and
severe methods. If a military coup were to take place or the Communists
were to return to power, it would not be long before they would make
known their manner of working throughout the country.[16]

But this creeping fusion of police and military forces is happening under a supposed democracy, not Communism. Indeed, the
FSB's spying on the armed forces has grown with the outbreak of
organized opposition to Yeltsin's belated and wildly incoherent
scheme of military reform. The FSB is now investigating investors
in Russia as well as the armed forces.[17]

As Rogov recently wrote, "There is still no system of checks and
balances in Russia, neither is there a genuine separation of executive and legislative branches of power."[18] Moreover Russians experience a steady process of diminished state control over the
bureaucracy, as the state loses its power to govern. Bureaucracies
operate in a vacuum where they are completely irresponsible and
unresponsive. Accordingly no one's civil rights are safe, and Lilia
Shevtsova and Scott Bruckner of the Carnegie Endowment report that
the Russian people had more influence on the government under
Gorbachev than they do now.[19] Clearly the effort to create a viable

mechanism for civilian and legal control over the various armed forces has totally failed. Describing the mechanism for control over the military, Rogov cited four distinct structures for the formation of defense policy. And sadly, they replicate late tsarist structures.

First is the Council of Ministers. The power ministries, which is the second structure or set of structures, and a component of this council, do not report directly to the council. It is no stronger an institution than it was under tsarism when tsars freely overrode it, as Yeltsin does now, which thereby serves to subvert any notion of cabinet or accountable and regular government. The ministers are merely a random collection of officials who are servants of the tsar or president, are routinely set against each other, and who serve the whim of the president.[20]

But neither the ministries nor Yeltsin are subject to public or parliamentary control or account. Since the power ministries are directly subordinate to Yeltsin, the Council of Ministers plays no real role in policy formation and implementation. The Security Council, the State Defense Inspectorate (GVI), and the Defense Council, which serve as the third set of structures within the government, are purely advisory bodies by statute or by decree. They also function as Yeltsin or other strong personalities acting in his place desire. Hence they can substitute for the Council of Ministers or individual ministers, be a block between Yeltsin and the ministers, or be merely one more ineffectual collection of officials designated by him, while real power and authority lie somewhere else, often in an unregulated institution.[21] Precisely due to the Security and Defense Councils' flexible status and composition, their missions are fundamentally unstable, irregular, and subject to the whims of personalities, not rules.

The fourth structure is the presidential administration and staff, who are utterly unaccountable to anything or anyone except Yeltsin. They are distinct from the Security and Defense Council. Before being appointed to head the Defense Council, Yeltsin's former presidential advisor on national security, Yuri Baturin, had nothing to do organizationally or formally with it or the Security Council, but afterward used his position to screen out Rodionov, a choice of Yeltsin's. Thus any of these presidential staffs, ministries, or administration groups can usurp each other's power. Any agency, armed with Yeltsin's approval, can make or unmake policy, and they do so constantly. For instance, the FSK (predecessor of the FSB) simply took hold of army divisions before Chechnya, without notifying Defense Minister Grachev.

Worse yet, the appointment of Minister of Interior General Anatoly Kulikov to be deputy prime minister in 1997 with the tax and customs agencies concentrated under him suggests the creation of a Ministry of the Interior that begins to resemble the dreaded NKVD of the 1930s under Stalin. His appointment also suggests a lack of policy other than the invocation of order and discipline to combat corruption and economic failings in tax and customs collection. This kind of policy is the last refuge of tired despots who cannot offer anything worthy of being called a program for development.

Kulikov's appointment signifies in many respects the end of creative policy, though the ministerial leapfrog will clearly continue for some time. Indeed, since then we have had endless intrigues between factions at the top, with one faction grouped around Chubais seeking to oust Kulikov and Prime Minister Viktor Chernomyrdin, and the reverse is also true. Throughout 1997 these factions waged what Russians call an "information war" against each other in the country's media, which they own. In the meantime, Yeltsin tosses one or another official overboard to preserve the balance. This fatigue, lack of imagination, and resort to order as an end in itself and not a means to an end, along with the emancipation of the secret police agencies from any legal controls replicates either late tsarist or Soviet practices, analogies that should give those proclaiming successful democratization some pause. Likewise Yeltsin's renewed promises of personal supervision over the entire government means that he will supervise nothing effectively and have to delegate to Chubais, Nemtsov, Chernomyrdin, and others, and whoever they appoint. In other words, a failed autocracy once again yields to despotic oligarchy masquerading as bureaucracy. In the end, these new creatures of Yeltsin will also have to be removed so that he can escape blame once again for failed policies.

Yeltsin's ministerial leapfrogs since 1992 have effectively decapitated defense and security policy. In appointing the ambitious former General Aleksandr' Lebed in 1996 to lead a revamped and greatly expanded Security Council, Yeltsin openly politicized the council and made it an instrument for the struggle to succeed him. By then firing Lebed and shifting most defense issues to the extralegally created Defense Council that he established to check Lebed, Yeltsin underscored the regime's personalism and continuing disarray. Any and all aspects of security policy will be further politicized. Hence, there is neither effective nor coherent defense policy. In light of this, however, we do see open insubordination, political infighting, and strategic incompetence of a rare order.

Kulikov ousted Lebed by trumping up charges that Lebed was plotting his own coup. He succeeded in getting him fired in October 1996. To do so, Kulikov launched his own coup by sealing off intercity communication across Russia, having Lebed followed, and mobilizing approximately two thousand of his own MVD troops. It should be noted that he did all this, including linking up with the FSB and the Federal Agency for the Protection of Communications (FAPSI), on his own authority.

Nor did Lebed's firing end matters. Instead, Chubais, then Yeltsin's chief of staff, reduced the Security Council's mandate, transferring it to the recently formed Defense Council. He also made sure that the new leader of the Security Council, Ivan Rybkin, would follow orders and accept the council's nonaccountability to the Duma. Rybkin's new deputy, Boris Berezovskii, then made it clear that the seven largest bankers, of whom he is one, launched a deliberate campaign to secure first Yeltsin's reelection in July, 1996, and then key government posts in economics and security policy to promote their own interests as Russia's interests.[22] He thus flaunted the privatization of the state's economic and security policy, which had become a cloak for the private interests who use the rhetoric of national interest to seize power and state assets for their personal or factional gain.

Since Lebed's firing, we have seen no systematic effort to alleviate these shortcomings in state building; rather, efforts to pit men and factions against each other continue. By November 1997 Yeltsin had fired Rodionov, the CINC of the Navy and the Army, Baturin, Berezovsky, and other officials in economic administration. While there have been major decrees of military reform, it is doubtful that much has actually changed or that the crisis of the military has dissipated; rather, they have probably deepened. All appointments and policies remain essentially a struggle for personal, private, factional, or sectoral interest, not national interest. No one knows who is responsible for what or the degree to which any interagency coordination should proceed. Worse yet, this confusion also afflicts state and military spending.

Even as far as the federal budget is concerned there is a certain confusion—the government sends one appropriations request for military expenditures, the Ministry of Defense lobbies for a distinctly different amount [invariably much higher than the government asks for or could afford-SB] while the Ministry of Finance appropriates money having still another vision of the situation.[23]

And then, neither the Ministry of Defense nor the government knows how many men are under arms or what happens to the monies that are allocated.[24] Likewise, since 1992, none of the hundreds of laws or ordinances promulgated to protect soldiers' and officers' rights have been enforced.

Therefore, the following system has developed in the defense sector. There are fifteen to twenty-four formally chartered organizations of armed forces, not counting the many private security or government guards hired out to guard big banks, businesses, and even major criminals. These various organizations comprise an estimated 3 to 4.5 million men—a broad range which indicates the government's ignorance of how many men are involved. Russia cannot afford to maintain or demobilize them and professionalize the army. Since the state cannot raise the taxes needed to support these men, it does not pay them. But the Ministry of Defense habitually spends money it does not have and runs up enormous arrears and debts to them and to contractors who are thereby expropriated. Therefore it is not surprising that the state's share of GDP in 1995 was 20 percent higher than in 1989 or that one cannot begin to compute the burden of the military upon the ruined economy.

The military exists in an intensely anomic and demoralizing limbo of embitterment, corruption, fractionalization, violence, and politicization, a volatile situation that could explode at any time. The armed forces are thoroughly corrupted and brutalized. Demoralization and anomic behavior increasingly typify the troops and officers' public behavior as soldiers starve, freeze, moonlight, beg, or commit crimes or suicide, while corrupt officers go free. And the absence of controls makes for a situation inviting the pervasive use of force at home, as Yeltsin himself admitted in his 1995 report to the Duma.

The institutions of state power have yet to accumulate sufficient weight to ensure **that force does not have to be applied to restore Russian sovereignty on their territory**. Today, the state has to resort to the exercise of its right to use strong-arm methods in order to preserve the country's integrity [bold in original].[25]

Meanwhile, each military formation has its own administration and chain of command that intersect only at Yeltsin. None of them account to any law or legal standard. Nor can they maintain themselves or effectively defend Russia from internal or external threats. They all exist, not on the basis of a regular state budget, but essentially from Yeltsin's, the cabinet's, or the public's largess because they habitually exceed the budget and come running back for more money, which they often get. Hence, the defense budgetary process is wholly politicized and beyond any legal control or accountability. Much defense and general state spending is off the budget or beyond the Parliament's authority to make appropriations. Meanwhile, the economy remains excessively militarized and the military's true spending and budget needs are hidden from public or legislative scrutiny.[26] Only three national-spending accounts and four items in the Ministry of Defense's budget are open to parliamentary discussion. The ministry resists legislative scrutiny, consistently demands more money without any explanation, and remains addicted to closed processes and spending habits that foster corruption among the brass and their cronies.[27]

This explains much of the resistance to parliamentary scrutiny. Another reason is that the military still has no concept of public accountability or people who believe it necessary to submit their budgets to scrutiny or who wish to, or know how to, talk to the Parliament. Accordingly there is reason to believe that it still gets too much money and resources (which are stolen or misdirected) rather than not enough, even though the budget cuts of 1994 through 1996 are real and painful. Or, one could argue that the government simply does not know what it is doing when making up the military budget and administering the military economy. Sadly, these explanations are not mutually exclusive.[28]

Forces are rewarded to the degree that their political reliability is essential, or it is in question. While the army starves, the MVD forces and the Presidential Guard (the GUO) are lavishly rewarded. The Ministry of Defense was thoroughly and deliberately politicized under the former minister, General Pavel Grachev, who oversaw repeated election campaigns for Yeltsin and for military candidates to the Duma to create a promilitary bloc. The various secret-police formations also played key roles in the 1996 election campaign.[29] This tradition continues as the succession struggle heats up. Thus all contenders—Luzhkov, Lebed, Chernomyrdin, and Chubais—seek or sought to win personal control over the various armed forces and key state agencies in order to politicize them. Serving officers play partisan politics, run for the Duma, form coalitions with regional politicos, and attack their CINCs with impunity.[30]

Nor are they immune from the debilitating effects of the privatization of the state. Whole sections of the fleets live off public charity.[31] Despite Rodionov's humiliation in February 1997, in October 1997 the ministry was still seeking private assistance.[32] All the rival military–political–economic agencies fight with each other, often pursuing their own policies. Here the army's demoralization set in rapidly, with many reports that the armed forces were the main providers of weapons to the Chechens.

Meanwhile, Moscow cannot collect taxes, organize a sustainable federal relationship with its component parts, or advance beyond sclerotic, premodern, tsarist-like institutional structures. It responded to the crisis of military payments by creating new extralegal and extraconstitutional commissions that usurp existing state functions, calling for a dictatorship of the state to provide for a democratic society, and playing bureaucratic games like firing the cabinet, rather than confronting the problems.

This terrifying picture characterizes all state policy. Kevin O' Prey and Mikhail Molchanov respectively confirm this. O'Prey writes,

People who decry the gridlock in [the] U.S. government would be in a shock if they were to look at the situation in Russia. In Moscow there is no gridlock. Rather, on bad days there can be five new law or decrees issued, some of which are contradictory and few of which are obeyed. Beyond the pulling and hauling of competitive bureaucracies, the Russian policymaking process appears to have no rules. Decrees are occasionally issued by aides to the president in his name but without his knowledge. The government at times issues decrees despite the opposition of the president. The new legislative branch—the Duma and the Federation Council—in the meantime is still getting accustomed to its proper role. Further complicating matters, many of the initiatives churned out by Moscow are totally ignored by regional governments and the enterprises. As a result, the government can stumble into armed conflicts like that with the separatist Chechen region without consulting with the legislative branch or, for that matter, many of the relevant ministries.[33]

And Molchanov wrote,

All Russian mysteries can be easily explained by: (a) thinking in terms of specific social groups and their particular interests; (b) examining the relative socio-economic positions of these groups with respect to both one another and the state; and (c) analyzing the specific means at the groups disposal that can be used in the continuing struggle for redistribution of the national economic pie.[34]

Other scholars corroborate this picture.[35] Why such processes remain intrinsic to Russian politics merits investigation, but in the current context, this means that no unified state policy is possible at a time of massive, wrenching, and concurrent socioeconomic and political crises.

STRATEGIC INSOLVENCY

Yet withal, Moscow, like its previous incarnations, insists on imperial overextension to retain its sense of statehood, nationhood, and power. Thus Russia again confronts the abiding strategic dilemmas of the late tsarist period when it faced a constant conflict in its own policies between "the lure of something erotic in the empire" and the financial poverty of the state and the nation. And like those governments, this one has opted for strategic overextension and insolvency, overstraining the economy, society, and polity who are bleeding profusely, and even in some places, starving. Baturin's January 1997 published draft of military reform, which became the basis for subsequent decrees, explicitly assumes that the other members of the CIS are in Russia's defense space and partake of its unwanted extended deterrence. All military reform is based on these axioms that are taken for granted, even though Russia cannot even afford its own defense.[36]

Meanwhile, a weak state coexists with or controls an even weaker yet politicized series of multiple armed forces, which may be useful for political street fighting, but for little else. Yet these forces are still tasked with guarding the CIS's and Russia's borders, peace operations throughout the periphery of the CIS and Russia, the occupation of Moldova, and the "defense of the realm" at home. They may also be called upon to confront NATO enlargement and a Taliban-sponsored Islamic threat issuing from Afghanistan that is above and beyond the problems posed by Tajikistan's endless civil war. They can obstruct the creation of, though they cannot themselves create, a durable, peaceful order.

Furthermore, influential sectors of the armed forces believe that Russia already and for some time has been embroiled in an information and psychological war with the United States, which takes place within and without Russia, and which Russia has, of course, lost since 1985, due to both superior Western technology and internal betrayal.[37] And virtually every threat assessment and the state's procurement policy since 1991 are premised on multiple threats up to and including intercontinental nuclear war! As some current scenarios suggest, important military elements feel that Russia is already at war, but there is a more widespread belief that the state, as such, is under siege from within and without. The concatenation of all these missions and threat assessments (leaving aside nuclear weapons) adds up to a doctrine of threats *a tous azimuts*, within which there is no priority. Everything or everyone is an equal and compelling threat, and strategy loses any touch with the political dimension from which it must be formed. As Vladimir Ivanov of the Institute of World Economy and International Relations and the USA–Canada Institute in Moscow noted, the 1993 defense doctrine showed that "foreign policy cannot unquestionably be considered a factor that sets the context and requirements for the military policy of Russia." Military policy and a doctrine of national interests based on it is moving to the forefront of Russian security policy.[38] Interests, capabilities, and objectives remain disconnected in the Russian policy, which pursues unattainable goals with the mindset of the era of empire and Cold-War bipolarity.

Obviously the triumph of this view as policy would lead to a search for enemies at home and abroad as well, as the internal and external militarization of the like seen in 1917, and with equally tragic repercussions. And we see that key sectors of the military demand forces and funds that are radically incommensurate with the means at the state's disposal. Russian security policy still sees security mainly in military and zero-sum game terms, where Russia must be an equal and opposing pole of the United States. Russia, in this view, also did not lose the Cold War and remains a great global power by virtue of its potential. Hence, it is entitled to a seat at all "presidium tables" of world politics, even though it cannot even defend itself either economically or militarily.[39]

This martial outlook is not confined to the armed forces, nor do all military men promote it, but it is linked to and aggravates the fundamental structural defects of Russian policy because it inhibits a rethinking of security policy and domestic reform. Although economics is regarded as the foundation of national power, it takes a back seat to *Realpolitik* and to exaggerated claims for Russia based on a Hobbesian perception of the world and of threats to Russia. Economics exists only to serve classically conceived security interests, not national prosperity. For instance, in early 1997, Foreign Minister Yevgeny Primakov urged the Duma to support Yeltsin's program for integration and unification with Belarus. When it dissented due to the economic folly of the plan, he argued that long-term strategic interests outweighed economic interests, a view that Rodionov shared.[40] Nor was this an isolated example. As one analysis of trends in Russian geopolitical thinking concluded,

However, beneath the recognition of the changes that economic and technological development, particularly in Europe and Asia have wrought on geopolitics, for Russians the concept of Eurasia remains rooted, as it has been historically, in control and defense of territory. It should, in this sense, be seen not only as the current means of binding the country together against the internal and external forces that may threaten its unity, but also the continuing basis of Russia's great power aspirations.[41]

Kulikov wrote that virtually all of Russia's neighbors and other interested powers actually—or potentially—threaten Russia's integrity, especially in conjunction with their alleged support for internal insurgent or other destabilizing movements. Therefore, the main basis of threat assessments must remain the geopolitical one, which emphasizes the use of force in response to and support of the "war for Russia."[42]

Adherents of this outlook demand equality with the United States in all political issues; Russia's equal status to the United States entitles it to receive great power preferences and compensations equal to those of the United States. Moreover, Moscow holds that the West "owes it something." Russian security policy suffers from this entitlement psychology. Major General Anatoly Bolyatko (retired) wrote that the United States must compensate for Russia's reduced military power in Asia by reducing and dissolving its own power in a compensating mechanism of a regional security system. That system would be based on a series of multilateral, regional security structures and confidence-building mechanisms to lessen the threat of war.[43] The debate over NATO's enlargement reveals the same mind-set. Russia demanded a veto in NATO, equality with the United States worldwide, compensations for NATO's internal decisions, and a free hand for itself in its own CIS and near-abroad sphere of influence.[44] Highlighting another aspect of this militarized worldview, Alexei Zagorsky and Frank Umbach have both observed that the armed forces were in fact not committed to true military reform, had changed relatively little in their anti-Western outlook since 1991, and hoped to restore Russia's great power status.[45]

Russian threat assessments and planned military procurements confirm this, as they remain wedded to the threat of a great power war with the United States and its allies. For example, an air force threat assessment in 1994 argued that Japan could launch a combined-arms attack against the Kuriles and Sakhalin with U.S. help to seal off those islands and the Russian Pacific Fleet and to destroy Russian installations and forces in the Far East. It is bizarre to think that Russian nuclear and conventional forces could not deter such an attack. But Russian planners used this scenario, and threats of a NATO invasion and a Russo–Chinese war, to demand an air fleet of two thousand planes.[46]

Alexei Arbatov observed that this threat assessment reflects the armed forces' natural tendency to retain the maximum number of traditional strategic roles and operational missions, while giving only lip service to new security realities. He notes that Russian armed forces' military requirements are still driven by contingency planning for major war with the United States, its NATO allies, and/ or Japan. Therefore he charged that "nothing has really changed in the fundamental military approaches to contingency planning." The military's interest in self-preservation, and not in threat analysis that determines the true needs of the armed forces, drives its threat assessment, force structure, and deployment policy.[47]

New force deployments also suggest the continuing primacy of major conventional, if not nuclear, warfighting in doctrine and policy. A recent threat assessment published in Russia's main military journal, *Voennaya Mysl'* (Military Thought) openly accused

NATO of planning military aggression against Russia through enlargement and stated that

A number of political scientists are of the opinion that there can be seen in relations between the West [note not just the United States, but the West as a whole] a "slow creeping into a semblance of standoff which threatens serious losses both for international security and security of individual countries, and for Russia." It is caused by a whole number of factors. First, there is the apparent incompatibility of Russia's and the United States' current potentialities on the world scene which makes the prospects of their relations on a parity basis illusory [and] for which reason Russia is hardly going to settle for the role of junior partner.[48]

Even though parity is an illusion, Russia is evidently determined to chase after this mirage, regardless of cost. Naturally, the pursuit of such a security policy based on rivalry and equality with the United States and the West must presage another disaster for Russia. But Russia's leading military policy makers seem oblivious to this elementary truth. Accordingly, ever quieter submarines, SSBNs and SSGNs (nuclear-powered attack submarines with conventional ordnance and missiles) with greater attack ranges, are being produced at a steady rate and are tracking the U.S. fleet for the first time in years.[49] Naval threat assessments continue in this vein. In 1995, Rear Admiral Valery Aleksin of the Naval Academy advocated a building program through 2015, giving Russia 440 oceangoing warships: nuclear-powered submarine destroyers with cruise missiles, frigates, missile patrol boats, small guided-missile ships, amphibious ships, and minesweepers. This figure omits antisubmarine ships, aircraft carriers, coastal missile forces and marines, and the investment in infrastructure needed to sustain this force and defend against all enemies, not just the United States.[50] This demand was made to prepare for a time when the U.S. Navy will have about 330 projected ocean-going ships! Aleksin has been forced to scale down this quantitative requirement due to economic stringency and political pressure. But his revised analysis still calls for a fleet the size of the U.S. fleet in 2015.[51]

Aleksin's threat assessment also presumed returning to Soviet practices of working from worst-case scenarios and readiness for every conceivable contingency. He observed that

Calculations show the reliable performance of tasks by the naval strategic forces of homing antisubmarine rocket weapons systems in the Northern and Pacific fleets in a state of constant readiness, with no less than 15–20 units having a total of up to 240 ballistic missiles and about 1000 warheads. Only this will guarantee the stability of the Nuclear Strategic Forces of Russia under the most varied versions of the development of conflicts of any intensity.[52]

He argued that in wartime, Russian forces must be able to strike throughout the enemy's entire depth of force disposition to terminate hostilities.[53] Aleksin called for a Russian worldwide oceanic strike force against every major naval power and imaginable contingency. Even if Russia could afford this burden, the program would unite all the major naval states against it.

Aleksin's first-strike scenario postulates a massive land, sea, and air-based missile attack from hundreds, if not thousands, of miles away from Russia. In that scenario, Russia's enemies would possess new generations of sea-launched cruise missiles (SLCMs) that can strike Russia from the entire northern Atlantic and Indian Oceans and in the Pacific from as far away as Guam and Midway. Therefore the navy must deny those "sanctuaries" to the enemy. Russian SSNs with SLCMs are the best weapons to counteract enemy delivery systems, followed by naval aviation. Accordingly, he recommended a force that will not only fight across the world's oceans but can also achieve superiority over "probable coalitions" in wartime and peacetime deterrence.[54]

Aleksin was not alone in confirming that reliance on worst-case scenarios persist. Bolyatko also conceded that worst-case scenario planning for Asian military contingencies continues in the army and Strategic Nuclear Forces.[55] The conformity to Aleksin's approach is not accidental. Military spokesmen consistently reiterate that the real threat is U.S. naval, air, and strategic superiority. If the United States would just reduce its arms and adhere to Russia's concept of Asian collective security, all would be well.[56] The aforementioned article in *Voennaya Mysl'* duly concludes that, "As before, the most important is readiness to carry out the tasks of deterrence 'on all azimuths.' In the event the strategy of deterrence fails, the task is to protect sovereignty, territorial integrity, and the other permanent vital interests of the country."[57]

Obviously such militarized approaches to security and bizarre strategies are not merely confined to Asia or naval theaters. German defense analyst Reiner Huber recently observed that Russian models of offense and defense in Europe are based on frankly paranoid calculations. Russia's current models state that to feel secure in this theater, Russia requires a potential successful defense of at least 90 percent in a purely conventional war with NATO forces. And this calculation excludes Russia's nuclear retaliatory capability![58] As Huber rightly observes,

This underscores the deep mistrust still prevailing in Russia vis-à-vis NATO and the United States. For example, if we were to assume that the success of defense is equivalent to the failure of aggression, the defense sufficiency principle suggests that the Russians believe NATO will attack even if the chances of success were only about 10 percent. Obviously NATO and the United States are perceived as being quite reckless.[59]

Yet the economic, war-planning, and political requirements that flow from such a paranoia and demand for absolute security at everyone else's expense are ruinously unsustainable. Efforts to obtain security on this basis will destroy the material foundations of Russian military and economic power, and trigger new international hostilities, as has happened before and for the same reasons. Obviously this discrepancy between strategic ends and means is a recipe for disaster that could engulf all of Eurasia.

Thus an outstanding symptom of the crisis of the various armed forces is the amazing and even paradoxical fact that in 1997, the burden of the various militaries upon the economy is probably proportionately greater than it was under Soviet rule, when it was widely believed that that burden was crippling, excessive, and a fundamental cause of the Soviet collapse. Certainly, cognitive change has been distressingly slow compared to political and economic change, leaving Russia with armed forces that refuse to reorient their thinking to current realities. Consequently, aligned to a state that is distinguished by its irresponsibility, we have military forces who are equally deluded. Therefore, to grasp the multiple points where a scenario of state and military failure may occur, we must go deeper into the state and military's crises.

IS RUSSIA A FAILING OR FAILED STATE?

If unchecked, Russia's protracted crisis of the state will bring it perilously close to the condition of a failing, or failed, state. In many aspects, its security profile corresponds in far too many ways with that of the typical failing state. As described by Pauline Baker and John Ausink, failing states are recognizable as having the following pathologies:

Major demographic pressures. While Russia's population is declining absolutely and is aging rapidly, Muslim populations to its south and China are undergoing rapid population growth and on the verge of major water, energy, and ecological crises. They must find adequate sources of energy, food, and water, to survive and flourish in the next century and those resources are not, for the most part, in their home countries or readily accessible.

Massive refugee movements, largely of Russians leaving the CIS and returning to Russia, are taking place as a result of wars like Chechnya or of anti-Russian pressures in the new states. This war could exemplify the syndrome of failed states with perennial internal violence if Russia fails to consolidate the peace settlement there. Similarly, Russia is engaged in other wars or faces potential conflicts, like Tajikistan where its forces are engaged in a worsening situation, and across the North Caucasus where there are strong ethnopolitical tensions at work. If any of those governments collapse, that could cause new wars to spread along with mass migrations to Russia.

Uneven regional or ethnic economic development is clearly happening across Russia and greatly stimulates regional governments' disaffection with Moscow and pressure for more control over their resources. This disparity among regions takes many forms, e.g. Moscow, St. Petersburg and the Far East alone receive 50% of foreign direct investment to Russia. Meanwhile Moscow is imposing unequal terms of trade and transportation tariffs on the Russian Far East with ruinous consequences for the regional economy.[60]

A fourth precondition of state failure is a legacy of vengeance-seeking groups or group paranoia. Chechnya is only the most visible of many examples, not excluding paramilitary organizations like the various Cossack hosts, the new ethnic militias in Dagestan and Ingushetia, or the Black Sea Fleet in Ukraine, or Russian Parliamentary claims on Ukrainian territory or on North Kazakstan if Russians there get into trouble. If Russia commits itself against the Taliban should they conquer Afghanistan, this could be another example of accepting an unnecessary provocation for protracted war. And it would also represent the acceptance of this risk in order to try and bind Central Asia more firmly to Russia.[61]

In conjunction with this last possibility, the rise of ethnic identification is a particular threat in a multiethnic Russia. First of all, this model of state failure presumes that where the state is increasingly unable to serve the basic needs of the people, the identification of people with their ethnic group grows. Second, in an economy like Russia's, rent seeking is the main occupation of the elites, which denotes a redistributive, rather than growth-oriented, economy whose inertial tendency is toward stagnation. Thus ethnic elites, already inspired by a "we-versus-they" mentality, find ample justification to carve out regional, ethnic enclaves of the economy that are equally prone to rent-seeking. They thereby add competitive and nonproductive economic structures and attitudes to other sources of ethnic animosity.

This trend, already visible in regional "baronies" in the Russian economy and Chechnya, is particularly dangerous because statistics point to a rising self-identification among all ethnic groups and a growing trend toward residential segregation among nationalities in the Russian Federation where non-Russians are moving out of largely Russian areas and Russians out of minority areas.[62] In short, conditions that can be associated with impending ethnopolitical conflict are already visible across the Russian scene.

The criminalization or delegitimization of the state is another major factor making for breakdown, something which is certainly widespread in Russia. Indeed, the criminality and venality of the topmost sectors of the state are on regular public display, and Duma members are regularly bribed. Thus the penetration of the state and the regular economy by criminal forces is growing in the face of the virtual defenselessness of the state against this plague. Observers also noted a trend in the 1995 Duma elections towards a fusion of criminal, political, military, and economic elites.[63] Elite criminalization undermines the legitimacy and authority of the laws and of all branches of government and provides opportunities or pretexts for the concentration of very large military or paramilitary and police forces under one authority on the grounds of fighting crime.

The next factor is sharp economic distress or economic crisis. As continuing economic crisis is imminent, according to the more honest economic officials, and there is neither a growth strategy, a tax-and-revenue basis for stabilization, or the resources for stabilization followed by investment, Russia is unlikely to escape from its terrible economic condition for quite some time. Neither is it going to make sense of its defense economy and defense economic policy any time soon.[64]

Furthermore, the general economic crisis now coincides with a banking crisis. Numerous banks face the danger of collapse. Naturally this situation aggravates every sociopolitical point of stress and could trigger a general crash of the state. Russia's forced response to the crash in Southeast Asia in late 1997 underscored that vulnerability. It preemptively devalued the ruble and raised interests rates, strangling growth for 1998 to satisfy bondholders and foreign investors, but once again shortchanging domestic needs. Then talented people flee the country, causing a "brain drain," the rule of law, which is already a fiction, is further undermined, and we find the security apparatus operating as a state within a state, which has been the case for some time and may be expected to continue under Yeltsin's, Chubais's, Chernomyrdin's, and Kulikov's control.

While the presence of all these conditions does not mean an inevitable breakdown, the absence of reliable governing institutions compounds their effect and heightens their impact on the polity as a whole. Stagnation puts Russia further behind its peers and rivals and builds up unfulfilled and volatile pressures for reform and for great-power competition, until something explodes.

Excessive stress on more than one of the many vulnerable points in Russian economic and political life, not including a collapse of the armed forces, could be the triggering factor. Historically, protracted war has always strained the Russian state to its utmost and even in victory, triggered massive phenomena of sociopolitical unrest. Defeat, economic stagnation, domestic coups led by politicians commanding essentially privatized armed forces, and the inability to construct viable and representative governing institutions—all are traditional signs of the collapse of state order in Russia. Another very possible factor is the break away, either de facto or de jure, of outlying regions from a central government that cannot fulfill its responsibilities toward them. These provinces could then assume the attributes of state power, such as issuing money and conducting foreign relations. Or they could come under the effective de facto sway of Russia's neighbors, who may then be tempted to seek their own sphere of influence in the Commonwealth of Independent States and Russia. Should these scenarios come to pass, the unreformed army would be hard pressed to counter them.

THE COMPARATIVE AND HISTORICAL DIMENSION

This is not a uniquely military or even Russian crisis. One may find, by examining current comparative trends in world politics, a stagnation occurring in the global process of democratization.[65] Many states are in danger of falling apart as they lose control over domestic violence.[66] Furthermore, as some Western analysts, who remember that Russia had a history before Gorbachev, have come to realize, the *Krizis Verkhov* (elite crisis) of today eerily resembles that of late tsarism. Peter Stavrakis has written about "ministerial feudalism," and Vladimir Shlapentokh has devoted whole articles to the analogy of today's Russia and early feudalism.[67] Most tellingly, Eugene Huskey, in chronicling the development of the State–Legal Administration, finds it necessary repeatedly to trace institutional development and state building in Yeltsin's Russia to late tsarist antecedents.[68] We should compare current realities to Baron A. P. Izvol'skii's remarks on the eve of his appointment as Minister to the Quai D'Orsay. He stated that "despotism" always bore the same fruits: "incoherence if not contradiction in the conduct of affairs which are treated simultaneously by various departments which ignore each other—and which obtain from the supreme leader detailed decisions which are irreconcilable in fact: the Russo-Japanese war came from this."[69] Since this insight accurately captures the rivalries among the players in defense policy, effective, civilian-based, democratic control of a purely professional and politically impartial armed force and police force is not in the cards for a long time to come.

At the comparative level, Russia's main challenge resembles that of Third World states: building effective states under enormous internal and external pressures that today are magnified by the fact that state sovereignty is under attack from international economic and financial institutions. To the degree that Russia's government has to follow guidelines to get the money necessary to survive, it cannot be fully a master of its own house. Having outlined the pathologies of failing states, we can see from such examples what the nature of the civil–military relationship is and how eerily these failing states resemble Russia's condition.

In many states, such as in Nigeria, "There are no civil–military relations—in the sense of discrete military and civilian institutions with a structured relationship." However this pathology is a symptom of a deeper malignancy, the system of political economy that makes power and wealth coterminous.[70] That relationship is, of course, the hallmark of feudalism, and both Vladimir Shlapentokh and Stavrakis have described Russia's regime rightly as such, because for it power and wealth are coterminous as well. Furthermore, where states have broken down, and warlordism has taken over, that may not necessarily be a regression to chaos (although it certainly could be described as such). Warlordism here represents the emergence of an alternative system in response to the government as a failed state. Accordingly, in Sudan, "The state had not so much collapsed as attempted to compensate for its economic weakness by dividing and manipulating civil society."[71] This is a fair description of the socioeconomic results of the vast expropriation of wealth that state policy has crafted over the years in response, as in Sudan and elsewhere in Africa, to the demands of the International Monetary Fund and the international community.

In Chechnya the collaboration of Russian forces with the Chechens has analogies all over the Third World: In Cambodia, Peru, and Sierra Leone, where the regular soldiers and the rebels seem to be in cahoots to depopulate resource-rich areas, divide the spoils between them, and terrorize the civilians, it is not unlike Chechnya during the war.[72] War in much of Africa and the Third World is now privatized, a search by warlords and assorted *condo-*

tierri for loot and personal power. This trend is discernible in the wars of the Transcaucasus and in Yugoslavia's wars of 1991 through 1995.[73] States that cannot protect their population thereby forfeit the monopoly of legitimate force; this is happening in Russia as private security and mafia-type forces grow out of state control, and regular military formations like the Northern Fleet and the Black Sea Fleet are forced to live off the charity of the Russian public, the municipal authorities, or the banks.[74]

In a situation of failing government capability, people fall back into ethnic or racial patterns of solidarity, at the expense of any supraethnic collectivity like the Russian government. The government's recent attempt to incite the Cossacks against the Chechens or to flirt with another war on the Afghan–Tajik frontier, even as the Tajik civil war carries on, exemplifies the Russian government's strategic rashness in flirting with such centrifugal forces as the unleashing of protracted ethnic war for the second time to maintain order and its own integrity.

CONCLUSION

Two harbingers of state collapse are confronting Russia. One is stagnation of the current situation. The other is the galloping privatization or deregulation of the state and the means of war.

In the first instance, stagnation means no exit or a very slow and uneven one from the current economic crisis. Further regional or class economic polarization will occur in a "no-or-slow" growth economy that remains technologically backward, beholden to foreign institutions, and bereft of the means of collecting taxes or, more broadly, devising coherent economic policies for recovery. The crime issue and corruption will remain at high levels, if not actually increase, and state capacity will continue to stagnate if not decline. Although some have postulated stagnation or muddling through as an option, this is not viable because the accumulated unanswered grievances of the system will inevitably trigger an explosion along the many fault lines that the current crisis and stagnation expose.

The second alternative is taking place now, since the state's inability to fund military reform or perform its other duties is leading to desperate efforts to find alternatives, such as the banks paying for the armed forces or for their legislatively mandated social benefits. Continuing privatization of the state, its assets, ministries, and levers of power, if not arrested, will accelerate the present stagnation and plunge Russia into a situation of domestic rivalry and warlordism, if not civil war. The African examples cited above are harbingers of something more terrible: the privatization of warfare outside anyone's effective control and in the form of a virus whose nature and manifestations mutate along uncontrollable and ever-changing lines.[75] This is the disaster that will surely come about if stagnation is not reversed, but this government and its supporters at home and abroad are not the men for the job.

As in past instances of state collapse in Russia, the consequences are unpredictable, and the international order cannot remain aloof. By virtue of American and world investment in Russia and in light of its nuclear capability, we will be obliged as in 1918 to intervene somehow, if not necessarily with force. But it is hardly clear that in the second act of post-Communism, we will better understand what we are doing and with whom than we did in the first act of the drama. Following Chekhov, we may note that if the gun is hanging on the wall in Act I, it will be used in Act II. But if the actors cannot resist temptation and use the gun in Act I, but fail in achieving desired results, then what will happen in Act II?

NOTES

1. Moscow, *Rossiyskaya Gazeta*, in Russian, February 17, 1995, Foreign Broadcast Information Service Central Eurasia (henceforth FBIS-SOV), 95-034-S, February 21, 1995, pp. 9–10.

2. Moscow, NTV, November 16, 1997, from Johnson's Russia List, david johnson@erols.com, No. 1395, November 25, 1997. David McLaren McDonald, *United Government and Foreign Policy in Russia, 1900–1914* (Cambridge: Harvard University Press, 1992) demonstrates what late Tsarist foreign policy was like, and the resemblances to Yeltsin's court are striking.

3. Alexander Bykovskiy, "Country Awaits Change," *Sel'skaya Zhizn'*, October 28, 1996; Marshall Ingwerson, "For Yeltsin's Top Aide, Can-Do May Be Ticket to Power in Kremlin," *Christian Science Monitor*, November 1, 1996. Both are from Johnson's Russian List, davidjohnson@erols.com, November 1, 1996.

4. Anders Aslund, "The State of Transition Economies," *Demokratizatsiia* 5, no. 4 (Fall 1997): 502.

5. E. G. Timothy Shaw and Clement E. Adibe, "Africa and Global Developments in the Twenty-First Century," *International Journal* 51, no. 1 (Winter 1996): 1–26; Mohammed Ayoob, *The Third World Security Predicament: State Making and the International System* (Boulder, Colo.: Lynne Rienner, 1995).

6. Michael Bratton, "Deciphering Africa's Divergent Transitions," *Political Science Quarterly* 112, no. 1 (Spring 1997): 88.

7. Ibid., pp. 88–89.

8. Richard Sakwa notes that a central feature of Russian development "is that the invasive state is marked, paradoxically, by the extraordinary underdevelopment of modern forms of institutionalization of state power."

Richard Sakwa, "Russia, Communism, Democracy," in *Developments in Russian and Post-Soviet Politics*, ed. Stephen White, Alex Pravda, and Zvi Gitelman, 3d ed. (Durham, N.C.: Duke University Press, 1994), p. 291. Likewise, S. Frederick Starr observes that despite the enormous expansion of Russian bureaucracy, to the point where its numbers eclipse those of Gorbachev's Soviet bureaucracy, Russia remains undergoverned. S. Frederick Starr, "The Paradox of Yeltsin's Russia," *Wilson Quarterly* 99, no. 3 (1995): 66–73.

9. Sergei M. Rogov, *Civil–Military Relations in a Democratic Society* (Moscow: Institute of USA and Canada Studies, Center for National Security and International Relations, 1996), pp. 9–10.

10. This view is not only the author's—indeed it is obtaining general approval by other authors, such as demonstrated by the writings of Michael McFaul, "When Capitalism and Democracy Collide in Transition: Russia's 'Weak' State as an Impediment to Democratic Consolidation," working paper, series no. 1, program on New Approaches to Russian Security, Davis Center for Russian Studies, Harvard University, Cambridge, Mass., September 1997, pp. 4, 16–23.

11. E-mail transmission by Peter Heinlein for the Voice of America, October 14, 1996; Chrystia Freeland, "Russia: Banker Offers to Pay Civil Servants," *Financial Times*, September 4, 1997, p. 2; *Radio Free Europe/ Radio Liberty*, December 11, 1997 (henceforth RFE/RL).

12. "Rodionov Plays the Banker," *Kommersant-Daily*, February 28, 1997, from *Johnson's Russia List*, davidjohnson@erols.com, March 1, 1997; Moscow, *Kommersant-Daily*, March 1, 1997, FBIS SOV, 97-041, March 4, 1997.

13. Pauline Baker and John A. Ausink, "State Violence: Toward a Predictive Model," *Parameters* 26, no. 3 (Fall 1996): 19–31, and Robert Dorff, "Democratization and Failed States: The Challenge of Ungovernability," *Parameters* 26, no. 2 (Summer 1996): 20–23.

14. Jeffrey Simon, *NATO Enlargement and Central Europe: A Study in Civil–Military Relations* (Washington, D.C.: Institute for National Security Studies, National Defense University Press, 1996), pp. 26–28.

15. This goes back at least to 1995, if not earlier. For example, see the law on the FSB, Moscow, *Rossiyskaya Gazeta*, in Russian, April 12, 1995, FBIS-SOV, 95-076, April 20, 1995, pp. 19–28; Moscow, *Segodnya*, in Russian, February 16, 1995, FBIS-SOV, 95-033, February 17, 1995, p. 19. For the current situation, see Konstantin Preobrazhensky, "FSB–Army Relations a Well-Kept Secret," *St. Petersburg Times*, December 16–20, 1996.

16. Ibid.

17. Moscow, *RIA, Novosti*, July 19, 1997, translated in *Johnson's Russia List,* July 19, 1997, davidjohnson@erols.com.

18. Rogov, *Civil–Military Relations*, p. 10.

19. Ibid., pp. 16–17; Lilia Shevtsova and Scott Bruckner, "Toward Stability or Crisis?" *Journal of Democracy* 8, no. 1 (January 1997): 18.

20. Rogov, *Civil–Military Relations*, pp. 16–17.

21. Ibid.

22. McFaul, "Capitalism and Democracy," pp. 21–22.

23. Rogov, *Civil–Military Relations*, pp. 16–17.

24. Ibid.

25. FBIS-SOV, February 21, 1995, pp. 9–10.

26. For an examination of Russia's incredible defense economy, see *OMRI Daily Digest*, October 30, 1996; Vitaly Shlykov's articles, "Russkaya Ruletka ili Soldatskaya Kasha is Topora," *Sreda* 4 (September 1996): 67–75, "Biudzhet i Armiya," *Nezavisimoye Voennoye Obozreniye*, May 16, 1996, "Voennyi Kamuflazh Rossiyskoi Ekonomiki," *Sreda* 2 (1996): 19–24, "The Budget and the Army," *Russian Politics and Law* 35, no. 5 (September–October 1997): 56–76; and "Economic Readjustment within the Russian Defense–Industrial Complex," *Security Dialogue* 26, no. 1 (1995): 19–34; and Sergey Rogov, *Military Reform and the Defense Budget of the Russian Federation* (Alexandria, Va.: Center for Naval Analysis, 1997).

27. Ibid. See also Pyotr Yudin, "Lawmakers Decry Secrecy," *Defense News*, January 6–12, 1997, pp. 3, 26.

28. Ibid.

29. Stephen J. Blank, "The Code and Civil–Military Relations: The Russian Case," *Cooperative Security, the OSCE, and Its Code of Conduct*, ed. Gert de Nooy (The Hague: Kluwer Law International, 1996), pp. 106–109; Francoise Dose, "The Army in Parliament, 1989–95," *Russian Politics and Law* 35, no. 5 (September–October 1997): 77–88.

30. Moscow, *Nezavisimaya Gazeta*, in Russian, September 13, 1996, FBIS-SOV, 96-179, September 13, 1996, pp. 24–25. If anything, this situation worsened in 1997 when General Lev Rokhlin, who was at the same time deputy chairman of the Duma Defense Committee, openly organized a movement to unseat Yeltsin and his government on the grounds that Yeltsin's military reform threatened the interests of the army and the state and that he had refused to consult the Duma in preparing the reform.

31. Heinlein, Freeland, p. 2, RFE/RL, December 11, 1997.

32. Moscow, *Krasnaya Zvezda*, in Russian, October 17, 1997, *Foreign Broadcast Information Service Military Affairs* (henceforth FBIS-UMA), 97-293, October 20, 1997.

33. Kevin P. O'Prey, *A Farewell to Arms?: Russia's Struggles with Defense Conversion* (New York: The Twentieth Century Fund Press, 1995), p. 52.

34. Mikhail Molchanov, "Russian Political Culture: Any Hope for the West?" *Reconstructing Russia: Perspectives from Within*, ed. Heyward Isham (New York: Institute for East–West Studies, 1996), p. 36.

35. Mikhail Tsypkin, "The Politics of Russian Security Policy," in *State Building and Military Power in Russia and the New States of Eurasia*, ed. Bruce Parrott, vol. 5 of *The International Politics of Russia* (Armonk, N.Y.: M. E. Sharpe, 1995), pp. 12–43.

36. Moscow, *Nezavisimaya Gazeta*, in Russian, January 22, 1997, FBIS-SOV, 97-015, January 24, 1997. See also Andrei A. Kokoshin, *Reflections on Russia's Past, Present, and Future*, Project on Strengthening Democratic Institutions, Harvard University, Cambridge, Mass., 1997, p. 31.

37. Stephen J. Blank, *The Russian Army on the Brink of Reform* (Carlisle Barracks, Pa.: U.S. Army War College, Strategic Studies Institute, 1998).

38. Vladimir I. Ivanov, "Russia's New Military Doctrine: Implications for Asia," in *Asia in the 21st Century: Evolving Strategic Priorities*, ed. Michael D. Bellows (Washington, D.C.: Institute for National Security Studies, National Defense University, 1994), p. 223. This point was made in 1993, and it still is valid.

39. E-mail from Darrell Hammer, *Johnson's Russia List*, davidjohnson @erols.com, February 5, 1997; Dmitry Trenin, "Transformation of Russian Foreign Policy: NATO Expansion Can Have Negative Consequences for the West," *Nezavisimaya Gazeta*, February 5, 1997; J. Michael Waller, "Primakov's Imperial Line," *Perspective* 7, no. 3 (January–February 1997): 2–6, and "Primakov: Setting a New, Tougher Foreign Policy," *Current Digest of the Post-Soviet Press* 49, no. 2 (February 12, 1997): 4–7.

40. For Primakov's views, see "Primakov Denies Split With Yeltsin on NATO Issue," *Current Digest of the Post-Soviet Press* 49, no. 19 (June 11, 1997): 4–6.

41. David Kerr, "The New Eurasianism: The Rise of Geopolitics in Russia's Foreign Policy," *Europe–Asia Studies* 47, no. 6 (1995): 987.

42. Anatoly Kulikov, "Russian Policy in the Sphere of National Security: Essence and Magnitude of Inner Threats to Stability and Order," paper presented at the Conference on Russian Defense and Security Policy, Kings College, London, May 16–18, 1995; also *European Security* 6, no. 3 (Autumn 1997).

43. Anatoly V. Bolyatko, "Russian National Security Strategy and Its Implications for East Asian Security," in *Russian Security Policy in the Asia–Pacific Region: Two Views*, ed. Stephen J. Blank (Carlisle Barracks, Pa.: Strategic Studies Institute, U.S. Army War College, 1996), p. 29.

44. Stephen J. Blank, *NATO Enlargement and the Baltic States: What Can the Great Powers Do?* (Carlisle Barracks, Pa.: Strategic Studies Institute, U.S. Army War College, 1997), pp. 5–21.

45. Alexei Zagorsky, "The Post–Cold War Security Agenda of Russia: Implications for Northeast Asia," *Pacific Review* 8, no. 1 (1995): 95; Frank Umbach, "The Role and Influence of the Military Establishment in Russia's Foreign and Security Policies in the Yeltsin Era," *Journal of Slavic Military Studies* 9, no. 3 (September 1996): 467–500.

46. Alexei Arbatov, "Russian Air Strategy and Combat Aircraft Production: A Russian View," in *The Arms Production Dilemma: Contraction and Restraint in the World Combat Arms Industry*, ed. Randall Forsberg CSIA Studies In International Security, no.7 (Cambridge, Mass.: MIT Press, 1994), pp. 27–29, 31–49.

47. Ibid., pp. 49–60.

48. A. F. Klimenko, "Mezhdunarodnaya bezopasnost' i kharakter voennykh konfliktov budushchego," *Voennaya Mysl'* 1 (1997).

49. U.S. Office of Naval Intelligence, *Worldwide Submarine Challenges* (Washington, D.C.: U.S. Government Printing Office, 1996).

50. Ibid.

51. Moscow, *Morskoi sbornik*, in Russian, No. 3, March, 1995, *Joint Publication Research Service Military Affairs*, 95-020, May 2, 1995, p. 36.

52. Ibid., p. 34.

53. Ibid., p. 30.

54. Ibid., pp. 34–36.

55. For a discussion of this strategic concept, see Stephen J. Blank, "We Can Live Without You: Rivalry and Dialogue in Russo-Japanese Relations," *Comparative Strategy* 12, no. 2 (1993): 184–189.

56. Bolyatko, *Russian National Security Strategy*, p. 34. For an earlier article, see A. B. Bolyatko, "Voenno–politicheskaya situatsiya i problemy formirovaniya novoi struktury bezopasnosti v severo–vostochnoi azii," *Voennaya Mysl'* 2 (February 1994): 6.

57. Klimenko, "Mezhdunarodnaya bezopasnost'," pp. 8–9.

58. Reiner Huber, "NATO Enlargement and CFE Ceilings: A Preliminary Analysis in Anticipation of a Russian Proposal," *European Security* 5, no. 3 (Autumn 1996): 396–403.

59. Ibid., p. 400.

60. Evidence of this can be found in Moscow, *Izvestiya*, in Russian, November 29, 1995, FBIS-SOV, 95-231, December 1, 1995, pp. 39–41.

61. Baker and Ausink, *State Violence*, pp. 19–31. The aspects of state failure are taken from their list.

62. William G. Thom, "An Assessment of Prospects for Ending Domestic Military Conflict in Sub-Saharan Africa," *CSIS Africa Notes* 177 (October 1995): 3–4; "More RF Citizens Identify With Ethnic Subgroups," *Current Digest of the Post-Soviet Press* 49, no. 44 (December 3, 1997): 10–12.

63. Blank, "The Code," pp. 108–109.

64. See the sources listed in Note 26.

65. Larry Diamond, "Is the Third Wave Over?" *Journal of Democracy* 7, no. 2 (Summer 1997): 20–37.

66. Thus, as of late 1997, the following states all were menaced by the breakdown of control over violence and have witnessed or are witnessing the increased use of force or the potential for it to resolve domestic disputes: Colombia, Albania, Haiti, Algeria, Pakistan, and Yugoslavia's former republics, including not only Bosnia but also Kosovo.

67. Vladimir Shlapentokh, "Early Feudalism: The Best Parallel for Contemporary Russia," *Euro–Asia Studies* 48, no. 2 (1996): 391–411; Peter Stavrakis, *State-Building in Post-Soviet Russia: The Chicago Boys and the Decline of Administrative Capacity*, occasional papers of the Kennan Institute for Advanced Russian Studies, No. 254, 1993; and "The Russian State in the Twenty-First Century," paper presented at the Eighth Annual Strategy Conference of the U.S. Army War College, Carlisle Barracks, Pa., April 22–24, 1997.

68. Eugene Huskey "The State–Legal Administration and the Politics of Redundancy," *Post-Soviet Studies* 11, no. 2 (1995): 115–143.

69. This citation from the French diplomatic archives is reported in David M. McDonald, "A Lever without a Fulcrum: Domestic Factors and Russian Foreign Policy, 1905–1914," in *Imperial Russian Foreign Policy*, ed. and trans. Hugh Ragsdale (Washington, D.C.: Woodrow Wilson Center Press, 1993; Cambridge: Cambridge University Press, 1993), p. 281.

70. Kent Hughes Butts and Steven Metz, *Armies and Democracy in the New Nigeria* (Carlisle Barracks, Pa.: Strategic Studies Institute, U.S. Army War College, 1996), pp. 16–17.

71. David Keen, "Organised Chaos: Not the New World Order," *The World Today* (January 1996): 15.

72. Ibid., pp. 15–16.

73. Charles Fairbanks, "The Postcommunist Wars," in *Civil–Military Relations and Democracy*, ed. Larry Diamond and Marc F. Plattner (Baltimore, Md.: Johns Hopkins University Press, 1996), pp. 134–150.

74. In Chechnya the main source of weapons for the Chechens was Russian soldiers, who sold them off, if they did not lose them in battle. In the former Yugoslavia by 1993 there were at least seventeen different military formations participating in the wars.

75. Keen, "Organised Chaos," pp. 15–16.

10

Altering the Icon: The Americans and Guerrilla War

Anthony James Joes

The disastrous experience in Viet Nam overshadows American thinking about counterinsurgency. But in fact Americans have achieved notable successes against guerrillas, under circumstances both diverse and difficult. This chapter calls attention to those successes and suggests that they need to be incorporated into the American understanding of how to deal with guerrilla insurgency.

It is close to a certainty that, because of humanitarian impulses, the desire to spread or uphold democracy, or the compulsion to participate in so-called UN and NATO peace operations, U.S. military personnel will sooner or later encounter hostile insurgents. This is a disheartening prospect for those who believe or suspect that "the United States does not understand low-intensity conflict nor does it display the capability to adequately defend against it," and that "our defeat in Viet Nam has taught us nothing."[1]

Viet Nam remains a nightmarish memory. Even so, U.S. forces in cooperation with their allies defeated the guerrillas. That is why the final conquest of South Viet Nam had to be carried out by the PAVN, at the time one of largest and best equipped armies on the planet.

This chapter has two principal aims. The first is to alter the icon of American counterinsurgency—the disaster in Southeast Asia—by recalling other guerrilla conflicts in which the United States achieved its main purposes. The second is to draw some empirical lessons from those successful episodes. The conflicts to be reviewed fall into two categories. The first consists of two guerrilla conflicts in which U.S. ground combat forces participated directly: the Philippines (1899–1902) and Nicaragua (1912–1932). The second includes three cases in which the United States supported a government under attack by insurgents without committing ground combat units: Greece (1947–1949), the Huk War (1946–1954), and El Salvador (1979–1992). Although it differs in important respects from the preceding cases, we will also look at the Afghan insurgency (1979–1988). In that conflict the United States was on the side of the insurgents, and may well find itself in a similar posture, on the same continent. Besides, the Soviet war in Afghanistan is such an excellent example of how *not* to wage counterinsurgency that a review of its main features will help to test the validity of some of the conclusions reached about U.S. counterinsurgency experiences.

THE AMERICANS VERSUS AGUINALDO

The Americans achieved a complete victory over guerrillas in the post-1898 Philippine War—a victory after which all sides were able to live with each other and with themselves. It is the American equivalent of the British victory in Malaya.

The Philippine archipelago has an area of 116 thousand square miles, about the size of Arizona. There are seven thousand islands, only half of which have names. Spain had imposed political unity on the islands for the first time in their history. In 1896 a major rebellion against Spanish rule broke out, organized by a secret society called the Katipunan. This rebellion was still unresolved when the United States and Spain went to war, and Commodore George Dewey won his overwhelming victory against the Spanish fleet in Manila Bay (May 1, 1898). Dewey brought home from exile Emilio Aguinaldo, the thirty-year-old leader of the Katipunan, who proclaimed himself provisional dictator of an independent Philippine Republic. He apparently expected American recognition. But President McKinley believed with good reason that the islands would be unable to preserve their independence in the face of Japanese and German imperialism. Hence he chose to retain control in the Philippines for the time being. Clashes between U.S. forces and Aguinaldo's troops began on February 4, 1899.

At first employing conventional military tactics, Aguinaldo soon realized that only guerrilla war had any chance of success. His men dug pits with sharpened spears at the bottom and set booby traps with poisoned arrows. They avoided combat except where they had great numerical superiority, and severely punished all Filipinos who showed themselves friendly to Americans. Between actions they assumed the role of peaceful villagers.

In the early months of the fighting, American forces were not numerous enough to simultaneously garrison all the main towns and pursue the guerrillas. They also suffered from tropical illnesses.[2] But the Americans had a most powerful weapon: a vigorous policy of preemption. Setting out to win the Filipinos by good works, they opened free schools, often with officers as instructors, attacked the deplorable sanitation problems in Manila and outlying areas, and reformed the atrocious penal system. The army provided free inoculations against the scourge of smallpox and waged a largely successful campaign against malaria. Despite Aguinaldo's dire warnings that the Americans had come to enslave the Filipinos and destroy Catholicism, it was clear to all that at the very least, the rule of the Americans was immeasurably better than that of the Spanish.

Of equal importance, as early as March 1899, President McKinley sent civilian commissioners, headed by the president of Cornell University, to pledge repeatedly that the United States recognized the right of the Filipinos to achieve eventual independence and would work toward that goal.

Military Factors in the American Victory

The American counterinsurgency in the Philippines illustrates the potentially decisive influence of geography. Fighting in an archipelago, Aguinaldo had no international border to retreat across in times of difficulty. His guerrillas received no offer of assistance from any other power (although elements in the Japanese military had strongly expressed their conviction that such aid should be sent), and in any event, the U.S. Navy would have seriously hindered any efforts toward such assistance. Against guerrillas lacking both protective borders and outside aid, even the most uninspired counterinsurgency tactics would have been effective over time. But in fact American tactics, first under General E. S. Otis and then under General Arthur MacArthur, were basically sound. Local commanders exercised much initiative and authority.[3] Rather than trying to kill guerrillas, American units concentrated on holding territory and creating local zones of safety, often with the help of the inhabitants. In some areas of high guerrilla activity, the Americans gathered the rural population together into the nearest town. The American army also gave a cash bounty or released a prisoner of war to any Filipino turning in a gun, no questions asked.

These tactics had the long-term effect of isolating the guerrillas and making their cause seem hopeless.[4] And they provided time for American political efforts against the guerrillas to take effect.

Political Factors in the American Victory

Four major political factors profoundly influenced the outcome of the struggle. First, Aguinaldo was unable to mobilize the power of Philippine nationalism, because for the most part it did not yet exist. Regional, ethnic, linguistic, and religious divisions among the Filipinos undercut the potential for a truly national uprising, and indeed the Americans found it was very easy to recruit personnel among the minority peoples of Luzon and other areas. Second, the other potentially powerful card in the hands of the rebels was an appeal to social revolution, but the conservative Aguinaldo rejected such a course (yet even then, the upper classes of Philippine society generally supported the Americans as the best guarantors of social order). Third, Aguinaldo claimed that he was fighting for the independence of the Philippines, but the Americans also had pledged themselves in writing to that very goal; a devastating war over the mere timing of that independence appealed to few Filipinos. Fourth, and not least, many Filipinos felt that American policies in education and health care were powerful arguments in favor of at least a temporary accommodation.

More Americans (4,200) lost their lives in repressing the Aguinaldo insurgency than in fighting the Spanish–American War. The American soldiers were culturally alien, far from their native land, less numerous than they needed to be, and without imperial experience to guide them. They had no tanks to deploy and no air force to call upon. In spite of all these handicaps (or more likely *because of* some of them), they were completely victorious. And the victory over the guerrillas was won in such a way as to lay the basis for lasting cooperation and friendship between the Filipinos and the Americans; even Aguinaldo himself eventually became reconciled to American tutelage.[5]

NICARAGUA

Endemic civil war characterized Nicaragua's first hundred years of statehood. In 1912, in response to a plea from President Adolfo Diaz, two thousand U.S. sailors and marines landed in Nicaragua.[6] They established a semblance of peace at the cost of thirty-seven marine casualties. The marines remained in Nicaragua most of the time until 1925, although after 1912 there was usually no more than a one-hundred-man detachment guarding the U.S. legation in Managua, a miniscule force to "occupy" a country that is the size of Pennsylvania with 700 thousand inhabitants.

There were two decisive reasons for the U.S. to have an interest in Nicaragua. First, it wanted security for the Panama Canal; violence in Central American states often spilled across borders, and might invite European or Mexican intervention.[7] Second, the Americans wished to prevent the Germans or the Japanese from building any future interoceanic canal in Nicaragua.[8]

In 1923 the U.S. State Department announced that the legation guard in Managua would be removed following the 1924 elections. The Liberal Party emerged victorious in "the most nearly honest elections in the history of the country."[9] The last marines embarked from Nicaragua that summer.

The next year, civil strife blazed again. The Mexican government sent weapons and volunteers to the Liberals.[10] Consequently, marines again landed to protect the lives and property of Americans and other foreigners. The American-supervised elections of 1928 were close to impeccable.[11] At the insistence of the Conservative Party, the United States oversaw the elections of 1930 and 1932 as well. The fairness of the marine supervision in these elections is suggested by the fact that they were all won by the anti–U.S. and pro-Mexican Liberal Party.[12]

The Guardia

The State Department and the Nicaraguan government agreed on a plan for a nonpartisan constabulary. After a false start, fresh recruiting for a *guardia nacional* began in May 1927 under the supervision of Marine Colonel Robert Rhea.[13] The United States hoped "to transform Nicaragua's armed forces into a nonpolitical force, dedicated to defending constitutional order and guaranteeing free elections."[14] But no faction in Nicaragua, then or thereafter, accepted the nonpartisan purpose of the constabulary, which is an essential reason why things went fundamentally wrong.

Almost all the officers in the Guardia were marine NCOs. "The marines did surprisingly well, transforming their raw recruits within a few months into the best trained, disciplined and equipped force in Nicaraguan history."[15] Regular pay, uniforms, food, medical treatment, and the respect for Nicaraguan fighting qualities that many marine officers developed made their service attractive for most recruits.

Sandino

By the 1927 Peace of Tipitapa, the leaders of the Liberal and Conservative parties agreed to stop fighting. Thirteen Liberal generals signed the accord, but not General Augusto Sandino, who disliked the arrangements for U.S. supervision of the 1928 elections.[16]

Within two months of the peace, the marine presence was reduced to only 1,500 men. On July 16, 1927, six hundred Sandino followers made a dawn attack on the thirty-nine marines and forty-seven guards at Ocotal. The defenders repulsed the attack, but suffered six casualties. In perhaps the first dive-bombing action in history, five marine aircraft attacked their opponents.[17]

Sandino "was one of the precursors of modern revolutionary guerrilla warfare—the process used to seize political control of an entire country by guerrilla action, without resort to conventional military operations except perhaps in the final stage of the struggle when the guerrilla army has acquired many of the characteristics of a regular army." Sandino was certainly no communist; he boasted of how he frustrated efforts of Farabundo Marti to take over his movement "for the Comintern." As he stated, "There is no need for the class struggle in Nicaragua because here the worker lives well; he struggles only against the American intervention."[18]

Between the attack on Ocotal and the spring of 1929, Guardia patrols made at least 13 contacts with Sandinistas, mixed marine–guardia patrols 32 contacts, and solely marine patrols another 59. During that period the marines suffered 70 casualties.[19] In 1930, Sandino divided his army into eight columns of seventy-five to one-hundred men. In response, the marines trained an elite guardia battalion to carry out extended patrols; such tactics frightened Sandino, but this was not enough to overcome guerrilla advantages and marine handicaps. Sandino's men were as well armed as the marines. They could escape pursuit in the northern wilds or across the Honduran border. The marines and the guardia lacked sufficient numbers to hold fixed posts and at the same time hunt the guerrillas effectively. Their food, equipment, and fodder for their horses had to be carried on muleback, for the countryside was too poor for foraging. The marines were better trained and better marksmen than the guerrillas. They also had the advantage of aircraft, which could provide them with close combat support, emergency supplies, and medical evacuation, and help for small groups of marines in the field to stay in contact with their headquarters. But aircraft over a given area also alerted the guerrillas to the possible presence of marines. Besides, the guerrillas learned how to counter marine air support by restricting daylight movements, refraining from firing at airplanes, and camouflaging their camps. Casualties were not numerous, but encounters were often grisly. The insurgents executed prisoners in cruel ways; their official seal pictured a Sandino soldier beheading a prostrate marine.[20]

In 1932, leaders of both Nicaraguan parties requested that the marines remain; they "symbolized order in a disorderly society."[21] But Congressional criticism grew ever more strident, and President Hoover was well aware that U.S. military victory in Nicaragua would not be possible unless several thousand more troops were sent there. Washington accordingly announced that the marines would leave after Nicaragua's 1932 elections.[22] Once again, the Liberals won a clear victory.

Handing over command to their Nicaraguan successors on January 1, 1933, the last marines sailed from Corinto the following day. In more than five years of fighting, seventy-five national guards and forty-seven marines had lost their lives in combat. Another eighty-nine from both groups had died of disease, accident, or suicide. Ten mutinies in guardia units had resulted in the deaths of seven marine officers. Adding in figures from Haiti and the Dominican Republic, the marines had lost seventy-nine officers and men killed in action or dead of wounds in the entire Caribbean area.[23]

Lessons

Sandino was never able to deploy even one out of a thousand Nicaraguans. The insurgency survived because of the Honduran sanctuary, help from Mexican dictator Plutarco Calles and his hand-picked successors, and above all because of the inadequate numbers of the marines and national guards.[24]

The marines learned a lot in Nicaragua about counterinsurgency. Constant training was absolutely necessary. Big search-and-destroy sweep operations were generally useless. Sustained patrolling was much more effective: twenty men, carrying very little with them, could cover up to thirty miles a day. "Nothing upsets a guerrilla band more than to be chased by a compact, fast-moving patrol of soldiers who are familiar with the people and terrain of the area of operations, and are willing to stay in the field until decisive contact is made."[25] And the marines also found that the most effective response to ambush was a great volume of automatic-weapons fire.[26]

The marines were quick to take advantage of Indian dislike of ethnic Nicaraguans. They fielded mixed units, in which guardia members received on-the-job training while the marines learned the nature of the countryside and its inhabitants. "American officers shared with Nicaraguan enlisted men the hardships and dangers of life on the trail, and more often than not formed bonds of comradeship with the native soldiers. Together they trudged through sweltering valleys, endured torrential downpours, forded swirling rivers, inched their way up precipitous mountainsides, and shivered through the night in rain- or sweat-soaked clothing—lying in hammocks rocked by tropical breezes that could seem as cold as an arctic blast."[27]

They also discovered the value of close air support: "Marine aviation came of age in its support of ground troops in Nicaragua."[28] Above all, the marines "learned that a successful operation was one in which the enemy suffered casualties and they had none."[29]

Out of their experiences in Nicaragua and the Caribbean, the marines distilled principles of counterinsurgency for their *Small Wars Manual* of 1940. Among the most notable of these:

"The occupying force must be strong enough to hold all the strategical points of the country, protect its communications, and at the same time furnish an operating force sufficient to overcome the opposition wherever it appears. . . . While curbing the passions of the people, courtesy, friendliness, justice, and firmness should be exhibited."

"When the patrol leader demands information, the peasant should not be misjudged for failure to comply with the request, when by doing so, he is signing his own death warrant."

"In small wars, caution must be exercised, and instead of striving to generate the maximum power with forces available, the goal is to gain decisive results with the least application of force and the consequent minimum loss of life."

"In small wars, tolerance, sympathy and kindliness should be the keynote of our relationship with the mass of the population."[30]

GREECE

Greece was the scene of the first armed confrontation between the Western and Communist blocs. It called forth the Truman Doctrine, launched the Containment policy, and ended in the complete defeat of the insurgency.

In December 1942 the Greek Communist Party created a guerrilla force, ELAS. Fifty-one-thousand square miles in area, the size of Virginia and Maryland, covered with mountains, crossed by few highways, with a long tradition of resistance to invaders, Greece was good country for guerrilla warfare. Nevertheless, ELAS did little fighting against the Germans, conserving its strength for a postwar showdown.

The Civil War

On the heels of the retreating Germans, British and Royal Greek Army elements landed in the Athens area. In December 1944, ELAS attacked these forces, and also executed thousands of civilian hostages. Churchill himself spent Christmas Day in the beleagured city. In February 1945 ELAS agreed to a truce. But the communists boycotted the 1946 elections and embarked upon guerrilla war. Now calling themselves the Democratic Army, they held some big cards. Greece's communist northern neighbors provided ELAS with munitions and training camps; hard-pressed guerrilla units could find sanctuary across any of several borders. In addition, the Royal Greek Army suffered from antiquated equipment, political interference in appointments, tactics of static defense, and communist penetration.

In March 1947, as victory for the Greek communists appeared all but inevitable, President Truman declared that "it must be the policy of the United States to support free peoples who are resisting attempted subjugation by armed minorities or by outside pressures." By 1948, the United States had shipped 174 thousand tons of military supplies to Greece; soon it would be spending about $10,000 to eliminate each guerrilla.[31]

American Troops to Greece?

The Truman administration emphasized from the start that U.S. military personnel in Greece would have solely an advisory role.[32] The first members of U. S. Army Group Greece reached Athens in May 1947. An internal State Department memorandum noted that "Greek officials are obsessed with the idea of getting the United States so deeply committed in Greece that it will be unable to withdraw if the Greeks themselves lie down on the job."[33] Key Greek politicians wanted a small number of U.S. combat troops to bolster Greek morale.[34]

In the gloomy winter of 1947–1948, the administration contemplated the expansion of its military commitment to Greece. The State Department advised in December 1947 that if Greece's communist neighbors recognized a guerrilla counterstate within Greece or introduced their own troops into the fighting, the United States should at least call on the United Nations to authorize the dispatch of armed forces to assist the legitimate government.[35] Major General A. V. Arnold declared that sending two U.S. divisions to Thrace could make a vital contribution to ending the war, but George Kennan thought that the Peloponnesus might be easier to defend.[36]

Nevertheless, powerful opposition arose to any proposal for send-ing U.S. ground combat units to Greece. Republican spokesman John Foster Dulles rejected the idea.[37] U.S. Ambassador Lincoln MacVeagh believed that the Greek Army could achieve control of the situation with better tactics and leadership.[38] And Dwight Griswold, in charge of U.S. aid to Greece, wrote, "Defeat of Com-munism is not solely a question of military action as demonstrated in Germany, France and elsewhere. In Greece, the military and economic fronts are of equal importance." Therefore he "would op-pose the use of even a single American officer or soldier against the Greek bandits."[39] In the fall of 1948 the State Department warned that the introduction of American combat units might serve the Kremlin as an excuse to send Soviet forces into Yugoslavia.[40] Gen-eral Marshall returned from Athens convinced that the Greek Army needed improvement, not expansion.[41]

Effective opposition to deploying American combat troops to Greece came from the U.S. military.[42] In September 1947, Undersecretary of War Kenneth Royall told Marshall that such deployment would be "disturbing and provocative." Major General Stephen Chamberlin, heading a special military mission to Greece, stated that the Greek Army should be able to cope with the guerril-las, provided there was no overt intervention from the north.[43] Marshall feared that sending U.S. combat troops to Greece might result in both a buildup of forces larger than the United States should commit to one place and possibly their withdrawal under unpropitious circumstances.[44] To Major General A. M. Harper, Greece was a strategic "mousetrap."[45] Even if American forces were stripped from other theaters to go to Greece, they would be nu-merically inferior to what the Soviets or Greece's communist neigh-bors could commit.[46] (In mid-1947 U.S. armed forces totalled less than 1.6 million.[47]) The joint chiefs went on record against such a deployment unless it was preceded by national mobilization, which was hardly a likely prospect. Besides, the Berlin Blockade began in the spring of 1948, and the NATO Treaty would soon greatly ex-tend U.S. commitments. Finally, the British informed Washington in early 1948 that they would keep a considerable number of troops in Greece. Thus D.C.I. Souers told the National Security Council that "the United States should not now send armed forces to Greece as token forces or for military operations."[48]

By September 1948, almost a year and a half after the proclama-tion of the Truman Doctrine, 450 U.S. military advisors were in Greece (three of whom would lose their lives).[49] Knowing little and caring less about the nuances of Greek politics, these Americans brought more strictly military considerations to bear on operational planning than Greek officers had been accustomed to.

Communist Defeat

In light of the guerrillas' many advantages, why did they lose? One might begin with Guevara's dictum that one cannot make a revolution against a democratic or quasi-democratic government, and Greece, with its parliament and its multiparty system, was at least the latter. But four factors easily stand out as decisive in the communist defeat.

First, in December 1948, the communists prematurely adopted conventional tactics, thereby exposing the insurgents to attack from the air and encirclement on the ground. At that very moment, internal reforms and U.S. assistance were making the Royal Greek Army a much more effective force, with 150 thousand men, plus 50 thousand militia and 25 thousand paramilitary gendarmerie. All of these were now under the supreme command of the able General Alexander Papagos. The guerrillas counted about 25 thousand. In the summer of 1949, the communists conveniently assembled fully 12 thousand fighters in the Grammos mountain area for the Greek army to attack. The insurgents lost at least two thousand; the remainder scuttled into Albania.

Second, the guerrillas alienated the peasantry. Greek mountain folk had been willing enough to help guerrillas against the German invaders, but not against fellow Greeks. The communists were overwhelmingly petit bourgeois intellectuals or else social marginals like students, tobacco farmers, and seamen, unrepresentative of the social group among whom they operated. The hard-core party leaders were ashamed of the Greek peasantry; in their brave new world, peasants would not exist. At the same time, because they were receiving supplies from across the borders, the communists did not feel a great need for peasant support. As the war went on, communist policy toward the peasantry hardened, with executions, seizures of foodstuffs and hostages, and the destruction of villages to create refugees that the hardpressed Greek government would have to care for. In addition, the party forcibly sent 28 thousand children to communist states in East Europe. At the same time, the insurgency had little support in Athens or the Peloponnesus.

Thus the Greek Communists deliberately violated the two most fundamental rules of guerrilla insurgency: (1) don't fight unless you are certain to win, and (2) make friends with the rural folk.

Third, in July 1949 the Yugoslavians closed their border, trapping thousands of guerrillas inside Yugoslavia, and isolating several thousand more in Thrace.

These factors, however, would not have come to fruition if Greece had collapsed in 1948. This did not happen because of the fourth main factor: *the United States provided valuable assistance.* American help allowed the Greek government to expand and properly equip its army without unduly disrupting the economy, and U.S. military advisors pressured the Greek army to improve its practices.

In November 1949, President Truman informed Congress that the Greek conflict was over. The Greek armed forces had suffered 17 thousand killed and 40 thousand wounded or missing; the guerrillas had executed at least 4 thousand civilians and burned 12 thousand homes. Government forces had killed 37 thousand guerrillas and captured another 20 thousand.

THE HUKS

Origins of the Huks

During the Japanese occupation of the Philippines (1942–1944), the People's Army Against Japan arose; its Tagalog acronym—"Hukbalahap"—produced the nickname "Huks." By late 1943 there were 10 thousand of these Huks, and sometimes they attacked American-led guerrilla units. During the liberation, the Huks were well armed with Japanese and American weapons. Their stronghold was Luzon, an area of 40 thousand square miles, and about the size of Kentucky, which for generations had been the scene of agrarian unrest. Soon they were fighting the new Philippine Republic's forces.

The Huks did not wage a self-consciously Maoist-style war, because that model had not yet become prominent. The leaders were largely urban, including several former university professors.[50] Their major activity was robbing banks, payroll offices, and trains. Against them the government deployed the Philippine constabulary, with a paper strength of 25 thousand. Poorly trained and equipped, its usual tactics were encirclement and sweeps, which the guerrillas easily evaded. The constabulary also systematically robbed the peasants they were supposed to protect, fueling the rebellion.[51]

When Mao triumphed in 1949, the Philippine insurgents changed their name to the People's Liberation Army. That same year they backed the successful reelection bid of President Quirino, believing that his inept administration was their guarantee of ultimate victory. The election of 1949 was corrupt even for the Philippines. The "dirty elections of 1949," seemed to prove that there was no peaceful path to change. By mid-1950 the Huks had 25 thousand fighters, carrying out spectacular raids in the very outskirts of Manila.

Yet, the tide was just about to turn. Contrary to classic Leninist tactics, the Huks failed to form a broad front with other disaffected groups. Peasants learned to fear the many common criminals in the Huk ranks. Within the organization punishment for infractions was severe, and the insurgents lost support through such sense-less acts as the murder of the widow of former President Quezon. In September 1950 a thoroughly alarmed President Quirino ap-pointed as secretary of defense a congressman named Ramon Magsaysay.

Magsaysay Defeats the Huks

A World War II guerrilla, Magsaysay had clear insights into the nature of the Huk challenge.[52] He moved vigorously to halt abuses by the constabulary and army, set up a telegraph system whereby for a nominal fee any villager on Luzon could contact him, ended useless sweep operations, and insisted on incursions into hitherto unmolested guerrilla areas to disrupt their food supply and deprive them of rest. He made unexpected visits to the field in his small airplane, descending upon shiftless or venal local commanders like a *diabolus ex machina*. He greatly improved the supply of intelli-gence, partly through offering fabulous rewards for the capture of guerrilla leaders, who were accused of some specific crime such as murder or rape at a particular place and time. Realizing that many younger Huks had no place to go if they accepted amnesty, he be-gan a resettlement program. Perhaps most important, Magsaysay deployed army units to ensure the honesty of the 1951 congres-sional elections. The opposition won in a landslide. This demon-stration of an alternative route to change did as much as anything to deflate the Huk movement.[53] In 1953 Magsaysay easily won the presidency. The next year, the surrender of Luis Taruc, the most famous Huk leader, effectively ended the conflict in which 10 thou-sand Huks had died, 4 thousand were captured, and 16 thousand surrendered.[54]

The Question of U.S. Combat Involvement

The United States had a deep emotional stake in the postwar Philippines, wishing them to become the showcase of democracy in East Asia. President Truman sent American officers to help train the Philippine Army, and President Quirino was anxious to have U.S. combat troops deployed against the Huks.[55] But until 1950, Washington believed that a Huk victory was improbable, and, be-sides, was otherwise preoccupied with China, Greece, NATO, and the Marshall Plan.

In April 1950, the U.S. Embassy in Manila identified the sources of Huk strength as maldistribution of land and fraudulent elec-tions, and the passive tactics of the Philippine armed forces and their alienation of the peasantry, aggravated by an overreliance on artillery, weapons that obliterated the distinction between guerrillas and civilians. "The employment of United States troops against Filipinos outside our bases should probably be considered only as a last resort. Such action would provide our enemies all over Asia with valuable propaganda and might be expected to cause many Filipinos to regard us as invaders and to join forces with the Huks." The embassy was suggesting that the Americans should do what they had done in Greece: send well-prepared U.S. advisors in larger numbers.[56]

The deteriorating situation in early 1950 alarmed President Truman: "Failure of the Philippines experiment which all Asia watches as evidence of American intentions and abilities could only have the most unfortunate repercussions for the United States both abroad and at home."[57] A few months later, North Korean troops crashed across the 38th parallel. Soon U.S. forces were fighting for their lives around Pusan. Later that year the Chinese communists intervened massively. At the same time, Washington was assuming ever more responsibility for the supply of French and Vietnamese forces fighting the Viet Minh.

Yet even in those desperate circumstances, U.S. Ambassador to Manila Cowen stated his belief (September 29, 1950) that the United States should at least consider sending a reinforced division to the Philippines.[58] And a "top secret" draft paper by the deputy director of the Office of Philippine and Southeast Asian Affairs (dated January 19, 1951) read, "It is assumed that the United States is determined, regardless of the cost and despite any eventualities, as part of its Pacific policy to retain the Philippines within the orbit of the democratic powers and to deny it to the Soviet orbit. This is the irreducible minimum of American security and interests in the Pacific and the Far East."[59] The author of the secret document approved the idea of sending two American divisions to the Philippines. But a National Security Council staff study had concluded in November 1950 that the Philippine armed forces, if well trained and adequately equipped, would defeat the Huks, provided that the latter received no important outside aid.[60]

Washington analysts focused on the need for leadership and land reform. A Department of State paper of June 1950 stated, "Since the tragic death of President Roxas in 1948, Philippine leadership has been discouragingly weak and short-sighted." A National Security Council staff study noted that "leadership of the Philippine Government has been largely in the hands of a small group of individuals representing the wealthy propertied classes who, except in isolated instances, have failed to appreciate the need for reform and the pressures generated among the less prosperous and more numerous groups of the population." Secretary of State Acheson had a particularly unfavorable opinion of President Quirino. Washington was also aware that the fraud and violence of the 1949 presidential election increased the attraction of the Huks.[61]

In February 1951 U.S. Ambassador Cowen stated that land reform, including resettlement of landless peasants, would defeat the Huks. He also reminded Washington that everyone who was killed by U.S.–supplied arms had relatives who might consequently support the communists. Acheson shared this general stance: "We strongly believe that the only way to beat the Communists is to show our ability to carry out under democratic processes those reforms they advocate which are worthwhile. Land redistribution is one such reform."[62]

Accordingly the Truman administration moved toward making assistance to Manila contingent on internal political, military, and economic reforms.[63] Philippine leaders, however, felt that they could ignore such pressures, since in the last analysis the United States would save them. Acheson wrote to President Truman, "If there is one lesson to be learned from the China debacle it is that if we are confronted with an inadequate vehicle it should be discarded or immobilized in favor of a more propitious one." Yet if the U.S. government encouraged the removal of President Quirino, it would resound all over Asia, to the detriment of U.S. policy aims.[64]

Among the least anxious to get involved in the fighting were the leaders of the U.S. armed forces. General George Marshall told Philippine statesman Carlos P. Romulo that he "did not wish to have the same experience that he had in China in supplying arms to an Army which was guided by political interests."[65] On September 6, 1950 the Joint Chiefs of Staff advised Secretary of Defense Johnson that "intervention would require, in light of the present world situation [fighting in Korea and building up NATO] a considerable increase in the extent of mobilization currently envisaged." Instead, the United States should increase shipments of military materiel, augment the number of security personnel on U.S. installations there, and raise its military mission in Manila to thirty-two officers and twenty-six enlisted.[66] U.S. advisors already in the islands opposed the direct assignment of American officers to Philippine combat units.[67]

The joint chiefs believed that "the basic problem [in the Philippines] is primarily political and economic. Military action should not be an alternative for a stable and efficient government based on sound economic and social foundations." Inequities in land ownership constituted the roots of the Huk rebellion, as well as the preference for guerrilla life that some men had acquired under the Japanese occupation. Therefore "direct United States military intervention in the Philippines would be justifiable, from a strategic point of view, only if there remained no other means of preventing Communist seizure of the islands."[68] And well before the end of 1951, it had become clear that the Huks were not going to win.[69] Thus the United States did not commit combat troops to the anti-Huk struggle.

EL SALVADOR

In December 1980, several Salvadoran insurgent groups gathered in Havana to organize the Farabundo Marti National Liberation Front (FMLN), named after a Salvadoran communist contemporary of the Nicaraguan Augusto Sandino.

The insurgency in El Salvador arose during an anxious period for the United States. Saigon had finally fallen to the North Vietnamese army in 1975, mobs in Tehran had taken the American embassy staff hostage in 1979, Pol Pot was devastating Cambodia, the Soviets had invaded Afghanistan, and Cuban troops were fighting in Angola. The presence of Cuban forces in neighboring Nicaragua made the Salvadoran situation more alarming to Washington; the FMLN was going to pay dearly for the Sandinistas' close ties with Havana and Moscow.[70]

Mao's writings suggest that the small size of El Salvador should have been a serious disadvantage to guerrillas. But along its border with Honduras, both countries had no-entry zones for their troops, and these areas provided the insurgents with convenient sanctuaries. In addition, the rebels received much help, including combat training, from neighboring Nicaragua, and from the USSR, Cuba, Bulgaria, East Germany, and Viet Nam.[71]

In 1980 the Carter administration concluded that the United States must assist the Salvadoran government against the insurgency. U.S. aid was probably not the decisive factor—it was certainly not the *only* factor—in the defeat of the insurgency.[72] Nevertheless, President Carter's decision was one of the most important events of the entire conflict.[73] At the time, the Salvadoran government and army seemed on the verge of collapse. The guerrillas numbered ten to twelve thousand fighters, many more than either the Fidelista or Sandinista insurgencies had commanded. In January 1981 the FMLN launched its "final offensive." Scoring some impressive gains at first, by the end of the month it was receding. Thus, before any appreciable American aid had reached El Salvador, it was clear that the government was not going to fall.[74] Notably, the popular uprising which the FMLN called for in conjunction with its January offensive was a resounding flop, the first major indication that support for the insurgents was not as wide-spread as many outside El Salvador liked to claim.

President Reagan dispatched a small number of U.S. military advisors to El Salvador; army officers from that country began counterinsurgency training at Fort Bragg. Out of these efforts would arise a more competent Salvadoran army. Improvement was sorely needed in light of that army's peculiar shortcomings, which included (1) the "tanda" system, whereby an entire class of officers received promotion at the same time, negating any concept of merit; (2) structural corruption, whereby officers profited from government payments for nonexistent soldiers and sold goods at inflated prices to their troops; and (3) a reluctance on the part of many officers to see the war end, because U.S. aid would then also end.

In 1984 the influential Kissinger Commission offered the following observations. "The roots of the crisis [in El Salvador] are both indigenous and foreign. Discontents are real, and for much of the population conditions of life are miserable. . . . But these conditions have been exploited by hostile outside forces—specifically by Cuba, backed by the Soviet Union and now operating through Nicaragua—which will turn any revolution they capture into a totalitarian state. . . . As a mainland platform, therefore, Nicaragua is a crucial steppingstone for Cuban and Soviet efforts to promote armed insurgency in Central America. . . . The use of Nicaragua as a base for Soviet and Cuban efforts to penetrate the rest of the Central American isthmus, with El Salvador as the target of first opportunity, gives the conflict there a major strategic dimension."[75]

The war had become a stalemate, with the scales increasingly tipping toward the government. Now the FMLN's internal fissures began to widen. The FMLN was an alliance of five different guerrilla armies, each suspicious of and even hostile to the others. In 1985, with the war not going well and regular elections taking place, the most hardline of the guerrilla groups, the ERP, radicalized its tactics. The guerrillas made the destruction of the country's economic life their central goal.[76] They forcibly recruited peasant youths into their units.[77] Government officials and their relatives became the target of assassination; the rebels killed the most popular and honest officers, politicians, and administrators (as the Viet Cong had done in South Viet Nam).[78] By thus embracing terrorism ("urban guerrilla warfare"), the FMLN lost prestige and popular support and alienated the less intransigent elements of its own membership. In 1989, leading FMLN figures publicly renounced revolution in favor of political participation. And in the March presidential election of that year, witnessed by the international press, the ARENA party candidate, Georgetown University graduate

Alfredo Cristiani, won 53.8 percent of the vote in a large turnout, against 36.6 percent of the vote for the candidate of the Christian Democrats. The inauguration of Cristiani was the first handover of power by a civilian president to a civilian leader of the opposition in the country's history. Shortly thereafter most of the FMLN leadership entered into negotiations with ARENA. These talks collapsed in November 1989, and the FMLN launched another offensive. Their most ambitious military effort ever, it failed nonetheless.[79] The FMLN's strategy was bankrupt.

Greece, not Viet Nam

The ending of the Cold War put pressure on both sides: FMLN support from communist countries was drying up, while army leaders realized that the United States now felt itself in a position to be able to cut off aid. Accordingly, in January 1992, the Cristiani administration and the FMLN signed peace accords in Mexico City. The FMLN agreed to disarm under UN supervision and to transform itself from a guerrilla army into a political party.

Thus, contrary to fashionable predictions (and hopes), El Salvador never turned into "another Viet Nam." And why should it have? The differences between the wars in El Salvador and Viet Nam were, or ought to have been, much more impressive than the similarities. Consider that El Salvador had one-eighth the area and one-fifth the population of South Viet Nam. Consider further that Washington is closer to the South Pole than to Saigon, but San Salvador is closer to Houston and San Diego that either of those cities is to New York. And there is no communist China in Central America.

Presidents Carter, Reagan, and Bush worked to strengthen the Salvadoran army, significantly upgrading its capabilities.[80] Despite continuing shortcomings, that army's treatment of civilians indisputably improved; thus, if the United States had not intervened, the El Salvador conflict would almost certainly have been much more ferocious. U.S. pressure also brought free elections to El Salvador in 1984, which, as in the Philippines in 1951, deprived the insurgents of their powerful argument that there was no peaceful way to change an intolerable situation. FMLN threats against potential voters only served to increase its isolation. Guevara's thesis—that violent revolution cannot succeed against a democratic or even a pseudodemocratic government—received new confirmation.[81] In El Salvador as elsewhere, "the ballot box . . . has proven to be the coffin of revolutionary movements."[82]

If the elections were free and honest, why didn't FMLN win? FMLN calls for a massive popular uprising had repeatedly failed; its vote totals in internationally supervised elections, especially in

1994, were unimpressive. All this suggested that FMLN's authoritarian Marxism and terrorist tactics had made it increasingly unattractive to broad strata of Salvadoran society. FMLN defeat, on the battlefield and at the ballot box, resulted from the failure of its leaders to imitate the Cuban and Nicaraguan models by forging a broad coalition behind a program of democratic revolution, thereby isolating the regime and avoiding American intervention. Meanwhile, the Salvadoran upper and upper-middle classes were united in "the strongest anticommunist sentiment in Latin America."[83] Conservative forces, moreover, were able to attract or purchase considerable support among workers and peasants: Thus the rightist ARENA party won the internationally supervised presidential elections in both 1989 and 1994, and obtained 44 percent of the vote in the 1991 Legislative Assembly elections.

Unable to mobilize a sufficient mass in society, the FMLN had no path to power but force. But American help was increasing the size and competence of the Salvadoran army. Then, foreign help for the FMLN began to diminish. The Soviets lost interest in El Salvador, and the unexpected electoral debacle of the neighboring Sandinista regime in March 1990 gave the coup de grace to whatever vision of military victory the guerrillas may have still entertained.

In summary, El Salvador's government, legitimizing itself through democratic elections, retained the support of most of the country's middle classes, along with substantial segments of the peasantry and the town workers, and of the U.S. government. In these ways the Salvadoran case *contrasts fundamentally and decisively with the Cuban and Nicaraguan experiences.* Instead of "another Viet Nam," El Salvador was more like a return to the Greek model: The United States furnished economic and military aid, along with a quite limited number of military advisors, providing time for its ally to clean up its more egregious shortcomings. And in El Salvador, as in Greece, the insurgents had already failed strategically even before they lost their sanctuary.

Like the campaign against Aguinaldo, the conflict in El Salvador deserves a great deal more dispassionate scrutiny than it is likely to receive.[84]

A DIFFERENT CASE: AFGHANISTAN

Afghanistan is the size of Illinois, Indiana, Ohio, Michigan, and Wisconsin combined. Covered by mountains, with no railways and few all-weather roads, the country had a preinvasion population of 16 million, divided into many ethnic, religious, and racial groups, united only by Sunni Islam. In April 1978 a bloody coup in Kabul resulted in a regime controlled by the tiny Afghan communist party, the PDPA. This group's bloodthirstiness, contempt for the peasantry, and hatred of Islam soon provoked widespread insurrection. On the eve of the Soviet invasion, twenty-three of Afghanistan's twenty-eight provinces were under rebel control.[85] On December 24, 1979, Soviet airborne troops descended on Kabul.[86] The Soviet invasion of Afghanistan called forth the "largest single national uprising in the twentieth century," enmeshed the Soviets in their longest war, illustrated the pitfalls awaiting even a major power confronting guerrillas, provided the Americans with the opportunity to even several scores, and contributed to the most radical alteration of the world balance of power in this century.[87]

The Resistance

The disparity between the world's mightiest military power and the backward buffer state was tragicomic. But the resistance movement had cards to play. It was so amorphous that one or two blows could not destroy it. The insurgents had a sanctuary in Pakistan. Most of all, they had high morale: as *mujahideen* (warriors of God), they were certain of eventual victory over their profane enemies. By 1985, the guerrillas numbered between 80 thousand and 150 thousand. Confronting them were 30 thousand Afghan army troops (down from 100 thousand since the invasion), 50 thousand unreliable local militia, and 115 thousand Soviet soldiers. Thus the invader and his allies enjoyed at best a ratio of 5 to 2 over the guerrillas—which was utterly inadequate. The strategy of the *mujahideen* was to make the costs of occupation too high for the Soviets; by the sixth year of the war they had achieved a stalemate.[88]

Soviet Strategy

Among the unpleasant surprises that greeted the Soviets was the inability of their Kabul clients to build an effective native army. Most of the officers of the preinvasion army who had not been killed, fired, retired, or exiled by the PDPA had joined the resistance. Surrender, desertion, and defection were common; great quantities of army weapons were handed over to the guerrillas. The PDPA offered very high pay, accelerated promotions, and high school and university credits for army service; it commissioned officers after only three months of training; and it lowered the draft age to sixteen, and then to fourteen. All this availed little; the Kabul army never exceeded three-tenths of 1 percent of the population. Thus, Soviet troops had to bear most of the burden of serious fighting against the *mujahideen*.[89]

The Soviet army that went into Afghanistan had not experienced serious combat since the 1940s. It lacked a serviceable doctrine of counterinsurgency. The number of troops in country was grotesquely inadequate to their mission.[90] Predictably, the Soviet forces relied on ineffective sweeps by roadbound units. It was this combination of insufficiencies—of doctrine, of experience, of numbers, and of tactics—that led the Soviets to resort to the systematic destruction of the country and its inhabitants. The campaign against crops, animals, and people eventually made it impossible in many areas for the guerrillas to obtain food. Especially determined to empty the provinces along the borders with Pakistan and with the USSR, the Soviets used poison gasses and dropped small explosive devices shaped like toys, designed to kill or maim children.[91] By 1988 this program of "migratory genocide" had created fully four million refugees, the largest number on the planet.[92] Civilian deaths resulting from Soviet policy numbered at least 1.3 million, proportionately equivalent to the deaths of 20 million Americans.

Domination of the air by the helicopter gunship was the Soviets' most effective weapon. When the guerrillas obtained surface-to-air missiles in 1983 and Stingers in 1986, the war changed profoundly. Now the guerrillas were able, by depriving convoys of air cover, to halt land travel between major cities for extended periods. They had penetrated the Kabul government and army so thoroughly that surprise operations of significant size became nearly impossible. And life became ever more perilous for PDPA members and the Soviet community in Kabul itself: Assassinations, explosions, and rocket attacks occurred with increasing frequency.

The United States and Afghanistan

In 1953, the Joint Chiefs of Staff had advised President Eisenhower that "Afghanistan is of little or no strategic importance to the United States."[93] Afghanistan was in the "Soviet sphere of influence"; no amount of U.S. aid could change that.[94] With Secretary of State Dulles supporting Pakistan (a Baghdad Pact ally) in its border disagreements, Kabul turned to the Soviets. The Russians built the Bagram airport north of Kabul, and the Salang Pass through the mountains near the Soviet–Afghan border, both highly useful in the invasion of 1979.

The Kremlin anticipated little trouble from the United States over Afghanistan.[95] This was in part because the Soviets expected no effective resistance from the Afghans.[96] But in a notable hyperbole, an aroused President Carter called the Soviet invasion of Afghanistan "the greatest threat to peace since the Second World

War."[97] For the administration, the invasion was extremely ominous; this first Soviet military movement outside the Soviet bloc carried the Red Army close to major Western and Japanese oil sources. "If the Soviets could consolidate their hold on Afghanistan," Carter wrote later, "the balance of power in the entire region would be drastically modified in their favor, and they might be tempted toward further aggression."[98] President Carter postponed consideration of the Salt II treaty by the Senate, proclaimed a U.S. boycott of the 1980 Moscow Olympics, imposed a wheat embargo on the USSR, asked the United Nations to condemn the Soviets, initiated legislation aiming at a reintroduction of the military draft, called for greatly increased aid to Pakistan, sent his secretary of defense to Beijing, and began the flow of military and financial assistance to the *mujahideen*.[99] And in his State of the Union message on January 23, 1980, the president issued this warning: "Let our position be absolutely clear: An attempt by any outside force to gain control of the Persian Gulf region will be regarded as an assault on the vital interests of the United States of America, and such an assault will be repelled by any means necessary, including military force."[100]

The Central Intelligence Agency received the responsibility to aid the insurgents, the largest "covert" CIA operation since Viet Nam.[101] CIA often supplied the *mujahideen* with Soviet weapons in order to mask their origin.[102] Much of this aid never made it out of Pakistan.[103] But in view of the eventual effect of the Afghan conflict on the Soviet Empire, the Americans surely got their money's worth.

The Soviets Depart

After seven years of war, the resistance was unable to take and hold any major city. But the Soviets controlled little beyond those cities, two airports, and the main road from the USSR to Kabul. And they had lost their domination of the air.

The Soviets had disastrously overestimated their ability to prevent outside help reaching the rebels. They had alarmed the West and offended the Islamic world. They had suffered 50 thousand casualties, of which 15 thousand were fatal. They had lost more than one thousand aircraft, six hundred tanks, and thousands of other vehicles. The conflict helped President Reagan pry big defense budgets out of Congress, and was bringing Washington and Beijing closer together. The USSR's 50 million Muslim subjects, living in territories conquered relatively recently, were witnessing the stalemating of the mighty Red Army by Islamic peasants—the Red Star eclipsed by the Crescent—Lenin tamed by Mohammed. This was some spectacle. And to reach the traditional 10 to 1 ratio of troops to guerrillas, the Soviets would have had to put at least 900 thousand soldiers into Afghanistan, eight times the size of their actual commitment.

Why—and how—was Gorbachev obliged to carry on with this catastrophic imbroglio of Brezhnev's? Thus, in April 1988 Pakistan and the PDPA signed accords at Geneva, with the United States and the Soviet Union as guarantors; the Russians began their UN–monitored withdrawal one month later.[104]

RUSSIA'S VIET NAM

In the 1980s one often heard references to the Afghanistan war as "Russia's Viet Nam." Some obvious similarities between these two conflicts ought not to obscure fundamental differences. First, Afghanistan bordered the USSR, while Washington, as was mentioned previously, is closer to the South Pole than to South Viet Nam. Second, the Soviet system was ideally suited to the conduct of a destructive war aimed at civilians: no intrusive media, no embarrassing congressional hearings, and no troublesome Amnesty International interlopers. Third, though the *mujahideen* were brave and tenacious, as a fighting force, they simply were not comparable to the North Vietnamese Army; relatively speaking, the Soviets had it easy.

Afghanistan was not Russia's Viet Nam: It was much more devastating than that. For the first time since the fall of Hitler's Berlin, the vaunted Soviet military machine had been halted. The common folk of Afghanistan, bombed and gassed and hounded from their ruined villages by the world's mightiest army—this remote and martyred people—inflicted an undeniable military reverse on what had so often been called the historical inevitability of Marxism–Leninism. Afghan resistance contributed directly to the gathering forces of disintegration within the Soviet Empire: The cries of battle in the Afghan mountains had their echo in the shouts of freedom on the Berlin Wall.

SOME IMPLICATIONS

In the twentieth century American troops have served effectively as counterinsurgent forces on foreign soil, in both the Philippines and Nicaragua. The American record in those conflicts needs more study. Nevertheless, for many Americans, the insurgencies whose outcomes were most satisfactory undoubtedly were those in which the United States provided financial help and military equipment and advice, but not combat troops: Greece, the Huk war, El Salvador, and Afghanistan.

Counterinsurgency is not a subset of conventional war. In an insurgency Clausewitz's center of gravity is the civilian population, and more specifically, the loyalty or at least the secure control of that population. Successful counterinsurgency, therefore, will not aim to destroy guerrillas but rather to marginalize them by the application of long and widely tested politico–military principles.

One such principle is to *isolate the battlefield.*[105] Failure to do this was a major cause (at least) of the frustration of the Americans in Viet Nam and the Soviets in Afghanistan; the small size of Nicaragua and El Salvador meant that the guerrillas were never far from international borders.[106] Isolation of the insurgents from outside aid was easy to achieve in the Philippines (both times), mainly because of geography. But where geography is not so accommodating, human effort can compensate. In the Boer War and in Chiang Kai-shek's campaigns against the communists before World War II, lines of small blockhouses confined guerrillas to an ever-shrinking space. The French built effective barriers running for hundreds of miles along Algeria's borders; the Moroccans carried out similar works in the Western Sahara. The South Vietnamese tried to change the geography of their state by retrenching into Military Regions III and IV in 1975; this was a good idea, but much too late.

The second principle is to *display rectitude.* Peasant populations are fundamentally conservative; their tendency is not to oppose authority, unless exasperated. The French in the Vendée and in Spain, the Japanese in China, the Germans in Yugoslavia, the Soviets in Afghanistan, as well as the guerrillas in Greece—to cite only a few instances—testify to the folly of mistreating the civil population. Improving the behavior of the forces of order was a fundamental and fruitful concern of Magsaysay, while in contrast Huk behavior toward the peasantry deteriorated. A similar phenomenon occurred in El Salvador. Several implications for counterinsurgency flow from this principle of rectitude: Use the lowest possible level of firepower; forbid body counts and quotas of dead guerrillas; commit enough forces so that the troops are not constantly exhausted, frustrated, and fearful; and ensure that the troops have the requisite training (if American troops are involved on the ground, such training should include familiarity with the language and culture of the disputed region on the part of at least some junior officers). Besides avoiding the gratuitous creation of sympathy and recruits for the guerrillas, rectitude pays off in two other vital areas: the gathering of intelligence and the exploitation of ethnic differences among the guerrillas. The Soviet failure to accomplish much on this score in Afghanistan is revealing—actually stunning. Rectitude is worth many battalions.

Third, and not least, *provide a peaceful road to change.* Guevara's aphorism that one cannot make revolution against a democratic or an apparently democratic state has much validity; failure to heed his own advice cost him dearly.[107] However regrettable its shortcomings, Greek parliamentary democracy continued to operate all during the civil war. Both Magsaysay and Duarte restored honest elections, to the grave detriment of the insurgents. Offering the insurgents inclusion in the political process is probably the easiest way to separate the diehards from the mass of their followers. The ballot box has often served as the coffin of insurgency.[108]

But perhaps the most important conclusion to be drawn is that American experience of guerrilla war is far broader and richer than the conflict in Viet Nam. This experience needs to be brought out of the mothballs, studied, debated, and inserted into the conciousness of U.S. political and military leaders, so that American objectives may be achieved and American lives may be saved.

NOTES

1. Report of the Joint Low-Intensity Conflict Project, Fort Monroe, Va., August 1, 1986; Philip B. Davidson, *Viet Nam at War: The History, 1946–1975* (Novato, Calif.: Presidio, 1988).

2. U.S. forces peaked at 70 thousand early in 1901.

3. In addition to John Morgan Gates, *Schoolbooks and Krags: The United States Army in the Philippines 1898–1902* (Westport, Conn.: Greenwood, 1973), some good studies of U.S. military efforts in the Philippines are Brian McAlister Linn, *The U.S. Army and Counterinsurgency in the Philippine War 1899–1902* (Chapel Hill: University of North Carolina, 1989); Glenn Anthony May, *Battle for Batangas: A Philippine Province at War* (New Haven, Conn.: Yale University, 1991); and Joseph L. Schott, *The Ordeal of Samar* (Indianapolis, Ind.: Bobbs-Merrill, 1965).

4. Gates, *Schoolbooks and Krags.*

5. Emilio Aguinaldo, *A Second Look at America* (New York: Robert Speller, 1957).

6. See discussion of U.S. Navy and Marine personnel going to Managua in *Foreign Relations of the United States 1912* (Washington, D.C.: U.S. Government Printing Office, 1919), pp. 1037ff (hereafter designated as *FRUS 1912*).

7. Whitney T. Perkins, *Constraint of Empire: The United States and Caribbean Intervention* (Westport, Conn.: Greenwood, 1981), p. 21.

8. Thomas W. Walker, "Nicaragua: The Somoza Family Regime," in *Latin American Politics and Development,* ed. Howard J. Wiarda and Harvey F. Kline (Boston: Houghton Mifflin, 1979), p. 321.

9. Neil Macauley, *The Sandino Affair* (Chicago: Quadrangle, 1967), p. 24.

10. Lester D. Langley, *The Banana Wars: The United States Intervention in the Caribbean, 1898–1934* (Chicago: Dorsey, 1988), p. 186.

11. For the request by President Diaz to President Coolidge on May 15, 1927 for help in supervising the elections of October 1928, see *Foreign Relations of the United States 1927* (Washington, D.C.: U.S. Government Printing Office, 1942), 3: 350 (hereafter designated as *FRUS 1927*).

12. Richard Millett, *Guardians of the Dynasty* (Maryknoll, N.Y.: Orbis, 1977), p. 106.

13. See the May 1927 agreement on establishing the Guardia Nacional (at a strength of 93 officers and 1,064 enlisted) in *FRUS 1927*, 3: 435–439.

14. Millett, *Guardians,* p. 70.

15. Ibid., p. 71.

16. Ibid., pp. 63–64.

17. Allan R. Millett, *Semper Fidelis: The History of the United States Marine Corps* (New York: Macmillan, 1980), p. 247.

18. Macauley, *Sandino Affair*, pp. 9, 211, 226.

19. Millett, *Semper Fidelis*, p. 254.

20. See explicit descriptions of these executions in Macauley, *Sandino Affair*, pp. 147, 212–213.

21. Macauley, *Sandino Affair*, p. 234; Langley, *Banana Wars*, p. 190.

22. Macauley, *Sandino Affair*, pp. 183–184; Henry Stimson, *On Active Service in Peace and War* (New York: Harper, 1948), p. 182 and passim.

23. Millett, *Semper Fidelis,* p. 262. On the activities of the marines in Haiti, see Millett, *Semper Fidelis*; Langley, *Banana Wars*; James H. McCrocklin, *Garde d'Haiti 1915–1934* (Annapolis, Md.: U.S. Naval Institute, 1956); and Hans Schmidt, *The United States Occupation of Haiti, 1915–1934* (New Brunswick, N.J.: Rutgers University, 1971).

24. Langley, *Banana Wars*, p. 206.

25. Macauley, *Sandino Affair*, p. 269; Langley, *Banana Wars*, p. 212.

26. Langley, *Banana Wars*, p. 212.

27. Macauley, *Sandino Affair*, p. 175.

28. Millett, *Semper Fidelis*, p. 252; and see Vernon Megee, "The Genesis of Air Support in Guerrilla Operations," *United States Naval Institute Proceedings* 91 (June 1965).

29. Macauley, *Sandino Affair*, p. 174.

30. United States Marine Corps, *Small Wars Manual* (Washington, D.C.: U.S. Government Printing Office, 1940), pp. 1–14, 1–16c, 1–16d.

31. C. M. Woodhouse, *The Struggle for Greece 1941–1949* (London: Hart-Davis, MacGibbon, 1976), p. 248.

32. Lawrence S. Wittner, *American Intervention in Greece, 1943–1949* (New York: Columbia University, 1982), p. 223.

33. *Eastern Europe and the Soviet Union*, vol. 4 of *Foreign Relations of the United States 1948* (Washington, D.C.: U.S. Government Printing Office, 1974), p. 57 (hereinafter referred to as *FRUS 1948*).

34. *The Near East and Africa*, vol. 5 of *Foreign Relations of the United States 1947* (Washington, D.C.: U.S. Government Printing Office, 1971), p. 469 (hereinafter referred to as *FRUS 1947*).

35. *FRUS 1947*, p. 460.

36. *FRUS 1946*, pp. 466–469.

37. Wittner, *American Intervention in Greece*, p. 236.

38. *FRUS 1947*, p. 273.

39. *FRUS 1947*, pp. 361, 363.

40. *FRUS 1948*, p. 208.

41. Wittner, *American Intervention in Greece*, p. 247.

42. Howard Jones, *"A New Kind of War": America's Global Strategy and the Truman Doctrine in Greece* (New York: Oxford University Press, 1989), pp. 94–99, 132–133, and passim.

43. *FRUS 1947*, p. 335, 383.

44. Wittner, *American Intervention in Greece*, p. 239.

45. *FRUS 1948*, p. 65.

46. Jones, *"A New Kind of War,"* chap. 5.

47. John Lewis Gaddis, *Strategies of Containment* (New York: Oxford University Press, 1982), pp. 22, 62.

48. *FRUS 1948*, p. 95.

49. Wittner, *American Intervention in Greece*, p. 242. See also the brief discussion in Jones, *"A New Kind of War,"* pp. 90–94. By August 31, 1949, the U.S. military mission in Greece consisted of 191 officers and men: Ibid., p. 221.

50. See Luis Taruc, *He Who Rides the Tiger* (New York: Praeger, 1967), and *Born of the People* (Westport, Conn.: Greenwood, 1973).

51. Taruc, *Tiger*, p. 134.

52. Magsaysay also benefited from the friendship and advice of the legendary Edward Lansdale. See Edward G. Lansdale, *In the Midst of Wars* (New York: Harper and Row, 1972), and Cecil B. Currey, *Edward Lansdale: The Unquiet American* (Boston: Houghton Mifflin, 1988).

53. In 1953 Magsaysay ran against President Quirino and defeated him handily.

54. Boyd T. Bashore, "Dual Strategy for Limited War" in *Modern Guerrilla Warfare*, ed. Franklin Mark Osanka (New York: The Free Press, 1962), p. 198.

55. *Asia and the Pacific*, vol. 6 of *Foreign Relations of the United States 1951* (Washington, D.C.: U.S. Government Printing Office, 1977), p. 1536 (hereinafter referred to as *FRUS 1951*).

56. *East Asia and the Pacific*, vol. 6 of *Foreign Relations of the United States 1950* (Washington, D.C.: U.S. Government Printing Office, 1976), pp. 1433, 1435–1438 (hereinafter referred to as *FRUS 1950*).

57. *FRUS 1950*, p. 1443.

58. *FRUS 1950*, p. 1495.

59. *FRUS 1951*, pp. 1498, 1501–1502.

60. *FRUS 1950*, p. 1517.

61. *FRUS 1950*, pp. 1403, 1442, 1462.

62. *FRUS 1951*, pp. 1507, 1537.

63. See National Security Council Statement NSC 84/2, "The Position of the United States with Respect to the Philippines," November 9, 1950.

64. *FRUS 1950*, pp. 1408, 1442–1443.

65. *FRUS 1951*, p. 1504.

66. *FRUS 1950*, pp. 1485–1489.

67. *FRUS 1951*, p. 1549.

68. *FRUS 1950*, pp. 1485–1489.

69. See *FRUS 1950* and *FRUS 1951*.

70. James Dunkerly, *Power in the Isthmus: A Political History of Modern Central America* (London: Verso, 1988), p. 338.

71. James LeMoyne, "El Salvador's Forgotten War," *Foreign Affairs* 68 (Summer 1989): 105–126.

72. The "final offensive" of the FMLN would fail in 1981 before any appreciable U.S. aid had arrived. Moreover, in neighboring Guatemala, a similar insurgency was beaten without U.S. help. See Timothy P. Wickham-Crowley, *Guerrillas and Revolutions in Latin America: A Comparative Study of Insurgents and Regimes since 1956* (Princeton, N.J.: Princeton University, 1991), pp. 282ff.

73. Nevertheless, there is hardly a mention of El Salvador in the memoirs of President Carter, his National Security Advisor Brzezinski, or his Secretary of State Vance. For that matter, President Reagan's Secretary of State George P. Schultz and Secretary of Defense Caspar Weinberger are almost equally reticent. See Jimmy Carter, *Keeping Faith: Memoirs of a President* (New York: Bantam Books, 1982); Zbigniew Brzezinski, *Power and Principle: Memoirs of a National Security Adviser 1977–1981* (New York: Farrar, Straus & Giroux, 1983); Cyrus Vance, *Hard Choices* (New York: Simon and Schuster, 1983); George P. Shultz, *Turmoil and Triumph: My Years as Secretary of State* (New York: Charles Scribner's Sons, 1993); and Caspar Weinberger, *Fighting for Peace: Seven Critical Years at the Pentagon* (New York: Warner, 1990).

74. Dunkerly, *Power*, p. 400.

75. *Report of the Bipartisan Commission on Central America* (Washington, D.C.: U.S. Government Printing Office, 1984), pp. 4, 87, 91, 126.

76. See "Concerning Our Military Plans: The Military Strategy of the FMLN," a document captured near Perquin, El Salvador, ed. and trans. Gabriel Marcella, U.S. Army War College, May 1986.

77. Enrique A. Baloyra, "Negotiating War in El Salvador: The Politics of Endgame," *Journal of Interamerican Studies and World Affairs* 28, no. 1 (Spring 1986): 132.

78. See Benjamin Schwarz, *American Counterinsurgency Doctrine and El Salvador: The Frustrations of Reform and the Illusions of Nation Building* (Santa Monica, Calif.: RAND, 1991).

79. It was during those turbulent days that Salvadoran army personnel executed six Jesuit priests, accusing them of being in sympathetic contact with the guerrillas, an episode that triggered great disquiet in the U.S. Congress.

80. American-supplied helicopters, for example, vastly improved the surveillance and response capabilities of the Salvadoran army.

81. Ernesto Guevara, *Guerrilla Warfare* (New York: Vintage, 1961).

82. Jeff Goodwin and Theda Skocpol, "Explaining Revolutions in the Countercountry Third World," *Politics and Society*, 17, no. 4 (1989): 495.

83. Wickham-Crowley, *Guerrillas and Revolutions*, p. 287.

84. See Max G. Manwaring and Court Prisk, eds., *El Salvador at War: An Oral History* (Washington, D.C.: National Defense University, 1988).

85. Tahir Amin, "Afghan Resistance: Past, Present and Future," *Asian Survey* 24 (April 1984): 380.

86. One of their first actions was to kill PDPA President Amin.

87. David Isby, "Soviet Strategy and Tactics in Low-Intensity Conflict," in *Guerrilla Warfare and Counterinsurgency: U.S.–Soviet Policy in the Third World*, ed. Richard H. Shultz, Jr. (Lexington, Mass.: Lexington Books, 1989).

88. Andre Bridgit and Olivier Roy, *The War in Afghanistan* (New York: Harvester-Wheatshaff, 1988); David C. Isby, *War in a Distant Country* (London: Arms and Armour, 1989); Grant M. Farr and John G. Merriam, *Afghan Resistance: The Politics of Survival* (Boulder, Colo.: Westview, 1987); Mike Martin, *Afghanistan: Inside Rebel Stronghold* (Dorset, U.K.: Blandford, 1984).

89. On the PDPA regime and army, see J. Bruce Amstutz, *Afghanistan: The First Five Years of Soviet Occupation* (Washington, D.C.: National Defense University, 1986); Anthony Arnold, *Afghanistan: The Soviet Occupation in Perspective*, rev. ed. (Stanford, Calif.: Hoover Institution, 1985); Craig Karp, *Afghanistan: Six Years of Soviet Occupation* (Washington, D.C.: U.S. Department of State, 1985).

90. For the Russian–Soviet effort, see Olivier Roy, *The Lessons of the Soviet/Afghan War*, Adelphi Paper 259 (Oxford: International Institute for Strategic Studies, 1991); Anthony Arnold, *The Fateful Pebble: Afghanistan's Role in the Fall of the Soviet Empire* (Novato, Calif.: Presidio, 1993); Geoffrey Jukes, "The Soviet Armed Forces and the Afghan War," in *The Soviet Withdrawal from Afghanistan*, ed. Amin Saikal and William Maley (Cambridge: Cambridge University, 1989); Anthony H. Cordesman and A. R. Wagner, *The Afghan and Falkland Conflicts*, vol. 3 of *The Lessons of Modern War* (Boulder, Colo.: Westview, 1990). For specifically Soviet treatments, see Oleg Sarin and Lev Dvoretsky, *The Afghan Syndrome: The Soviet Union's Viet Nam* (Novato, Calif.: Presidio, 1993); Gennady Bocharov, *Russian Roulette: Afghanistan through Russian Eyes* (New York: Harper & Row, 1990); Artyom Borovik, *The Hidden War* (New York: Atlantic Monthly Press, 1990).

91. See *The Christian Science Monitor,* October 26, 1988, p. 11; *The New York Times*, December 10, 1985, p. 30; Edward Girardet, *Afghanistan: The Soviet War* (New York: St. Martin's Press, 1985), pp. 213, 219–220; Claude Malhuret, "Report from Afghanistan," *Foreign Affairs* 62 (Winter 1984): 430; Anthony Arnold, *Afghanistan: The Soviet Invasion in Perspective*, rev. ed. (Stanford, Calif.: Hoover Institution, 1985); Henry Bradsher, *Afghanistan and the Soviet Union* (Durham, N.C.: Duke University, 1985), p. 211; and J. Bruce Amstutz, *Afghanistan: The First Five Years* (Washington, D.C.: National Defense University, 1986).

92. Louis Dupree, quoted in Joseph J. Collins, *Soviet Invasion of Afghanistan* (Lexington, Mass.: Lexington Books, 1985).

93. Leon B. Poullada, "Road to Crisis," in *Afghanistan: The Great Game Revisited*, ed. Rosanne Klass (New York: Freedom House, 1987), p. 48.

94. Thomas T. Hammond, *Red Flag over Afghanistan* (Boulder, Colo.: Westview, 1984), pp. 26–28.

95. Arnold, *Afghanistan*, p. 12.

96. Collins, *Soviet Invasion*, p. 134.

97. Former USSR ambassador to Washington Anatoly Dobrynin writes that the Soviet leadership found Carter's statement "incredible," and one believes him. Anatoly Dobrynin, *In Confidence: Moscow's Ambassador to Six Cold War Presidents* (New York: Random House, 1995), p. 448.

98. Jimmy Carter, *Keeping Faith*, p. 473. According to Ambassador Dobrynin, top Soviet military leaders had opposed sending troops into Afghanistan. Dobrynin, *In Confidence*, p. 444.

99. Carter, *Keeping Faith*, pp. 471–489; Vance, *Hard Choices* (New York: Simon and Schuster, 1982), pp. 386–396; Zbigniew Brzezinski, *Power and Principle*, chap. 12.

100. Carter, *Keeping Faith*, p. 483. "The Soviet intervention and the sharp response of the United States proved a final turning point in Soviet–American relations": Dobrynin, *In Confidence*, p. 449.

101. John Ranelagh, *The Agency: The Rise and Decline of the CIA* (New York: Simon and Schuster, 1986), p. 681; Amstutz, *Afghanistan: First Five Years*, p. 210.

102. Bradsher, *Afghanistan and Soviet Union*, p. 278; Amstutz, *Afghanistan: First Five Years*, p. 210. A real debate raged inside the U.S. government on the morality of giving weapons to Afghan guerrillas so that they could die in a hopeless struggle, especially in light of what had happened to America's trusting friends in South Viet Nam. See Ranelagh, *The Agency*, pp. 682–683.

103. Arnold, *Afghanistan*, p. 118. See also *The New York Times*, May 3, 1983, and November 28, 1984; *The Wall Street Journal*, April 9, 1984; *The Washington Post*, January 13, 1985; *The Economist*, January 19, 1985; Anthony H. Cordesman and Abraham R. Wagner, *The Afghan and Falklands Conflicts*, vol. 3 of *The Lessons of Modern War* (Boulder, Colo.: Westview, 1990), p. 20.

104. See the many illuminating articles in Amin Saikal and William Maley, eds. *The Soviet Withdrawal from Afghanistan* (Cambridge: Cambridge University Press, 1989).

105. See Peter J. Woolley, "Geography and the Limits of U.S. Intervention" in *Conflict Quarterly* 11 (Fall 1991).

106. True, the Greek war ended while the insurgents still had the Albanian border open to them; nevertheless, during most of that conflict the ability of the guerrillas to escape over the frontier from pursuing troops seriously undermined the morale of the latter for years. Besides, counterinsurgents cannot count on their opponents being as incompetent as the Greek communists.

107. "Where a government maintains at least an appearance of constitutional legality, the guerrilla outbreak cannot be promoted, since the possibilities of peaceful struggle have not yet been exhausted." Che Guevara, *Guerrilla Warfare*, 3d ed., ed. B. Loveman and T. Davies (Wilmington, Del.: Scholarly Resources, 1997), p. 51.

108. True, regular free elections did not end Sandino's rebellion in the 1930s, but one ought not to forget what small numbers of marines and national guards he confronted. Nor have regular elections brought peace to Colombia, but violence is not revolution.

Index

About the Editor and Contributors

Alfred R. Barr is a former Foreign Service Officer with experience in MACV headquarters in Saigon, as well as in Honduras and Nicaragua. He represented the State Department in drafting the NSDD on Low Intensity Conflict in 1986. He most recently wrote "The Good Neighbor Policy," in *Foreign Service Journal.*

Stephen Blank is the Douglas MacArthur Professor of Research with the Strategic Studies Institute at the U.S. Army War College. His recent works include *Imperial Decline: Russia's Changing Role in Asia, The Sorcerer as Apprentice: Stalin's Commissariat of Nationalities,* and *The Soviet Military and the Future.*

Frederick H. Fleitz, Jr., has studied and worked with the United Nations for many years. From 1981 to 1987, he held several positions, including president of the board of directors of the National Collegiate Conference Association, a nonprofit corporation which sponsors a college-level educational program on the United Nations. From 1985 to 1986, he was a program associate with the Center for War/Peace Studies, a New York-based think tank dedicated to UN reform. He also was a UN nongovernmental organization representative. Mr. Fleitz is currently an analyst with the Central Intelligence Agency.

Anthony James Joes is Professor of International Relations at Saint Joseph's University. His previous works include *Guerrilla Warfare: A Historical, Biographical and Bibliographical Sourcebook*; *Guerrilla Conflict Before the Cold War*; *Modern Guerrilla Insurgency*; *The War for South Viet Nam*; and *From the Barrell of a Gun: Armies and Revolutions*.

Max G. Manwaring, Colonel U.S. Army (Ret.) is Adjunct Professor of Political Science at Dickson College. His experience includes service with the U.S. Southern Command, the Defense Intelligence Agency, and the U.S. Army War College. His recent works include *Toward Responsibility in the New World Disorder: Challenges and Lessons of Peace Operations, Managing Contemporary Conflict: Pillars of Success*, and *Gray Area Phenomena: Confronting the New World Disorder*.

Thomas R. Mockaitis is Professor of History at De Paul University. His recent works include *British Counterinsurgency in the Post-Imperial Era* and *British Counterinsurgency 1919–1960*.

Enrique Obando is president of the Strategic Studies Institute in Lima, Peru. He is also associated with the Peruvian Center of International Studies and the Catholic University of Peru. Recent works include *Nuevas amenazas a la seguridad y relaciones civiles-militares en un mundo en desorden* and *Fuerzas armadas y constitucion*.

Caesar D. Sereseres is Associate Dean for Undergraduate Studies and Associate Professor in the School of Social Sciences at the University of California, Irvine. He has been a staff member in the Department of State and a consultant to the Bureau of Inter-American Affairs and the RAND Corporation. His main research interests concern U.S.–Latin American security issues.

Harvey Sicherman is President and Director of the Foreign Policy Research Institute. He has served as staff member and/or consultant with the State and Navy Departments. His recent works include *The Chinese Economy: A New Scenario, Palestinian Autonomy, Self-Government and Peace,* and *The Three Per Cent Solution and the Future of NATO*.

Stephen Sloan is Professor of Political Science at the University of Oklahoma. He specializes in the comparative study of political violence, international terrorism, and insurgency. His latest books include *The Historical Dictionary of Terrorism*, coauthored with

Sean Anderson, and *Low-Intensity Conflict: Old Threats in a New World*, coedited by Edwin G. Corr.

Peter J. Woolley is Professor of Comparative Politics at Fairleigh Dickson University, book review editor for *The Journal of Conflict Studies*, and a former Advance Research Scholar of Naval Warfare Studies at the U.S. Naval War College. His works include *Japan's Navy: Politics and Paradox, 1971–2000*, as well as articles in *Asian Survey, Strategic Review, Journal of East and West Studies*, and *The Naval War College Review*.